ENGLISH DIALOGUES *of the* DEAD

Frederick M. Keener

ENGLISH DIALOGUES
of the DEAD
A Critical History, An Anthology, and
A Check List

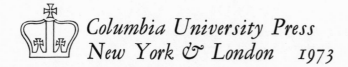 Columbia University Press
New York & London   1973

Library of Congress Cataloging in Publication Data

Keener, Frederick M   1937–
    English dialogues of the dead.

    Includes bibliographical references.
    1. English literature—History and criticism.
2. Dialogue.   3. Imaginary conversations.
I. Title.
PR618.K4   825'.06   73-1871
ISBN 0-231-03695-7

Preface

Congenial horrors, morbidity, necrophilia—these and
other gloomy topics, I must say directly, have little to do with the
subject of this book, the life and fortunes in the English language of a
classical genre now almost unknown but once, especially in the eighteenth century, quite commonplace, even popular, and deservedly so
in some cases. The long-unpublished, still neglected dialogues of Matthew Prior remain as delightful as Alexander Pope found them; dialogues by George, Lord Lyttelton, Mrs. Elizabeth Montagu, and others will, at the very least, repay attention and justify a short history of
this unusual literary form. To the history I have appended a
comparably short anthology, for the most part containing pieces difficult to find except in the best libraries. The third part, a chronologi-
cal check list, supplies the incidental advantage of lightening the burden of my text and footnotes: the date of a work mentioned in
passing will serve to locate it in the check list, which is no more than
that. As a glance at the variety of titles shows, you cannot tell a dialogue of the dead by its cover. I have lengthened the known bibliography of the genre and, I hope, included all works of any conse-

quence, but exhaustiveness seems unattainable. For my principal foothold I have used the one book bearing directly on the subject, Johan S. Egilsrud's *Le "Dialogue des morts" dans les littératures française, allemande et anglaise (1644–1789)* (Paris, 1934), despite severe shortcomings—some inevitable in so ambitious a task—a useful pioneer work. In *Essays on Fielding's Miscellanies: A Commentary on Volume One* (Princeton, 1961), p. 396*n*, Henry Knight Miller remarked that Egilsrud's study is much in need of amplification.

I am pleased to acknowledge the help afforded me by grants from the Columbia University Council for Research in the Humanities and from the School of General Studies of Columbia University, and I am grateful to the editors of the *Bulletin of the New York Public Library* for permission to reprint a part of Chapter II which appeared, in somewhat different, unamplified form, in that periodical (LXXIII [January, 1969], 13–23). A check list of kind acts by students, librarians, colleagues, and members of my family would run too long, but I cannot omit specific mention of my gratitude to Professor James L. Clifford and to the late Moses Hadas, who, at the first stage of my work, gave wise directions but of course bear no responsibility for whatever false steps I have taken on my own.

Frederick M. Keener

Columbia University
December, 1972

Contents

Part I

A CRITICAL HISTORY

But if death is the journey to another place, and there, as men say, all the dead abide, what good, O my friends and judges, can be greater than this? If, indeed, when the pilgrim arrives in the world below, he is delivered from the professors of justice in this world, and finds the true judges who are said to give judgment there, Minos and Rhadamanthus and Aeacus and Triptolemus, and other sons of God who were righteous in their own life, that pilgrimage will be worth making. What would not a man give if he might converse with Orpheus and Musaeus and Hesiod and Homer? Nay, if this be true, let me die again and again. I myself, too, shall have a wonderful interest in there meeting and conversing with Palamedes, and Ajax the son of Telamon, and any other ancient hero who has suffered death through an unjust judgment; and there will be no small pleasure, as I think, in comparing my own sufferings with theirs. Above all, I shall then be able to continue my search into true and false knowledge; as in this world, so also in the next; and I shall find out who is wise, and who pretends to be wise, and is not. What would not a man give, O judges, to be able to examine the leader of the great Trojan expedition; or Odysseus or Sisyphus, or numberless others, men and women too! What infinite delight would there be in conversing with them and asking them questions! In another world they do not put a man to death for asking questions: assuredly not. For besides being happier than we are, they will be immortal, if what is said is true.—Socrates, in *Apology* (Jowett translation)

Chapter I

The Dialogue and the Dead

Vis . . . animam superbam
ultoris Bruti, fascesque videre receptos?
——*Aeneid* 6. 817–18

They were not inattentive to precedent, the eighteenth-
century writers of importance here. They knew dialogues of the dead
had existed before any Englishman wrote them, knew who had developed the form, and in what directions. The genre had its classics, to
be embraced or resisted—the three authors mentioned time and
again: "Lucian among the Ancients, and among the Moderns Fenelon, Archbishop of Cambray, and Monsieur Fontenelle, have written
Dialogues of the Dead with a general Applause," as George, Lord
Lyttelton remarked in the preface to his own, the most celebrated English collection of the century. Hence, if one is to learn about the
genre, its techniques and uses, and also to understand what English
authors did with it, one must become acquainted with their models,
especially Lucian of Samosata. The Syrian rhetorician, who wrote in
Greek during the second century, not only composed the earliest dialogues of the dead known to us. More than any of his successors, he
plumbed the genre's resources, writing so sensitively and variously
that his dialogues of the dead may be said to anticipate the entire history of the form.

The dead are talkative in old books: narratives of descents into the underworld, missives from the dead to the living, dream visions, and so forth. But a dialogue of the dead is not just any work in which the dead speak. The genre Lucian established represents the conversations, in Hades and its environs, of shades and infernal deities. There is no narrative frame; the dead are overheard, an important point because it serves to separate the dialogue of the dead from the most prominent of the genres that resemble it, the narrative of a passage to the realm of the dead. Various reasons, mainly arising from the dialogue of the dead's tendency to be satirical, make works like the eleventh book of the *Odyssey* and the sixth of the *Aeneid* less important here, for purposes of comparison, than such works as the second book of Lucian's *True History,* the third book of *Gulliver's Travels,* and Fielding's *Journey from This World to the Next.* The dialogue of the dead, it may be thought, amounts to the equivalent of a conversation excerpted from these narratives, and in some cases that is true. But in general it is not, for the dead behave otherwise when alone and simply overheard than they do when consciously speaking to, or for the benefit of, the living.

The more inaccessible the place described in accounts of travel, the more remarkable the place tends to be, in part because of the temptations besetting imaginative travelers. That truism applies *a fortiori* to the descent narrative; it is a vehicle for revelations. Someone who has visited the dead tells us of the marvels he has seen and we cannot, and so much does the genre rely upon novelty for its effect that the shades seem at times to compete with each other in making surprising, even outrageous disclosures. In all three of the descent narratives just mentioned, for example, the narrator interrogates Homer. Lucian asks him why he began the *Iliad* with the matter of Achilles' wrath, and Homer's bland reply is that it just came to him to do it, without any forethought. Gulliver finds that Homer does not know any of his innumerable commentators; they dare not approach the man they have so misrepresented. And when Fielding's narrator asks which of the cities that proclaimed themselves Homer's birthplace really deserved the honor, the answer is a mere "Upon my soul I can't tell."

Each of these incidents amusingly separates the great man from his unworthy retinue, satirizing the epigoni, but descent narratives also incline toward ridicule of the renowned shades themselves; every facet of the establishment invites burlesque. Fielding's narrator finds Madame Dacier in Homer's lap, Philip of Macedon is a cobbler in Lucian's *Menippus,* and Xerxes sells mustard in the second book of Rabelais. A vestige of this generic trait may be seen in Gulliver's telling us that the ruler of Glubbdubdrib, a necromancer, can compel the dead to be his servants. The world of descent narratives has a penchant for turning upside down.

> Lucrece for half a crown will shew you fun,
> But Mrs Oldfield is become a Nun.
> Nobles and Cits, Prince Pluto & his Spouse
> Flock to the Ghost of Covent-Garden house:
> Plays, which were hiss'd above, below revive:
> When dead applauded, that were damn'd alive.[1]

In nearly all such works, the narrator behaves like a gossip columnist at a masquerade, dashing from celebrity to celebrity, identifying them, gathering tidbits of scandal, but seldom pausing to pursue and complete a conversation.

Scandal crops up in dialogues of the dead too. Yet if novelty had been the main quarry of Lucian and his successors, they would not have bothered to cast their work in the form of dialogues, a form traditionally devoted to the consideration of serious philosophical questions (though Herodes and others before Lucian had written short dialogues, or mimes, on less weighty matters). The prefix *dia-* has nothing to do with the number of speakers; rather, it suggests the method whereby dialogues are customarily developed, "through" reasoning and talking. In the standard history of the form, Rudolf Hirzel observes that a dialogue is more than just a transcript of any conversation. The dialogue is the literary embodiment of dialectic, a form that probes and dissects a topic from two or more points of view.[2] But

[1] Thomas Gray, "Lines Spoken by the Ghost of John Dennis at the Devil Tavern," ll. 42–47, *Complete Poems,* ed. H. W. Starr and J. R. Hendrickson (Oxford, 1966), p. 72.

[2] Rudolf Hirzel, *Der Dialog: Ein literarhistorischer Versuch* (Leipzig, 1895), I, 2–3.

the dialogue of the dead, though generally more serious in tone than the satirical descent narratives, is distinct also from the dialogue proper. One need not recruit the dead to populate dialogues.

Those who speak in dialogues of the dead are nearly all famous persons from history and legend, personages. That many are from ancient times, even in dialogues written just a few centuries ago, is a fact suggesting the extent of Lucian's influence upon his successors and testifying to the conservative bias of the genre, which always has recourse to the past; the renowned persons who speak in Lucian were all more or less ancient even when he wrote.[3] This trait of the dialogues will not endear them to the many present-day readers who know and care less about the remote past than earlier readers did. In the last hundred years or so, writers have practically ceased to draw upon the fund of exemplary personages which earlier authors found indispensable: Alexander, Xerxes, Cato of Utica, Lucretia. When Dickens' Slackbridge, in *Hard Times,* harangues the mob, "Had not the Roman Brutus, oh my British countrymen, condemned his son to death?" we immediately realize the words are empty; it is hard to imagine a modern context in which they could be affecting— indeed, many educated readers of today would not know whom Dickens is talking about. The practice of employing such personages has faded, become disreputable, and with it has passed a world of fine facts.

A few centuries ago, those facts could still provoke considerable interest and emotion; what Cato stood for, and how he did so, touched the hearts and minds of many. Pope could revise Chaucer's *Hous of Fame* adding many ancient exemplars, and Lucius Junius Brutus, who was called upon to speak in at least two dialogues of the dead, could be assumed the property of numerous readers—an assertion supported by passing references in *Gulliver's Travels* (III, vii) and *Tom*

---

[3] See J. Bompaire, *Lucien écrivain: Imitation et création* (Paris, 1958), pp. 161–203. Perhaps the best, certainly the most comprehensive book on Lucian, Bompaire is particularly helpful concerning the sources and analogues of the dialogue of the dead: mime, *chria,* idyll, comedy (especially Aristophanes' *Frogs*), etc. For the much-discussed question of Lucian's debt to the lost works of Menippus of Gadara, the cynic of the third century B.C. who is prominent in the *Dialogues of the Dead,* and also for a discussion of "Menippean satire," see pp. 365–78, 549–62.

Jones (IV, iv). It was not simply pedantry, a scholarly passion for history, nostalgia, or a taste for learned embellishment that made many eighteenth-century authors look backward before advancing. Contemporaries of Clarendon, Burnet, Hume, Robertson, and Gibbon depended heavily upon history for norms and ideals of human conduct, thought the past a laboratory for the present. Dryden, for a time historiographer royal, mined history for his poems and plays; Swift described Queen Anne's last years; Fielding confessed, in the preface to his *Journal of a Voyage to Lisbon,* that he "should have honoured and loved Homer more had he written a true history of his own times in humble prose, than those noble poems that have so justly collected the praise of all ages; for, though I read these with more admiration and astonishment, I still read Herodotus, Thucydides and Xenophon, with more amusement and more satisfaction"; Johnson's preference for biography above the rest of literature is well known; and Boswell, when of a mind to reform himself, would resolve to be like Addison or some other person of historical consequence.

Horace's best of fathers branded his lessons deep by censuring not just vices but the vicious.[4] Similarly, in the deep tones of that paternal authority which is the ground bass of an aristocratic culture, Pope filled his satires with explicit accusations against real people, who were sometimes accused doubly by being given the names of ancient malefactors. Or if praise were in order, to recommend virtue, he and many of his contemporaries heeded the advice of Cicero's Laelius: "Let us interpret the word 'virtue' by the familiar usage of our everyday life and speech, and not in pompous phrase apply to it the precise standards which certain philosophers use; and let us include in the number of good men those who are so considered—men like Paulus, Cato, Gallus, Scipio, and Philus—who satisfy the ordinary standard of life; but let us pass by such men as are nowhere to be found at all"[5]—namely, the theoretical models of impossible perfection that Stoics, like the sage in the eighteenth chapter of *Rasselas,* had set

---

[4] *Serm.* 1. 4. 105–6.

[5] Cicero *Laelius de Amicitia* 6. 21, in *De Senectute, De Amicitia, De Divinatione,* trans. William Armistead Falconer, Loeb Classical Library (London, 1923), p. 131.

well beyond the reach of even their own capacity for imitation. The common use of the term "neoclassical" to indicate the concern of many eighteenth-century authors for literary precedent seems too restricted; the term is also of service in defining their attitude toward all the public and private offices of life.

The dead, moreover, were not so remote then as they have become. Lyttelton's dialogues appeared in 1760, just after mysterious rappings and scratchings began to cause goose flesh in Cock Lane. "What an illustration of the age of reason!" Douglas Grant remarks, referring to Johnson's report for the committee that looked into the question of the ghost's existence: "The fashionable women, the men of reputation, the gullible clergy, the possessed child, the seriousness of the charges, the midnight descent to the vault, with the stacked coffins shadowily lit by the trembling flame of the lamp: the judiciousness of Johnson's prose cannot disguise the fantasy of the scene." [6] True, and yet hardly uncharacteristic of the period. Apart from the ruminations of "graveyard" poets and even before heightened sensibilities welcomed Gothic horrors, ghosts walked abroad: Pope's Unfortunate Lady, Defoe's Mrs. Veal are just two manifestations of a possibility entertained not merely in places so esoteric as the *Theosophical Transactions by the Philadelphian Society* (1697), or so susceptible as John Wesley's *Journal,* but also in the chief literature of the century. How frequently do fictional characters reveal their fear of ghosts: Crusoe astounded by the footprint, "as if I had seen an Apparition"; Partridge in *Tom Jones,* quivering at the entrance on stage of Hamlet's father; Pekuah cowering before the pyramid in *Rasselas.* Despite these examples, superstition did not confine itself to the foothills of society, and religion left the question of apparitions unresolved, at the least, while allowing the possibility of meetings after death with the good or bad of former years. Many people could share Socrates' joy at the end of the *Apology* in contemplating conversations to come with the likes of Hesiod and Homer, and hence the dialogue of the dead was not so fanciful a form as it has become.

[6] Douglas Grant, *The Cock Lane Ghost* (London, 1965), p. 72.

Assuming readers had at least a gentleman's acquaintance with history and mythology, authors found it unnecessary to provide biographies of the shades entering their dialogues. As the nineteenth century approached, however, and as the genre was exposed to more and more of what Fielding called "mere English readers," it became customary for authors to draw exemplars from more recent history, especially that of England—witness Gray, who substituted the names Hampden, Milton, and Cromwell for Cato, Tully, and Caesar while composing his *Elegy*.[7] Names at which the world grows pale, or used to, and other, less intimidating names draw after them a train of ethical attitudes and demonstrated consequences. When we see Croesus or Diogenes, or Charles XII, we can immediately and with assurance guess the part he is to play. The genre's characters define its range. Because the dialogue of the dead is related to the dialogue proper and employs characters of known intellectual dispositions, the reader can expect a somewhat developed conversation to take place, on a subject of some importance. But because such a dialogue shares the fantastic basis of descent narratives, depends upon the successful artistic equivalent of resuscitation, the reader cannot expect the conversations, on the whole, to be invariably serious or very long. After all, the real persons named are not speaking, and fantasy cannot bear much undisguised sobriety.

In degree of complexity, the dialogue of the dead may vary within certain limits and still retain its identity. The characters may remain virtually unelaborated—that is, almost as they come to mind when mentioned—and be used to demonstrate a simple, typically a moral point. Or they may be rounded with factual and invented details, to the extent that we begin to care for them as persons as well as representatives of readily identifiable attitudes. Lucian concentrated on the former sort in his *Dialogues of the Dead*. Most of the thirty dialogues in this collection run no more than two pages, a few pages less than what would become standard for the genre. Dialogue II, for example, in a little more than a page presents an argument between Croesus,

[7] Gray, p. 39*n*.

Sardanapalus, and Midas, on the one hand, and on the other the cynic Menippus, a virtually allegorical confrontation. As Maurice Croiset remarked, it is less one against three than Voluntary Poverty against Complacent Wealth.[8] This dialogue, and most of Lucian's, is like a five-finger exercise. Menippus is right, the others are deluded, and Menippus, the hero, tells them so. Significantly, he appears in eleven of these dialogues, Diogenes has a similar role in six more, and in Lucian's one dialogue of the dead apart from this collection, a piece entitled *Voyage to the Lower World,* there is a character named Cyniscus, a third satiric agent from the same company.

But Lucian also showed how the dialogue of the dead might become more serious and complicated, especially in Dialogue XII, where Alexander, Hannibal, and Scipio contend for military preeminence. This type, which may be considered a short dramatic version of the *Parallel Lives* form, would later become the favored vehicle of authors such as Fénelon and Lyttelton, both of whom wrote specifically to instruct, entertain, and edify the young. Like Phoenix holding up the example of yielding Meleager to obstinate Achilles in Book IX of the *Iliad,* these writers explored parallels in the biographies of famous men so as to isolate universal principles of morals, politics, and other subjects of aristocratic concern, an analogical approach to history common in the eighteenth century.[9] (Fénelon placed a maxim at the head of each dialogue, the moral Q.E.D. of the piece; Lyttelton's characters regularly utter comparable observations in italics.) The timelessness of the afterlife supports such universalizing, and in turn, such a purpose calls for the exercise of restraint in depiction of the underworld. It is significant that the trappings of Hades receive scant mention when a dialogue seems designed to be serious in every respect, when burlesque is out of order. An exception is the dialogue, like Lucian's eighteenth, which is meant to be taken as idyllic or ele-

[8] *Essai sur la vie et les oeuvres de Lucien* (Paris, 1882), p. 337.
[9] Page Smith, *The Historian and History* (New York, 1964), p. 26. See also Herbert Davis, "The Augustan Conception of History," *Reason and the Imagination: Studies in the History of Ideas, 1600–1800,* ed. J. A. Mazzeo (New York, 1962), pp. 213–29.

giac. There Menippus sadly contemplates the skeleton that was Helen
of Troy, and for once we find him without a quip to utter. A mood of
tempus edax prevails.

Samuel Johnson's comment on *Gulliver's Travels* may be adapted
to describe what has been said here until now about the genre Lucian
established: once an author has thought of making the dead speak to
each other, the rest is easy enough. In two ways, however, Lucian
went beyond the obvious, doing so admirably. One entails his use of
Hades, the other his dramatic techniques.

Lucian's boneyard Elysium is more substantial and more macabre
than might be expected. Judging by the best-known guidebooks to
the underworld, the *Odyssey* and the *Aeneid,* one would expect to
find it populated with spirits: Odysseus and Aeneas both tried three
times without success to embrace a parent there. And though Homer's
Hades is a frightful place, so much so that the Socrates of the *Republic* would have suppressed his account of it, Virgil's resembles a sum-
mer colony in some quarters. The blest enjoy a bright sky and lovely
fields, dancing and wrestling and banqueting. Moreover, the Elysian
isle of Lucian's *True History* combines a site like Virgil's with architecture recalling the New Jerusalem in Revelation. Not so the Hades
of the *Dialogues of the Dead,* which offers the shades no physical
pleasures, is lightless, and seems destined to remain thus forever. As
Diogenes says in the first dialogue, Hades is a place of absolute, dismal equality: "Auburn locks, eyes bright or black, rosy cheeks, are as
little in fashion here as tense muscles or mighty shoulders; man and
man are as like as two peas . . . when it comes to bare skull and no
beauty." [10] There is a separate place where malefactors are punished
in earnest, as we learn in the thirtieth dialogue, but those permitted
to range the Elysian Fields enjoy no more than the absence of bodily
pain.

Most of the shades, anyway. There is one consolation for a few,

[10] Quotations are from *The Works of Lucian of Samosata,* trans. H. W. Fowler
and F. G. Fowler, 4 vols. (Oxford, 1905): *Dialogues of the Dead,* I, 107–56; *Voyage to the Lower World,* I, 230–46.

those who on earth scorned attachment to material goods and those who suffered there as a result of others' luxury and avarice. In Lucian's extra dialogue of the dead, *Voyage to the Lower World,* the poor downtrodden cobbler Micyllus mockingly bewails his death: "Woe's me! Never again shall I sit empty from morn till night; never again walk up and down, of a winter's day, naked, unshod, with chattering teeth!" And for the cynics, Lucian's underworld approximates a paradise. Here Menippus, Diogenes, Cyniscus, and their colleagues possess what they valued on earth, "wisdom, independence, truth, frankness, freedom" (Dial. XI). Here they enjoy the cynical pleasure of deriding those less sagacious in life and death. "I detest these abject rascals!" shrieks Menippus in the second dialogue. "Not content with having lived the abominable lives they did, they keep on talking about it now they are dead, and harping on the good old days. I take a positive pleasure in annoying them." Menippus, in fact, committed suicide the sooner to begin his blissful afterlife, or so Lucian would have us believe. In the eternal subterranean Saturnalia, the cynics are underdogs triumphant, and to bark about their triumph gives them enduring pleasure.

Not even Pluto can silence Menippus on this occasion. Indeed, the gods suffer their share of abuse. Dialogue IV contains no shades at all, showing Hermes' efforts to regain the money he has lent Charon to keep the ferry in trim (Charon's difficulties are dramatized in many dialogues of the dead, including the one in Erasmus' *Colloquies*). To Hermes' demands, Charon replies with all the forthrightness of a *Beggar's Opera* scoundrel: "I can't just now, Hermes; we shall have a war or a plague presently, and then the passengers will come shoaling in, and I shall be able to make a little by jobbing the fares." Hermes understands; he laments the loss of the good old days, when gorebespattered heroes regularly thronged the ferry. "Nowadays, a man is poisoned by his slave or his wife; or gets dropsy from overfeeding; a pale, spiritless lot, nothing like the men of old. Most of them seem to meet their end in some plot that has money for its object." Here the satire cuts both ways, the impecunious speakers revealing themselves as less than godlike, and those spoken about, Lucian's contemporaries, being revealed as less than heroic. Only the cynics, who seldom expect anything better, can remain unaffected.

Lucian's station in time, when irreligion and new religions had eroded the foundations of Olympus, permitted full exploitation of Hades' resources. He could take a step backward and treat his setting and its inhabitants sympathetically, as he does in the elegiac dialogue concerning Helen, or he could trifle with them. Though references to conditions below are omnipresent in the dialogues, he clearly did not mean his readers to think his setting and its denizens real, just real enough to suit the action of the dialogues. Hades was a premier object for satire, and Lucian felt no reticence about undraping the cracks in its walls. How can skeletons speak? he must have known we would wonder; let Homer tell you, he implies. No "darkness visible" or other paradoxical accommodations for him. He even parades Hades' inconsistencies before us, as in Dialogue XVII, where Menippus explores the nonsensical predicament of Tantalus. Why does the water recede? Clearly eating and drinking are beyond the needs or abilities of skeletons, whatever the shades do in Homer; Chiron tells the reader so in Dialogue XXVI. Yet to make a satiric point Lucian has Pythagoras ask for beans in the twentieth dialogue— Pythagoras, who had forbidden his disciples to eat beans for fear, it was said, that through metempsychosis the beans might contain the souls of ancestors. Lucian strenuously upholds the reality of death and decay in these dialogues, but not the Elysian hypothesis.

Oddly enough, eighteenth-century authors seem to have encountered more difficulty in sporting with the infernal mythology, and not because it was so thoroughly a thing of the past. The gods were objects of curiosity in England, touchy ones too. Bayle, Fontenelle, English deists, and others studied them with a mind to comprehending and annihilating superstition, which for some was practically indistinguishable from religion; [11] the predecessors of Sir James Frazer were at work, and of course, the forces of reaction. "This second-hand machinery of heathen mythology," one reviewer of a dialogue of the

[11] See Frank E. Manuel, *The Eighteenth Century Confronts the Gods* (Cambridge, Mass., 1959).

dead remarked, "is very awkward in the hands of pious lords and reverend prelates." [12] He was not alone in thinking so. Lyttelton, evidently one of the pious lords in question, had signified his awareness of the anomaly by a statement in his preface that recalls Milton's invocation to Urania ("The meaning, not the Name I call"). "Elysium, Minos, Mercury, Charon, and Styx," Lyttelton explained, "being necessary Allegories in this way of writing, are occasionally used here, as they have been by Fontenelle and the Archbishop of Cambray: which (if it offended any critical or pious Ears) I would justify by the Declaration gravely annexed to the Works of all Italian Writers, wherein they use such Expressions: '*Se havessi nominato Fato, Fortuna, Destino, Elysio, Stige, &c. sono scherzi di penna poetica, non sentimenti di animo Catolico.*'" It seems significant that Lyttelton mentions Fénelon in his episcopal capacity, a sort of *imprimatur*.

Despite Lyttelton's proviso, he and other of his countrymen could not fully reconcile themselves to the genre's way of mingling trifling fictions with the most awful, sacred truths. Their dialogues tend to lean less heavily than Lucian's upon the myth of the underworld. Hades remains the setting for most (a few were zealously set in Heaven, where a person like Voltaire could be properly dealt with), but pious qualifications and unmistakably Christian sentiments sometimes intrude, "realistic" details about the setting become infrequent, and the gloom of Lucian's Hades is almost never invoked. This condition is not solely the result of authorial scruples, however, for many of the dialogues of the dead written in England are comparatively serious in subject and tone, less satires than dramatic meditations on history and ethics—like Lucian's dialogue (adapted from Livy 35.14) between Alexander, Hannibal, and Scipio, where one also finds small emphasis upon the setting. Also, there was the repressive threat of literalistic criticism, manifest in one reaction to a pleasing, genuinely Lucianic touch in Lyttelton's work, that of allowing a shade to complain of hunger. "Methinks," the critic remarked, "this making ghosts talk with so high a gout of good eating is not much unlike what it

---

[12] Anon. review of *A Dialogue in the Shades, between Mercury, a Nobleman, and a Mechanic, The English Review,* XXIV (July, 1794), 65.

would be to introduce two Italian heroes of the opera mutually complaining to each other of their unhappiness in not having lived in the time of Helen, Cleopatra, Thaiis, or Fryne." [13] In view of such reactions, it is not surprising that many eighteenth-century dialogues of the dead have all the animation of a Wedgwood frieze, and it is the more remarkable that many others are not so limited. Especially when the British dialogues lean toward comedy and satire, the props of Hades tend to reappear, sometimes the Lucianic spirit as well.

Besides illustrating the uses of Hades and the dead, Lucian also set forth the dramatic possibilities of the dialogue—if it is legitimate to speak of drama in this connection. On the page, a dialogue looks like a play; it has characters, the characters come into conflict, and so forth. But it is designed to be read or heard, not played, and this must have some effect upon its typical form and purpose.

One of the few critics to theorize about the dialogue, Herbert Read argued that it is at its best when not strikingly dramatic; that it ought to be used to represent the tranquil interplay of ideas discussed by characters who are less persons than the voices of differing opinions.[14] Since the dialogue only with difficulty tells about its setting or the physical actions of its characters, one must recognize its predilection for mental and vocal action, its inability to match the totality of representation available on a stage. And Read's theory suits one of his models, Berkeley, very well: the philosopher, with his imaginary Greeks conversing in English gardens, did indeed create exemplary dialogues in which an absence of realistic qualities and excitement complements the abstractness of his subject matter. Berkeley's dialogues approach absolute lucidity, transparency. But there is something Euclidian about the theory, which squares with the practice of a masterful writer yet can prevent us from relishing dialogues written in a different manner. Judging Lucian's performance by such a stand-

[13] Anonymous, *Candid and Critical Remarks on the Dialogues of the Dead: in a Letter from a Gentleman in London to His Friend in the Country* (London, 1760), p. 55.

[14] "The Dialogue," *Reason and Romanticism: Essays in Literary Criticism* (New York, 1963), pp. 139–57.

ard, as Read does, is a case of what Pope called "trying a man by the laws of one country, who acted by the laws of another."

Lucian's approach to the dialogue is best described with the help of a passage he wrote in a work called *The Double Indictment,* a passage useful also for description of the dialogue of the dead in general:

Nothing could be more unexpected than the charge Dialogue has brought against me. When I first took him in hand, he was regarded by the world at large as one whose interminable discussions had soured his temper and exhausted his vitality. His labours entitled him to respect, but he had none of the attractive qualities that could secure him popularity. My first step was to accustom him to walk upon the common ground like the rest of mankind; my next, to make him presentable, by giving him a good bath and teaching him to smile. Finally, I assigned him Comedy as his yokefellow, thus gaining him the confidence of his hearers, who until then would as soon have thought of picking up a hedgehog as of venturing into the thorny presence of Dialogue.[15]

Having small tolerance for abstractions, high seriousness, long-windedness, and the pale cast of thought (and also, it must be confessed, for the inevitable complexities of philosophy), Lucian and many others who wrote dialogues of the dead sometimes went out of their way to make their work concrete: to make their characters resemble people we might know, to give their settings tangibility, to keep their colloquies pointed and brief. They introduced a modicum of physical action through anecdotes and the exclamations of witnesses, and in Hades they found the most common ground of all. Instead of abetting the dialogue's tendency toward the abstract, they sought to compensate for it—a stratagem that may be seen as running against the grain, but need not be.

Despite its peculiarities and limitations, the dialogue is unquestionably a dramatic form, capable of incorporating a dramatic action. As Dryden had a character say in *An Essay of Dramatic Poesy,* "Every alternation or crossing of a design, every new-sprung passion, and turn of it, is a part of the action, and much the noblest, except we

[15] Lucian, III, 166.

conceive nothing to be action till they come to blows." [16] Most of Lucian's dialogues, and indeed most dialogues, set characters as well as ideas at cross purposes and result in some sort of resolution, either explicit or ironic. That is, most dialogues have a plot, but to find much of a plot in many of Lucian's brief dialogues would require excessive body-English. Some have none, an extreme case being Dialogue XI, in which Crates and Diogenes congratulate each other for living so wisely. The plot of others is minimal, dialogues in which there is conflict that is never resolved—or perhaps one should say never unresolved. When Menippus argues against Midas and his once-wealthy friends, the opponents refuse to give in, but the reader has no trouble deciding whom to favor. However, in several of the dialogues one finds complete little plots. The contest for supremacy between Alexander and Hannibal leads Scipio to propose himself as arbiter, suspense rising and then ending when Scipio, who defeated Hannibal and who defers to Alexander, rates Alexander first, himself second, and Hannibal third. In Dialogue XXIII, Protesilaus pleads with Pluto for permission to visit his bride, still alive; the pleas are in vain until Persephone intercedes. Again there is a measure of suspense, happily resolved by a reversal, and the product is a pleasant little comedy, the yoking of Comedy and Dialogue.

Though its imitation of conversation makes the dialogue an indirect means of presenting an author's own views, he can exploit this indirectness more or less fully. At one extreme, the simpler, he can use the dialogue merely to enliven prosaic matter or to camouflage his dogmatism. Especially if his purpose is the latter, the author will normally create a spokesman for himself, a character like Lucian's Menippus, whose comments alone would constitute a complete essay on the subject if some transitional statements were added. Whether or not the spokesman convinces the other characters hardly matters—they can be made to seem blind—but the anxious author will usually conclude the dialogue with assertions of enlightened general agreement. Much of the *Republic* works this way: a discourse by Soc-

[16] *Of Dramatic Poesy and Other Critical Essays,* ed. George Watson (London, 1962), I, 52.

rates that is spaced by his auditors' affirmations. Yet the form may be used more subtly, inviting and indeed requiring the reader to become a more than passive participant. Perhaps no spokesman is distinguishable, or perhaps the apparent spokesman confesses perplexity at the end, or seems overcome by his companions. In such cases the reader must follow the discussion intently, point by point, as he would a political debate, drawing his own provisional and final conclusions, assessing what the dialogue as a whole conveys. "You see it is a dialogue," wrote Dryden in the *Defence of An Essay,* "sustained by persons of several opinions, all of them left doubtful, to be determined by the readers in general," [17] just as the reader of Plato's early dialogues must interpret Socrates' confessions of ignorance and incompetence. In the *Meno,* for example, when Socrates throws up his hands over the question Meno has proposed, whether virtue can be taught, are we supposed to do so too? Probably not.[18] Such dialogues must be approached as one would the novels of Henry James, by maintaining utter vigilance and resisting casual acquiescence in any character's judgments. In many dialogues, what is shown is at least as important as what is told.

Some of Lucian's dialogues of the dead, brief as they are, operate in this way, for example the sixth and the thirtieth: Terpsion immediately stops complaining about his early death when Pluto tells him his earthly rivals, the would-be heirs of old Thucritus, will also die young while the wealthy old man grows older; the criminal Sostratus, sentenced to severe punishment, artfully lures his judge Minos across a series of slippery questions, finally pushing him into the admission that nobody deserves either punishment or reward in Hades: Fate determines everything. "Ah," sighs Minos, ". . . look closely enough, and you will find plenty of inconsistencies besides these." That is as far as Minos will go. He acquits Sostratus with the feeble admonition,

---

[17] *Ibid.,* I, 123.

[18] See Alexandre Koyré, *Discovering Plato,* trans. Leonora Cohen Rosenfield, Columbia Studies in Philosophy, No. 9 (New York, 1946), p. 17, and Elizabeth Merrill, *The Dialogue in English Literature,* Yale Studies in English, No. 42 (New York, 1911), p. 3.

"But mind, . . . you must not put it into other people's heads to ask questions of this kind."

These colloquies are dramatic in every sense, with actions standard in the drama, each concluding in an unexpected but well-founded turn of fortune. There is even something like what Aristotle called "recognition" in the behavior of Minos, who knows all the time what Sostratus is driving at but does not want to admit it—who finally, grudgingly gives in, driven to the wall by Sostratus' argument; indeed, what Aristotle classed as the fourth kind of recognition, that arrived at through reasoning,[19] is the dialogue's readiest means to dramatic development. And each of these two dialogues also says more than any character in them knows. Terpsion's experience makes the point that men are really unhappy only when suffering alone, a moral corollary to La Rochefoucauld's famous maxim and the verses it inspired Swift to write about his own death. Sostratus' experience demonstrates the absurdity of the classical afterlife, at least of the conjunction of belief in Fate with a system of posthumous reward and punishment, and ridicules Minos as a hypocritical, self-serving bureaucrat. Neither point is profound, but because the points are left palpably unsaid, for the reader to discover, they come home to him with force. Especially the point of the Minos-Sostratus dialogue, traditionally the last in the *Dialogues of the Dead;* Lucian destroying his sets, the insubstantial play finished.

In the light of these comprehensively ironic dialogues, I may slightly revise my description of Lucian's most typical pieces, those in which Menippus or one of his surrogates speaks out against the foolish and the corrupt. A central device, both of the dialogue and of comedy, is the confrontation of *alazon* and *eiron*,[20] of the boastful, self-deceiving man and the self-deprecating, intelligent man given to questioning and understatement, of a Meno and a Socrates. There is no lack of boastful, deluded characters in Lucian, but except in the

---

[19] *Poetics* 1455a.

[20] Northrop Frye, *Anatomy of Criticism* (Princeton, 1957), p. 172. For remarks on the dialogue of the dead, see p. 310.

Sostratus dialogue, the traditional ironic character is rare. Instead we have another boaster, a *justified* boaster, whose outspokenness must be distinguished from his rectitude. By earthly standards, the ones at our disposal, the cynics stand at a distance from the mean or the good, and hence even in the most straightforward of Lucian's dialogues it is the action of the whole, not just the words of the favored spokesman, that constitutes the dialogue's thesis. There is a measure of irony in the displacement of the traditional *eiron*. It gives Lucian's dialogues a tough, somewhat desperate over-all tone; we can hardly be expected to sympathize entirely with their comedy of derision, a comedy sometimes reminiscent of Molière's.

This quality of Lucian's dialogues of the dead is less evident in most of his other works and should be seen, I think, as a consequence of the genre itself: a shadow is bound to fall across characters thinking and speaking in the nether world. Lucian was no doubt aware that a looking-glass setting, especially an eternal, macabre one, emphasizes the complexity, impermanence, and inscrutability of phenomena. It turns a man back upon himself in his search for what is stable, encouraging him to settle for a simple, practical code: knowing oneself, accepting oneself, remaining "lowly wise," regulating one's desires by realistic expectations, being skeptical about intellectual panaceas, bearing and enduring. Such a world promotes irony, which shows that things are different from, usually inferior to, what they seem to be. A Happy Valley, if it exists on earth at all, lies within the patient, disciplined man, the man who can bring himself to return from Houyhnhnmland with equanimity. "To reason right is to submit," as Pope put it in *An Essay on Man*. This ethical attitude attracted many eighteenth-century writers, and the suitability of the dialogue of the dead for propagandizing it *sub specie aeternitatis* is perhaps the main reason for the widespread revival of the genre— not, as Johan S. Egilsrud says, the broader reason that the dialogue flourishes in periods of political and intellectual ferment.[21]

[21] *Le "Dialogue des morts" dans les littératures française, allemande et anglaise (1644–1789)* (Paris, 1934), pp. 23–24.

"And among the Moderns Fenelon, Archbishop of Cambray, and Monsieur Fontenelle"—they too must be mentioned here, as important forerunners of the English writers and especially as representatives of differing approaches to the genre. Bernard le Bovier de Fontenelle published the *Nouveaux Dialogues des morts* in 1683, a work comprising two sets of six "Dialogues des morts anciens," six "Dialogues des morts anciens avec les modernes," and six "Dialogues des morts modernes." As the divisions imply, some dialogues bear on the ancients-moderns controversy that would really erupt some years later; Fontenelle was not one to magnify the value of ancient accomplishments. He deliberately imitated Lucian in part, or so he says in the prefatory letter addressed "A Lucien aux Champs Elysées," explaining that he will copy Lucian's practice of making the dead moralize. But he will do without Charon, Pluto, and the infernal mythology, and also, unlike Lucian, he will use only facts in characterizing his shades. In short, the prefatory letter suggests that Fontenelle's will be a staid performance.

One need not read many of his dialogues to find out otherwise; the first serves for illustration, a dialogue between Alexander and Phryne the courtesan. Lucian had employed Alexander in three dialogues: the twelfth, in which Scipio pronounced him the world's greatest military leader; the thirteenth, in which Diogenes ridicules his inextinguishable pride and greed; and the fourteenth, in which his father criticizes him for comparing his own exploits with the gods'. The severe criticism of the latter two dialogues seems tempered by the praise of the first, but in Fontenelle's dialogue Alexander is abused. He needed mighty armies to conquer men, Phryne argues; she could conquer all by herself. And Phryne behaved constructively, offering to rebuild with her earnings the walls of Thebes which Alexander had destroyed. Here and throughout the *Nouveaux Dialogues* we are treated to recurrent, soon rather predictable exercises in intellectual burlesque—as Fontenelle seems to have realized. A year later, in 1684, he published a long, two-part narrative, *Jugement de Pluton sur les Dialogues des morts,* in which he anonymously and ironically attacked his work, at one point allowing Aristotle to object: "Dans les *Nouveaux Dialogues* c'est une règle infaillible que vous trouverez toujours tout renversé. Du moment que vous voyez ensemble un sage et un fou, assurez-vous que le fou sera au-dessus du sage." [22] There is truth in the complaint.

Paragons topple in Fontenelle's dialogues and with them practically all illusions about human greatness, even human dignity. Lucian, it is true, had set prickly plain-talkers in opposition to deluded men, and the latter were dealt with harshly. His cynics are not entirely attractive. But their message is clearly "Know thyself"— Menippus even says so in Dialogue II. In Fontenelle, on the other hand, we are as much as told that the more we know about ourselves, the unhappier we are likely to be. His basic technique in most of these capricious, ubiquitously paradoxical dialogues is very like that appropriate to the descent narrative: turning everything upside down. A shrewd realization of this affinity probably led him to eschew Hades' props, since themes like his were close to those of outright burlesque. To avoid it, he created sophisticated conversations on morals and manners, which, ending in unconventional "turns," would unsettle received opinions, promote skepticism, and entertain the enlightened.

A quite different purpose moved François de Salignac de la Mothe-Fénelon to write dialogues of the dead. Between 1689 and 1699, while responsible for directing the education of the young Duke of Burgundy, Fénelon wrote them occasionally as a teaching aid, not to be published: seventy-nine dialogues in all, though twelve have at least one "living" speaker. Four were published in 1700, an edition of forty-five in 1712, all not until 1823. Perhaps needless to say, they are graver than Fontenelle's, designed to affirm and refine traditional ideas about morals and our famous ancestors. The setting of Hades is prominent and characters like Charon and Mercury ap-

---

[22] "Jugement de Pluton," *Nouveaux Dialogues des morts,* ed. Donald Schier, University of North Carolina Studies in the Romance Languages and Literatures, No. 55 (Chapel Hill, n.d.), pp. 195–96.

Chapter II

Charon Disinterred: Seventeenth-Century English Dialogues of the Dead

See Cromwell, damn'd to everlasting fame!

—*An Essay on Man*

But where as he faineth to talke with the princes in
hel, that I am sure will be mislyked, because it is most
certayne, that some of their soules be in heauen.

—*The Mirrour for Magistrates*

Those splenetic partisans of modern learning, Richard
Bentley and William Wotton, provoked not just Swift's *Battle of the
Books* but also the first series of Hadean dialogues written by an Englishman: *Dialogues of the Dead. Relating to the present Controversy
Concerning the Epistles of Phalaris* (1699). The author, one of several with the same name, was William King (1663–1712), remembered now as a minor satirist and an associate of those who produced
numbers of the *Examiner* before Swift became its regular author. Another in that circle, Matthew Prior, was to write four dialogues of the
dead, but since Prior's collection remained unpublished until 1907, to
King belongs more of the credit for making this an English genre.
His popularity survived long enough for Johnson to include a brief
biography among the *Lives of the Poets;* the dialogues were reprinted
in King's *Miscellanies,* an undated volume of 1708 or 1709, and in

his *Original Works* (1776). There was at least one imitation, an alleged second part.

Why did King choose such an uncommon literary form? His works carry no explanation. Perhaps the idea came without much forethought, the way the beginning of the *Iliad* occurred to the Homer whom Lucian questions in the *True History*. It is tempting to say that Fontenelle's *Nouveaux Dialogues des morts* affected King's decision (none of Fénelon's colloquies had been published when King's appeared). But the English author, a learned man whom Oxford had granted a doctorate in Civil Law, may have drawn his inspiration directly from Lucian—or from certain Lucianic tendencies in seventeenth-century English writing, so nicely do they converge on the dialogue of the dead as King and later authors knew it. And the peculiar occasion of King's dialogues, the dispute with Bentley and Wotton, could itself have recommended a genre which permits the ancients to comment on modern affairs, which gives Phalaris an opportunity to discuss the authorship of the *Epistles*. In the pages that follow, before looking closely at King's dialogues, I shall attempt to trace the recovery of this ancient form in England during the years surrounding the Restoration.

That the English imported the dialogue of the dead from France is an inference promoted by the most comprehensive history of the form. Johan S. Egilsrud, who mentions no English works preceding King's, calls Fontenelle's dialogues "l'œuvre destinée à influencer le plus directement d'autres auteurs, tant étrangers que français, en désignant cette forme à leurs propres essais." [1] A prodigious reader, King must have known Fontenelle's work. King's editor, John Nichols, said that "nothing of the humourous kind escaped his notice," [2] and indeed, few English readers could have failed to notice the dialogues of Fontenelle. A partial translation was published in 1683, the year they appeared in France. The next year, another incomplete

---

[1] *Le "Dialogue des morts" dans les littératures française, allemande et anglaise (1644–1789)* (Paris, 1934), p. 43.

[2] *The Original Works of William King, LL.D.* (London, 1776), I, xxvii ("Memoirs of Dr. King").

translation came forth, as well as a continuation of the first.[3] The dialogues drew enough attention for the publisher of a 1688 translation of *Entretiens sur la pluralité des mondes* to advertise it, on the title page, as "by the Author of the *Dialogues of the Dead*," while in the short "Life of Lucian" Dryden composed during the 1690s he proclaimed Fontenelle the best imitator of Lucian in French, "in his *Dialogues of the Dead;* which I never read but with a new pleasure." [4] Swift read the dialogues too, at Moor Park, in about 1697.[5] And there can be no doubting Fontenelle's power to attract imitators: John Hughes's translation of the *Nouveaux Dialogues* (1708) contains two of the translator's own colloquies. But nothing inside or outside William King's *Dialogues of the Dead,* except its having been written later, implies any debt to Fontenelle.

The French dialogues found a cordial welcome in England, where Lucian's were already quite at home, in English as well as Greek. What may be called Lucian's "extra" dialogue of the dead, *Voyage to the Lower World,* was translated by Francis Hickes and published in 1634. Thomas Heywood's translation of five of Lucian's dialogues of the dead, in verse, came three years later, in 1637, and in 1638 Jasper Mayne put ten into English prose. But Mayne's translation was not printed until 1663, when it was published jointly with another edition of Hickes's. In 1684–85 appeared the first English version of Lucian's *Works,* the earlier of these years bringing forth a separate, miscellaneous collection, in verse, containing eleven of the dialogues of the dead.[6] As the seventeenth century waned, much evidence be-

---

[3] Benjamin Boyce, "News from Hell: Satiric Communications with the Nether World in English Writing of the Seventeenth and Eighteenth Centuries," *PMLA,* LVIII (1943), 431–32. *The Infernal Observator . . .* (1684) is still another translation of Fontenelle (unidentified as such by Boyce and attributed mistakenly to Luke Beaulieu) according to D. M. Lang, "Fontenelle and the Infernal Observator," *MLR,* XLV (1950), 222–25.

[4] *Of Dramatic Poesy and Other Critical Essays,* ed. George Watson (London, 1962), II, 211. The translation of *Entretiens* was John Glanvill's.

[5] A. C. Guthkelch and D. Nichol Smith, eds., *A Tale of a Tub . . . ,* by Jonathan Swift, 2d ed. (Oxford, 1958), p. lvi; cf. p. 365.

[6] Francis Hickes, trans., "The Infernall Ferrie, Or The Tyrant," *Certain Select Dialogues of Lucian . . .* (Oxford, 1634), pp. 71–88. Thomas Heywood, *Pleasant Dialogues and Dramma's,* ed. W. Bank (Louvain, 1903), pp. 123–39. Jasper

came available to confirm Robert Burton's assertion, in *The Anatomy of Melancholy,* that "almost all posterity admire Lucian's luxuriant wit." [7]

Posterity could read Lucian in Latin too. Erasmus' translation of thirteen of the dialogues of the dead circulated widely,[8] also his own *Colloquia,* where one finds a dialogue evidently derived from Lucian's fourth—with a twist. A disconsolate Charon figures in both, in Lucian lamenting the scarcity of passengers (really their fares) and in Erasmus complaining that the hordes killed in Christendom's wars have sunk his boat. This Lucianic colloquy was known to many seventeenth-century Englishmen: a translation of the entire *Colloquia* appeared in 1671, and later Sir Roger L'Estrange translated a selection, the edition of 1689 including the dialogue set in Hades.[9] Here is his rendition of a passage in which Alastor, like Lucian's Mercury, quizzes Charon:

> I thought you had carry'd Shadows only, not Bodies. What may be the Weight, I prethee, of a Cargo of Ghosts?
> *Charon.* Why, let 'em be as Light as Water-Spiders, there may be enow of them to do a bodies Work. But then my Vessel is a kind of a Phantome too.
> *Alastor.* I have seen the time, when you had as many Ghosts as you could Stow a-Bord; and Three or Four Thousand more hanging at the Stern, and your Barque me thought never so much as felt on't.

Mayne, trans., *Part of Lucian Made English from the Originall. In the Yeare 1638. . . . To which are adjoyned those other Dialogues of Lucian as they were formerly translated by Mr Francis Hicks* (Oxford, 1663), pp. 47–66. Ferrand Spence, trans., *Lucian's Works . . . ,* 5 vols. (London, 1684–85): "Dialogues of the Dead," I, 133–86; "The Tyrant: or the Infernal Ferry," II, 45–62. *Lucians Dialogues, (Not) from the Greek: Done into English Burlesque* (London, 1684), Part I, pp. 5–10, 13–20; Part II, pp. 1–2, 5–13; evidently based on Spence's translation (see Part II, p. iv).

[7] *The Anatomy of Melancholy,* ed. A. R. Shilleto (London, 1893), I, 84.

[8] Hardin Craig, "Dryden's Lucian," *Classical Philology,* XVI (1921), 141. C. R. Thompson, *The Translations of Lucian by Erasmus and St. Thomas More* (Ithaca, N.Y., 1940), pp. 16, 22.

[9] "Hell Broke Loose. Col. XXI," *Twenty Two Select Colloquies Out of Erasmus Roterodamus. . . . The second Impression . . . with the Addition of two Colloquies to the Former* (London, 1689), pp. 265–72. The earlier translation was *The Colloquies, or Familiar Discourses of Desiderius Erasmus of Roterdam, Rendered into English. . . . By H. M. Gent.* (London, 1671), where this dialogue occupies pp. 403–7.

Charon. That is all according as the Ghosts are: For your Hectical, phthisical Souls, that go off in a Consumption, weigh little or nothing. But
those that are Torn out of Bodies, in a Habit of Foul Humours; as in
Apoplexyes, Quinzies, Fevers, and the like: But most of all, in the
Chance of War: These, I must tell ye, carry a great deal of Corpulent,
and gross matter, along with them.

Alastor. As for the Spaniards, and the French, methinks they should not
be very Heavy.

Charon. No not comparatively with Others: And yet I do not find them
altogether so Light as Feathers, neither. But for the Brittains, and the
Germans, that are rank Feeders, I had only Ten of 'em a-Bord once,
and if I had not Lighten'd my Boat of part of my Lading, we had all
gone to the Bottom.

When Alastor asks whether Charon cannot build another boat, the
reader discovers that "the woods that were in Elyzium, are all destroy'd: Not so much as a stick left . . . with burning Hereticks
Ghosts." Shades, it turns out, are combustible as well as weighty!
This is an exemplary dialogue of the dead. As Thomas Brown said in
the preface to a later edition of L'Estrange's translation, Erasmus captured Lucian's "Graces with such Success, that 'tis difficult to say
which of the two is the Original" [10]—a comment addressed to the
Colloquia in general but fully pertinent to the conversation wherein
Charon speaks. Dryden, in the "Life of Lucian," called Erasmus the
best imitator in Latin.[11] Though many topical references date the colloquy, a spirit of playful, slightly macabre absurdity like Lucian's, as
in the passage quoted, animates the moralist's point.

No more than Erasmus did Englishmen need Fontenelle's example
to write dialogues of the dead. Long before Fontenelle wrote anything, even before his century of life began, an original dialogue of
the dead had been published in England: *A Description of the Passage of Thomas late Earle of Strafford, over the River of Styx, with
the conference betwixt him, Charon, and William Noy* (1641). Here,
in a congenial Hades, Strafford may reasonably anticipate relaxing in
what promises to be an eternity of lighthearted, mildly satirical con-

[10] "The Life of Erasmus," *Twenty Select Colloquies Out of Erasmus Roterodamus. . . . To which are added, Seven New Colloquies . . .* (London, 1699), sig.
b6ᵛ.

[11] *Of Dramatic Poesy and Other Critical Essays,* II, 211.

versation. The anonymous author wrote with Lucian in mind. At one point, when Strafford laments the abundance of "Mercury's"—that is, periodical writers—spewing forth lampoons on earth, Noye has some practical advice: "They may doe well to read Lucian, he will teach their Pamphlets wit and innocence."

But to write dialogues of the dead, an Englishman of Dryden's time need not have known the work of any foreigner—Lucian, Fontenelle, or Erasmus. The period teemed with controversy, much of it religious in one way or another and disposing satirists not just to ridicule or revile their enemies but to damn them, to drive them into Hell, and to dwell gloatingly upon their supposed behavior among devils and the scoundrels of former days.[12] The best known of such works, Donne's *Ignatius His Conclave* (1611), represents most in that the words of its speakers—Loyola, Machiavelli, and other contestants for supremacy among the damned—lie embedded in narrative, here the account of a dream. When men of the mid-seventeenth century chose to create outright dialogues on subjects infernal, their productions tended to resemble Donne's more than Lucian's; for example, the characters of *Cromwels Complaint of Injustice: or, His Dispute with Pope Alexander the Sixth, for Precedency in Hell,* published as late as 1681, also strive to become Satan's second in command. In this and other such vindictive, generally cheerless, thoroughly occasional dialogues, characters from classical mythology seldom appear, ancients never.[13] Almost all the speakers are English-

[12] Boyce's "News from Hell" is an admirable short history of such satire, though his long bibliography could be readily extended today with the aid of Donald Wing's *Short-Title Catalogue,* not published when Boyce wrote. In seeking to complement his article, I have concentrated on infernal satire in the specific form of dialogues; I have not reproduced information Boyce gives about works closely related to the dialogue of the dead, for example the brief poems like Herrick's "Charon and Phylomel." And one particular reply may be made: the issues Boyce examined of the periodical *Mercurius Infernus* . . . (1680), which he classified among "direct imitations of . . . Menippean dialogues" (p. 417), are such in subject only; they are not dialogues.

[13] *Bradshaw's Ghost: Being a Dialogue Between the said Ghost, and an Apparition of the late King Charles* . . . (n.p., 1659), *A Parly Between The Ghosts of the Late Protector, and the King of Sweden, At their Meeting in Hell* (London, 1660), *A Satyr, By way of Dialogue Between Lucifer, and the Ghosts of Shaftsbury*

men whose funeral meats have scarcely cooled, if, considering the near ubiquity of disinterred Cromwell, a still more disquieting image is not in order. The setting remains Donne's Hell, a medieval inferno with no tincture of Hades about it, and the prevalence of characters regarded as villainous emphasizes that fact even when the locale goes nameless or is loosely called Elysium.[14]

However, though closely related to these works, several dialogues of the mid-seventeenth century illustrate significant departures from them—not, it seems, because the innovators imitated Lucian directly but because they sought effects which the Hellish manner could not supply. Cromwell speaks in one, *A Dialogue Betwixt the Ghosts of Charls the I, Late King of England: and Oliver The late Usurping Protector* (1659), an eight-page pamphlet that gives Charles the opening words:

> Tell me who thou art that thus presumest to disturb the Ashes of one that hath been at rest this ten years.
> *Oliver.* It is he that sent thee to that Rest, who now would fain be at rest himself, but cannot.
> *Charles.* Ha! what doth mine eyes behold, that grand Rebell and Traitor which was the destruction of me and my Family, I command thee to be gone; Was it not enough that in my life time by thy open force, and thy cunning and secret Plots, thou and thy Emissaries took away my life, and extirpated my Family, and the Lord knows what ruine thou hast brought upon the poor Kingdomes, that I once happily Governed, but that thou must now pursue me after Death.

---

and Russell (London, 1683), and *A Dialogue Betwixt the Devil and the Whigs* (n.p., 1684) are all set squarely in Hell, the destination of everyone in *A New Meeting of Ghosts at Tyburn. Being A Discourse of Oliver Cromwell. John Bradshaw. . . .* (London, 1660). Additional examples might be given.

[14] Two dialogues in verse hover uncertainly between Hell and Hades: *Bradshaw's Ghost; A Poem: or, A Dialogue between John Bradshaw, Ferry-man Charon, Oliver Cromwel, Francis Ravilliack, and Ignatius Loyola* (n.p., 1660), where Bradshaw becomes "Lord President of Hell" but Charon has a prominent part and Pluto is mentioned; and *A Dialogue between Anthony Earl of Shaftsbury, and Captain Thomas Walcott, Upon their Meeting in Pluto's Kingdome* (London, 1683), where the setting is at one time called Hell, at another Elysium. A third poem, more securely set in Hades—*Pluto, the Prince of Darkness, His Entertainment of Coll. Algernoon Sidney, Upon His Arrival at the Infernal Palace. . . .* (London, 1684)—is a broadside ballad.

Oliver. O Sir, Pray forgive me, for you cannot imagine the tortures of conscience that I indure, when I call to mind all my ambitious and damnable Plots, to ruine you and yours, and to set my self in your stead; It was I that laid the Plot to draw your Subjects obedience from you, under pretence of Religion and Liberty; It was I that after we had Routed your Army . . . , by my dam'd Policy and Power, broke off the Treaty, and all to get the Government my self.

Crude though it is, this amounts to a dialogue of the dead as the genre was understood during the eighteenth century. Cromwell speaks here, as he does in other, more conventional dialogues of the years following his death, and he is clearly a damned soul. "Hold my pains come on me," he exclaims at the end; "I must leave you, and repair to my Station." But the dialogue is more than just an exercise in literary damnation. Cromwell does not speak with another of his kind; his companion is a good man. Hence the setting of the dialogue cannot be Hell, and accordingly, nothing is said about its identity; Cromwell and Charles speak in a vacuum, an unspecified place where two shades may converse without raising distracting questions in the reader's mind.[15] As noted in the preceding chapter, a like setting, or lack of it, occurs in many eighteenth-century dialogues, particularly those which are soberly "historical" in tone and subject. Styx, in modern times at least, runs toward burlesque: Lyttelton mentions the river, the ferry, Charon, the infernal judges in humorous dialogues like the one involving an English duelist and an American Indian, but in his most serious conversations, like that between Louis XIV and Peter the Great, he tends to ignore the speakers' surroundings. The seventeenth-century author, by choosing to make Cromwell confront the good, saved man he had wronged, achieved a measure of poignancy —a quality foreign to the Hellish manner. And the same may be

---

[15] Another, more spiteful and conventional dialogue of the same year has Charles in Heaven speaking with Cromwell in Hell: *The Court Career, Death Shaddow'd to life. Or Shadowes of Life and Death. A Pasquil Dialogue* . . . (n.p., 1659), with double-paneled frontispiece I wish I could reproduce here! Still another work, resembling the *Julius exclusus* often attributed to Erasmus, represents the celestial rejection of several souls later snatched by Rhadamanthus: *News from Heaven: or A Dialogue between S. Peter and the Five Jesuits last Hang'd* . . . (n.p., n.d.); dated 1679 by Boyce, "News from Hell," p. 430.

said of another, earlier dialogue of the dead, its title a generous account of the contents: *Strange Apparitions, or The Ghost of King James, With a late conference between the ghost of that good King, the Marquesse Hameltons, and George Eglishams, Doctor of Physick, unto which appeared the Ghost of the late Duke of Buckingham concerning the death and poysoning of King James and the rest* (1642). A slight tie with the prevailing manner of infernal satire—the use of a narrator—becomes apparent only in the last line of the last page.

These two works are not alone in displaying a potentiality for change within the Hellish tradition. Charles I had spoken with Henry VIII in a Latin dialogue of 1657, *Nvntius a Mortvis . . .*, attributed to the royalist divine Richard Perrinchief (1623?–1673) and translated in 1658 as *A Messenger From the Dead . . .*, which begins with Henry's exclamation: "Say! Who are thou that presumest by a Sacrilegious Impiety to disturb the ashes of a King, which so many years have been at rest?"—words too much like those beginning the dialogue between Charles and Cromwell for a reader to overlook the dependence of the 1659 work upon the earlier. Another dialogue of 1659, *A New Conference Between the Ghosts of King Charles and Oliver Cromvvell,* is a sequel to those works. It begins with Charles asking "How now! who's this that disturbeth my dust, at Rest now some years?" to which Cromwell replies, "I am one that gave thee no Rest when we lived together upon the Earth," and there are further clear echoes of the other dialogue between Charles and Oliver. More interesting than any line of influence, however, are the differences characterizing these pieces, for they were written to serve quite varying purposes. The first dialogue, antimonarchical in spirit, has Henry arguing that Charles's fall exemplifies the biblical lamentation about the visiting of a father's sins upon his children: Charles was not on the whole a bad man, had nevertheless to suffer, but— unlike Henry—will be saved. The first dialogue between Charles and Cromwell, as we have seen, somewhat sympathetically condemns the Protector for his sins; the second dialogue between Charles and Cromwell depicts both unfavorably, the one a fool and the other a knave, and ends with the speakers agreeing that some good has been accomplished in spite of them, as an unforeseen result of their machinations: Parliament has learned that it must never again permit the army to be controlled by one man, whatever his title. The anti-monarchical dialogue takes place in Windsor Chapel, casting a harsh religious light upon the sinfulness of Henry and of Charles. The more compassionate, royalist dialogue, set in neither Heaven nor Hell but implying the existence of both, allows damned Cromwell some respite in which to speak his repentance with relative spontaneity; actual torment would, traditionally, have hardened his heart. And the parliamentarian dialogue, crying plague upon the houses of both Charles and Cromwell, neither describes nor hints at the nature of its setting but accents its pragmatic political philosophy by concentrating almost wholly on secular affairs. Significantly, the most conventional and religious of these dialogues, Henry and Charles in Windsor Chapel, contains several interpolated passages of the author's narration. There is none in the other two pieces, where the speakers, temporarily or permanently emancipated from the dominance of religious standards, speak more or less empirically, for themselves.

Later, between the publication of Fontenelle's dialogues, in 1683, and that of King's, in 1699, several original dialogues of the dead were composed in England, but none may be traced with certainty to Fontenelle's precedent. Indeed, one work of this time seems to represent, as on a diptych, the transition from the seventeenth century's Hellish ways to those of Lucian, Erasmus, King, and the eighteenth-century writers: *Nuncius Infernalis: or, A New Account From Below. In Two Dialogues. The First From the Elizium Fields, Of Friendship. The Second From Hell of Cuckoldom, Being the Sessions of Cuckolds. By Charles Gildon, Gent. With a Preface by Mr. Durfey* (1692). In the second dialogue, patterned on Machiavelli's *Belphagor,* Lucifer briefly interrogates many of the newly dead—Italians, Spaniards, Frenchmen, beaus, parsons, poets—and learns that each incurred damnation somehow as a result of his wife's infidelity. Then, after dismissing the cuckolds to horrible quarters in Hell, Lucifer proclaims "a general Play-day and Jubilee" for the devils: "Let none therefore loiter away his time in tempting the Marry'd, for one Woman will out-do a Legion of you." Brimstone steams from these pages; from those of the first dialogue, however, the scent is of asphodels. Just returned from a transmigration during which he lived as an Englishman, Timon of Athens criticizes modern Europeans, concluding that true friendship is now impossible, whereupon he and Laelius reminisce about what friendship was in antiquity. "The First is the more gravely severe, and a nearer Imitation of Lucian (who is an Author esteem'd by all the Ingenious Worthy to be imitated)," Thomas D'Urfey commented, going on to compare the first dialogue with Lucian's employing Alexander and Hannibal, the twelfth in the *Dialogues of the Dead.* Somewhat more guardedly, Gildon observed in the dedicatory epistle that "Lucian himself . . . first gave me the Hint of introducing the Dead, as Interlocutors; and in that only have I imitated him."

But the "Ingenious" mentioned by D'Urfey, would they not have esteemed Fontenelle as well as Lucian? Did Gildon owe something to Fontenelle? The question calls for a complicated answer. In the dedicatory epistle, Gildon asserts that when he wrote he had yet to read —not Fontenelle, who goes unmentioned, but "the incomparable Boileau." Boileau had written a dialogue of the dead, *Les Héros de roman,* during the 1660s, and it had been published in 1688, in an unauthorized edition.[16] Pluto questions and embarrasses a train of affected characters from contemporary romances, much as Lucifer does the cuckolds in Gildon's second dialogue. But *Les Héros,* untranslated until 1700, not published in an authorized edition until 1713, was never to have much effect on English authors.[17] It is unlikely that Gildon had Boileau's dialogue in mind, for he goes on to say that "we

---

[16] Thomas Frederick Crane, ed., *Les Héros de roman: dialogue de Nicolas Boileau-Despréaux* (Boston, 1902), pp. 27, 37–38 (Introduction).

[17] Boyce, "News from Hell," p. 416; Crane, p. 165*n.* One possible exception, a long, dreary dialogue of the dead called *The Heroes of France: in a Dialogue between Monsieur De Lovois, Colbert, Seignelai, Montchevreuil, Sarsfield and Waldeck. Relating To the Present State of Affairs . . .* (London, 1694), seems to be a translation from the French; see *British Museum General Catalogue of Printed Books,* LXXVII (1961), 1167.

may perceive some Glimmerings of the Beauty and Witt of that Great Man, through the abominable Jargon of his Scotch Translator." Gildon, it seems, meant *The Infernal Observator* . . . (1684), a translation of Fontenelle with a title page identifying the author as "Mr. Boileau," the translator being one Alexander Fraser.[18] As for Gildon's disclaimer, I think it should be believed. His comments suggest only a slight acquaintance with Fontenelle's work, which he does not seem to have read in French, and there is no hint of Fontenelle in Gildon's "classical" dialogue. What is more, there is evidence that Gildon was independently drawn to Lucian: he contributed to the translation of Lucian's works, begun in the 1690s but not published until 1710–11, which contains the "Life" by Dryden.[19] As claimed, it was probably Lucian's example which prompted Gildon's use of dead speakers; in other respects, the dialogue between Timon and Laelius derives from Cicero's *Laelius,* with which it shares Cicero's eponymous character, the subject of friendship, the form of dialogue, and a solemn tone. *Laelius,* it may be observed, had been given some special prominence by a translation issued a year before Gildon's pamphlet.[20]

The last dialogue of the dead to be noticed before King's—and, except for several in his collection, surely the most memorable produced in England during the seventeenth century—is "The Calendar Reform'd: or, A pleasant Dialogue between Pluto and the Saints in the Elysian Fields after Lucian's manner. Written by Sir Fl. Sh——rd in the Year 1687," the title it bore when first printed, some six years after Fleetwood Sheppard's death, in 1704.[21] The author was a prominent courtier under Charles II; it was in quest of Sheppard that the Earl of Dorset came to the Rhenish Wine Tavern on the day he discovered young Matthew Prior.[22] But Sheppard had small affection

---

[18] Lang, pp. 222–25.   [19] Craig, p. 159.

[20] *Cicero's Lælius. A Discourse of Friendship. Together with a Pastoral Dialogue Concerning Friendship and Love* (London, 1691).

[21] For the suggestion that Thomas Brown may have retouched Sheppard's dialogue while editing this volume, see Benjamin Boyce, *Tom Brown of Facetious Memory: Grub Street in the Age of Dryden,* Harvard Studies in English, XXI (Cambridge, Mass., 1939), 17*n.*

[22] Charles Kenneth Eves, *Matthew Prior, Poet and Diplomatist* (New York, 1939), pp. 14–15.

for James—or James's religion, as "The Calendar Reform'd" makes plain. Written, it seems, during the year of *The Hind and the Panther,* Sheppard's dialogue wittily probes the more legendary recesses of Roman Catholic hagiography, and though the presence of so many patently Christian souls in his Elysium recalls older controversial pieces, outrightly Lucianic elements preponderate. Pluto examines the long-dead saints:

. . . Where were you Born?

St. George. Some say in Cappadocia, others in Coventry.

Pluto. Why truly Coventry lies very near Cappadocia. But what a plague, can't you tell where you were Born?

St. George. —And others have affirm'd, that Alexandria in Ægypt was the place of my Nativity: For my part I cannot precisely tell where I was Born, but that I was Born somewhere or other, I hope your Majesty has the Charity to believe.

English St. George's being here in addition to such as the hapless St. Ursula demonstrates that Sheppard's skepticism comprehended more than just the beliefs of the Roman Catholic party, that his purpose had something in common with the "Scoffer" Lucian's (an epithet Charles Cotton employed in the title of his 1675 burlesque of that author). Anyone familiar with Lucian's thirtieth dialogue of the dead, in which Sostratus cannily pursues Minos into the admission that his system of reward and punishment is absurd, will find little new in Sheppard's tactics. Though the statement about "Lucian's manner" in the title may be an editor's addition, it is accurate enough.

William King's *Dialogues of the Dead,* then, was not unprecedented in England. Nor is the later popularity of this seemingly obscure genre unaccountable: it flourished from traceable roots in seventeenth-century English writing, nourished by the eighteenth century's preoccupation with classical literature and the moral uses of history, with satire, eschatology, and the dialogue form. Over 1500 dialogues of various kinds were printed in England between 1640 and 1750,[23] while increasing disbelief in, or at least de-emphasis of, the doctrine

---

[23] B. V. Crawford, "The Prose Dialogue of the Commonwealth and the Restoration," *PMLA,* XXXIV (1919), 601.

of eternal damnation [24] moved writers to forsake Hellish satire and disposed readers to accept the literary rediscovery of Hades. It was Lucian's dialogues, more than Fontenelle's, that attracted English imitation. But chiefly, the genre exercised its own magnetism, inviting authors to show Cromwell repentant and saints incredible, and to allow Laelius and Phalaris a few posthumous observations at the expense of modern manners and learning.

Why William King wrote is plain enough, far more so than his reason for choosing Lucian's genre. He wrote to strike a blow against Bentley in the English phase of the international Quarrel of the Ancients and Moderns. Phalaris' epistles, those traditionally attributed to the Sicilian tyrant of the sixth century B.C., had been cited by Sir William Temple, in his *Essay upon the Ancient and Modern Learning* (1690), to support the assertion that "the oldest Books we have are still in their kind the best." Four years later, William Wotton's *Reflections upon Ancient and Modern Learning* contested the supremacy of the ancients. To the second edition (1697), Richard Bentley appended a treatise on the epistles of Phalaris and other classical figures, a work superseded in 1699 by Bentley's monumental, independently published *Dissertation upon the Epistles of Phalaris. With an Answer to the Objections of the Honourable Charles Boyle, Esquire,* in which he proved conclusively that the epistles were neither genuine nor so old as Temple had supposed. Rather, they were a "cheat" perpetrated by an anonymous "Sophist." [25] Charles Boyle, Bentley's chief opponent, had become a party to the quarrel by producing an edition of Phalaris' epistles (1695) which attacked Bentley, the keeper of the Royal Library, for recalling a manuscript before Boyle's collator had finished using it. When Bentley gave his own account of the matter in the 1697 dissertation, Boyle responded by publishing a volume called *Dr. Bentley's . . . Dissertation Examin'd* (1698), now re-

---

[24] See D. P. Walker, *The Decline of Hell: Seventeenth-Century Discussions of Eternal Torment* (Chicago, 1964).

[25] *Works,* ed. Alexander Dyce, 2 vols. (London, 1836–38), II, 127; I, 89. Subsequent parenthetical references in my text are to this edition.

membered as the spear which, according to the *Battle of the Books,* skewered Bentley and Wotton like a brace of woodcocks. Bentley called the volume a "rhapsody of errors and calumnies" (I, xlix).

Here King pricked Bentley's spleen. An advocate at Doctors' Commons, King had been appointed secretary to the then Princess Anne after defending the homeland of her consort with *Animadversions* upon Robert Molesworth's *Account of Denmark* (1694), had displayed his wit in a parody of Dr. Martin Lister's *Journey to Paris in the Year 1698,* and was an alumnus of Boyle's College, Christ Church, Oxford, which Bentley had not spared while excoriating the editor of the epistles (I, xlii). To Boyle's examination of Bentley, King contributed a letter illustrating the latter's "Pride and Insolence." [26] Aetna-like, Bentley addressed King in the 1699 dissertation: "But let us hear the Dr.'s testimony; the air and spirit of it is so very extraordinary; the virulency and *insolence* so far above the common pitch; that it puts one in mind of Rupilius King, a great ancestor of the Dr.'s, commended to posterity by Horace under this honourable character,

> *Proscripti Regis Rupili pus atque venenum*
> The filth and venom of Rupilius King." (I, xvii)

Bentley may even have suggested the mode of King's rebuttal when, in a passage directed against the Christ Church men, he called to mind Castelvetro's plight: refuted "by Pasquils, Lampoons, Burlesque Dialogues" (I, lxviii). Before the year was out, King had published his *Dialogues,* "in self defense" he said,[27] and there can be no doubt that the dialogues were largely written that year too, filled as they are with minute references to the amplified version of Bentley's dissertation.

King's first dialogue, like Lucian's, employs Charon and acquaints the reader with the setting, conditions, and tone of all ten pieces. The first blows are aimed no higher than the rest. Just a week ago, says Lycophron (an Alexandrian poet noted for abstruseness), Hades re-

---

[26] *Dr. Bentley's Dissertations on the Epistles of Phalaris . . . Examin'd by the Honourable Charles Boyle . . .* (London, 1698), p. 8.

[27] *Miscellanies in Prose and Verse* (London [1709?]), sig. a6^v.

ceived "the Works of the snarling Critick Bentivoglio"—Bentley's name in the dialogues.[28] Charon remembers that Bentley's works were so heavy they nearly sank the boat, an Erasmian touch, whereupon Lycophron reveals that the Phalaris controversy now rages in the underworld:

> . . . Rhadamanthus is their Umpire, who finding the case difficult, has taken a considerable time to deliberate concerning it.
> *Charon.* But pray, Sir, what do you say as to this Affair?
> *Lycophron.* Why indeed I am not wholly Impartial in this matter, for Bentivoglio has very much oblig'd me throughout his Works. He has imitated me even without reason, for as it was my choice, so his natural Genius leads him to be unintelligible. A Man may as soon understand his Latin as his English, and his English as my Greek; his Prose is as Fantastick as my Verse; and my Prophecies carry more light with 'em than his demonstrations.

Like Charon's boat, King's *Dialogues* bears a heavy load, of unrelenting animadversion. In a letter contributed to still another of Boyle's replies, King claimed to have read more than anybody in England except Bentley—"I have Read his Book all over"[29]—and the dialogues prove it, the margins buzzing with page references, the text inlaid with italicized quotations. Misquotations, I should say; King assiduously twisted passages—in a note at the end of Dialogue VIII, for example, making the scholar seem lascivious by telescoping several widely spaced remarks (I, 313–16), including an ancient passage in translation which Bentley thought spurious because of its indecency! Many more dishonest references could be listed here, to-

---

[28] Why, it is difficult to say, except that the name reflects sarcastically on Bentley's good will. The Italian name suits King's claim in the Advertisement that the dialogues "were written by a Gentleman residing at Padua, upon some intelligence he received there of one Bentivoglio, a very troublesome Critick in the world." Perhaps the name of Guido Bentivoglio was running in King's mind. The correspondence of the seventeenth-century Cardinal includes a letter addressed "A Monsignor Cornaro Chicrico di Camera, che fù poi creato Cardinale da Papa Urbano VIII," *Raccolta di Lettere Scritte dal Cardinal Bentivoglio* . . . (Venice, 1636), p. 74. King's "Dialogue, Shewing the Way to Modern Preferment," mentioned later in this chapter, has a character named Cornaro who is a papal functionary.

[29] *A Short Account of Dr Bentley's Humanity and Justice* . . . (London, 1699), p. 135.

gether with footnotes nonsensically citing Bentley's scholarly sources, and outright, more or less slanderous accusations of plagiarism, affectation, egomania, scurrility, stupidity, eccentricity, triviality, and imposture.

To begin to pardon such ferocity, the reader must put himself in King's place for a moment. True, as Johnson wisely said, King "was one of those who tried what Wit could perform in opposition to Learning, on a question which Learning only could decide," [30] but all the dust of combat had not settled when King wrote, and of course, whatever the provocation, Bentley *had* written abusively. The Charon-Lycophron dialogue meanders into a discussion of anapests, a subject whereon Boyle's comments had proved particularly irksome to Bentley; "I must freely own," he observed, ". . . that some little disdain rises within me, to see myself employed in confuting such stuff as he has brought forth on this occasion" (I, 191). Clearly, King was more concerned with Bentley's bad manners than with his discoveries; Bentley must have seemed himself a rude and arrogant Phalaris whose behavior violated the standards that humane learning was supposed to instill. But even the method of Bentley's scholarship troubled King, who a year later would publish a satire on the Royal Society's *Transactions.* Bentley, a member of the Society, was a pioneer of scientific, painstakingly empirical research, which scholar-gentlemen like King distrusted; [31]

> The critic Eye, that microscope of Wit,
> Sees hairs and pores, examines bit by bit . . .

as Pope would make Bentley boast shortly before the accomplishment of the *Dunciad*'s prophecies (iv, 233–34). King thought Bentley a new, more threatening species of virtuoso, one not content with groping in ditches for microbes but set upon muddying the Pierian spring.

[30] "King," *Lives of the English Poets,* ed. George Birkbeck Hill (Oxford, 1905), II, 27.
[31] Colin J. Horne, "The Phalaris Controversy: King *versus* Bentley," *RES,* XXII (1946), 297. Ernest Eugene Weeks describes King's various satires against scientific studies in an unpublished dissertation, "The Life and Times of William King" (Columbia, 1965), pp. 91–144.

Even Lycophron recognizes the danger: "Proserpine only knows the event of these Troubles; for till this matter be decided, Poetry must lye still, since in such dubious times no Person can make an Anapaestic Verse with any safety."

So particular and emphatic are the complaints lodged against Bentley in most of King's dialogues that often the dramatic potentialities of the form go unexplored, either because the irony issues from the broadest kind of blame-by-praise, as in the final two conversations, or because the author's spokesman is so thoroughly tailored for the reader's approval, as in Dialogues V through VIII, and his companion is so egregiously foolish. It is amusing, for example, to behold the extravagances of the sixth dialogue, in which Bentley's devotee Calphurnia defends her affectations, but from first to last the reader knows her to be the butt of the discussion; her modest, sensible companion Bellamira commands all just admiration. Comparably, the lexicographer Hesychius argues that all learning is contained in dictionaries (Dial. V), the astrologer William Lilly sings Bentley's attainments in chronology (Dial. VII), and Heraclitus laments the loss of much trivial information about the past (Dial. VIII), while their opponents—Gouldman the lexicographer, Helvicus the chronologist, and Democritus, respectively—reply moralistically or mockingly.

Greater ingenuity nourished the composition of Dialogues II–IV, in the first of which Phalaris speaks to none other than Bentley's Sophist. Since the dissertation crossed the Styx, the Sophist has been going about claiming he wrote the epistles, with a predictable effect upon the hot-blooded tyrant:

> Shall a Prince be . . . told to his Face that his Works are not his own? Daggers, Bulls, and Torments!
> *Sophist.* Not so Angry, good Sir, you know that here in the Shades all Persons are equal. Besides, Sir, it was always my Humour to Plume myself with borow'd Feathers. . . . And besides, Sir, though Bentivoglio took whole passages from Nevelet, and Vizzanius, yet they make no disturbance amongst the Shades, but here is such a stir because I am pleas'd to own your Epistles.

Phalaris. Were you in the other World, you would not have dar'd to have talk'd so to me.

Sophist. Nay, were you in the other World, Bentivoglio would not have spoke as he has done of you.

The Sophist is honest about his opportunism, but he does not relent in his claims. At Phalaris' request, he rehearses the arguments against Phalaris' authorship, including little points having to do with the date at which certain words were first used, points that seem utterly trivial out of context and in front of Phalaris. Of course, King does not mention Bentley's admission that chronology based on language is "commonly nice and uncertain," and that if such were his sole proof, "I myself, indeed, should be satisfied with that alone, but I durst not hope to convince every body else" (I, 91).

Phalaris can only cry, "Rhadamanthus grant me Patience." The Sophist has the final words, which contain an ironic triple comparison like those elsewhere in the *Dialogues,* one of King's favorite devices. (Indeed, the comparison is to dialogues what the apostrophe is to odes, practically an indispensable element, but King had to raise his comparisons to a higher power because of the need to bring the living Bentley into them.) "Stay, Sir," says the Sophist, "but one Word more; you say the Epistles are your own, I say they are my own, and that Bentivoglio has prov'd them to be so, by Arguments that are his own." What anarchy, if reliance on widely accepted traditions gives way to solipsism. Wit more than learning, but memorable wit evident through the unsettling conclusion of the dialogue, enabled King to arrange this confrontation of two cardinal figures in the controversy, in which the Sophist convicts himself and his champion. Another colloquy built along such lines is the fourth, where the modern critic Ricardo (one more version of Richard Bentley) endeavors to convince Narcissus that Bentivoglio's self-love has never been surpassed—no small victory, if Narcissus can be overcome, and the triumph is Ricardo's when he drives the youth away with a barrage of self-congratulatory statements culled mainly from the *Dissertation* (I, xlix–liii). Bentley had spent some five pages describing his professional qualifications, supported by testaments from eminent correspondents. In the context of seventeenth-century controversy, such self-praise does not seem excessive, especially in the prolegomenon to so ample a book. But compressed within a brief dialogue the remarks become blatantly prideful, enough to shame Narcissus.

To this point the progress of the dialogue is simple: Ricardo unconsciously ridiculing Bentley by subjecting him to fulsome praise, Narcissus the appropriate foil. The ending, however, becomes unexpectedly provocative. Narcissus gone, Ricardo contemplates his victory, and as he does so it pales, ludicrously completing the pattern: "Something still intervenes," he muses, "to Tarnish the lustre of our Triumphs. I may have gain'd the Better of Narcissus, but then I greive to think that after his Example, some day or other, even my Friend Bentivoglio's Self-Love may chance to be put out of Countenance." It was silly, in the first place, to compete with Narcissus, the boy destroyed by conceit; sillier, to exceed him in it; and inane for Ricardo to reflect sadly, like Cyrus at the pyre of Croesus, upon the impermanence of supremacy, when all along the contested distinction was foolish and immoral.

More intelligently, a London butcher haggles with Hercules in what is perhaps the best of King's dialogues, the third, satirizing the devotion of scholars to the most vulgar, horrid, and peripheral details once they have been purified by aging. In a sense, the dialogue is mock-heroic, juxtaposing the ancient and the modern somewhat to the disadvantage of both. To Hercules' claim of cleansing the Augean Stables and subduing the bull of Marathon, the butcher answers, "Was it not I that when Tom Dove broke lo [o] se, and drove the Mob before him, took him by the Ring, and led him back to the Stake, with the universal Shouts of the Company? Besides, I question whether you ever saw a Bull-dog." Hercules tries again a few lines later by extolling the "Stories" to be found in ancient history— anecdotes drawn from the *Dissertation,* that is. He describes Phalaris' cannibalism, to which even the tyrant's son was sacrificed, and the Butcher, at a loss for a more sensational rejoinder, can merely protest, "But I know when, and where the Fellow run for the great

Bag-Pudding, and eat it when he had done; and I am sure, if this Story was well told, it would seem the more probable." Besides exasperating Hercules, the remark specifically attacks one of Bentley's main arguments, his setting "a prevailing tradition about Phalaris's eating his own son when he was an infant" against the epistles' clear indication that Phalaris had but one son, who had grown to manhood, and whom his father loved (II, 106). Here, with recourse to the gentleman scholar's common sense, King suggests that Bentley's decrepit evidence will not bear such dogmatism.

But while making small, literal points, the dialogue makes larger ones. Hercules, enraged, turns to descriptions of ancient athletic prowess and of the more fabulous exploits he himself performed; in each matter the butcher tenaciously withstands him. At last the ancient departs, haughtily observing that he finds the butcher must "have the last word." The modern does, complaining that "our great Scholards are so much taken up with such Fellows as this Hercules, Hyllus the Wrestler, Cleanthes the Cuffer, Phalaris and Xerxes the Man-Eaters, that they never mind My Actions, nor several others of their own Country-Men." Again the whole dialogue says more than its hero, for the butcher's conclusion is only partly the reader's. The butcher wonders why scholars (dullards that they seem) neglect his exploits, while the reader, in tune with King's reactionary satire, silently asks why scholars do not neglect more, especially the trivial, the gruesome, and the fantastic—the diversions of ancient butchers.

King's collection resembles Lucian's in several important ways, the dialogue just discussed recalling Lucian's sixteenth, in which Diogenes ridicules Hercules. Indeed, King has some claim to being thought the "best imitator in English." It is true, as Benjamin Boyce has said, that King lacks his predecessor's sobering emphasis upon the fact of death; [32] King's concern with topicalities precluded it, though traces may be discerned in passages like the one that ends the conversation of Ricardo and Narcissus. Like Lucian, however, King wrote a series of varied, very brief colloquies remarkable for their direct, exuberant,

[32] Boyce, "News from Hell," p. 418.

occasionally strident ridicule of man's shortcomings, especially his pride. Not only do the two authors share the technique of employing favored spokesmen, immediately identifiable as such, to deride conspicuously fatuous adversaries; the adversaries in both are virtually alike. The partisans of King's *philologus gloriosus* derive from that company of boastful philosophers, heroes, and monarchs against whom Lucian took aim. In King the reader encounters Charon, in the same nether world the Greek dialogues uncover: the Charon who never appears in Fontenelle, a Hades both positively realized and entirely purged of Christian vestiges—unlike the setting of most earlier English dialogues of the dead. Here is a sample of Pluto's plenty, even a character resembling Lucian's Menippus and Diogenes, the Democritus who trifles with Heraclitus in Dialogue VIII.

King preferred badinage to death's heads, and did not try to combine them, but readers must not overlook the effect he gained simply by adopting this ancient genre, which itself places the dispute with Bentley in a perspective of some length. By using the form almost as Lucian had established it, King demonstrated his allegiance to traditional ways, much as Dryden, Pope, and Swift did by appropriating the heroic mode. King's last two dialogues, in fact, ought to be classed with "Mac Flecknoe" as forerunners of *The Dunciad*. They are King's only dialogues in which the speakers agree at the end, and there is something ominous, apocalyptic in their unanimity. In the ninth, a dialogue of the living directed mainly at Wotton, Moderno praises the new scientists who seek to locate the animal spirits of tadpoles; only the thoroughness of his companion's docility could make the reader suspect that it is false. In the tenth dialogue, the shades of Richard Flecknoe and Thomas Dekker project scholarly investigations into the dramatic achievements of strolling players and puppeteers. The use of these writers, it may be mentioned in passing, links King in some degree to the English tradition of infernal satire, for Dekker had written several, mainly Hellish pieces and Flecknoe had marked the death of Sir William Davenant with a pamphlet narrating his entry into Elysium.[33] Even if King did know Fontenelle's work, he

[33] Boyce describes the infernal satire of *News from Hell: Brought by the Diuells Carrier* (1606) and other works by Dekker (*ibid.*, p. 410). Flecknoe's narrative, *S*ʳ

had to write differently: King's virtuosi, his mock-heroic devices, his travesty of Bentley's scholarly apparatus—all these display unmistakable, familiar, Scriblerian loyalties and affinities. As much as the dialogue of the dead on the classical model seemed destined to be revived in England, he was the person to do it.

King did not make a career of such dialogues, though he wrote one more, "A Dialogue, Shewing the Way to Modern Preferment," during the decade following the publication of his collection. Relying upon perfunctorily gathered evidence and the assertions of John Nichols, scholars have said the dialogue came into being and was printed as early as 1690 or 1691, but a reference by one of the characters to "the late King of Spain's Will," together with other details, surely points to the events immediately preceding the War of the Spanish Succession. The dialogue could not have been written, or at least completed, until after the death of Charles II of Spain, in 1700, and the first recorded publication came nearly ten years later.[34] Unfortunately, the problems of dating become more engrossing than the work itself, in which the former minions of a cardinal, a pope, and a mufti debate each other's merits, the conversation abruptly stoppered with a sarcasm on "the readiest means to modern Preferments." King had written more thoughtfully in some of the other dialogues, and not without some modest effect upon his countrymen.

"What have we here! a Second Part of that silly Book, the Dialogues of the Dead?" a character explains in the preface, itself a dialogue, to the only work that certainly derives from King's: *Dialogues of the Living and the Dead: In Imitation of Lucian and the French* (1701). This, one reads, is a continuation of "that which came out in Ninety-nine," the author "a Doctor of the Civil-Law," but neither the historian nor the critic will find those assertions credible. Eight of the

---

William D'avenant's Voyage to the Other World . . . (1668), is reprinted in *Theatre Miscellany: Six Pieces Connected with the Seventeenth-Century Stage,* ed. C. H. Wilkinson (Oxford, 1953).

[34] Nichols' date of 1691, for composition and publication (King, *Original Works,* I, 182*n*, 186*n*), was accepted, give or take a year, by everyone until Colin J. Horne proved that the dialogue first appeared in King's undated *Miscellanies* of about 1709 and suggested that it was written no earlier than 1700 ("Dr. William King's *Miscellanies in Prose and Verse," The Library,* 4th ser., XXV [1944], 37, 43).

ten dialogues take place in Hades, where disputes over materialist philosophy have supplanted the Phalaris controversy. An owl refutes Lucretius in the third dialogue, and in the fifth—the most imaginative of the lot—Charon confronts an "Atheist" who ridicules the god for busying himself with conveying souls when, as "Mr. Hobs" has revealed, "there is no such thing." Although Hobbes might have been given an abler spokesman, the anonymous author did construct an efficient satirical showdown, the atheist and a god, the disembodied materialist and a spirit. Had the author learned something from King? perhaps from King's pairing of Phalaris and the Sophist? At this point the question seems both unresolvable and unimportant. Of note is Charon's reappearance in a set of English dialogues published so soon after King's, dialogues clearly addressed to the common mass of readers. The theater-manager Tom Killigrew chats with Molley, who turned prostitute "that I might be Gentile, though it went against my Stomach" (Dial. I), and the dramatist Nathaniel Lee appalls Shakespeare by describing the perversities of the contemporary stage (Dial. VII). For the amusement of learned gentlemen, William King had humorously attacked modernists with an ancient genre, turned a classical form against an irascible classics scholar. But King's obscure follower simply gave the public what he had reason to think it wanted. Talkative Charon had become a true-born Englishman.

Chapter III

Books Neither Lost nor Found:
Matthew Prior's Dialogues and Others
1700-1759

> A Dialogue between two Infants in the womb concern-
> ing the state of this world, might handsomly illus-
> trate our ignorance of the next, whereof methinks we
> yet discourse in Platoes denne, and are but Embryon
> Philosophers.
> —Sir Thomas Browne, *Hydriotaphia: Urne Burial*

In the preface to the first edition of his *Dialogues of the
Dead* (1760), Lyttelton observed that England had produced nothing
in the genre "worthy of Notice," a comment deleted in the fourth edition (1765); why, it is impossible to say. Perhaps he had become
aware of King's collection, or the success of his own had rendered the
comment invalid. Whatever the case, it is true that though a good
many dialogues of the dead were published in England between
King's and Lyttelton's, nearly all have only the faintest importance
and could have served, at best, only as cautionary examples for Lyttelton and his followers. A quick review of these dialogues may help the
reader to appreciate Lyttelton's achievement, but the heart of this
chapter concerns the best dialogues of the dead ever written by an
Englishman, Matthew Prior's, which unfortunately remained in manuscript until the beginning of the present century.

Dialogues of the dead were to be found along Grub Street in the early 1700s, and might have occupied more fashionable literary thoroughfares if the format of the periodical essay had been hospitable to the dialogue. Some pieces in the *Tatler* (No. 81) and the *Guardian* (No. 158), for example, would be dialogues of the dead if they were not narratives. The genre did appear among the works of Thomas, or Tom, Brown (1663–1704), the somewhat disreputable, popular satirist who had been a contemporary of William King's at Christ Church, who contributed the *True History* to the 1710–11 translation of Lucian, and who may have had a hand in the composition of Charles Gildon's Hellish dialogue.[1] A very businesslike, comprehensive attack on William III entitled "The Belgic Heroe Unmasked," Brown's one dialogue of the dead was published in 1704, but his best service to the genre was the printing, in his edition of Buckingham's *Miscellaneous Works,* of Fleetwood Sheppard's "Calendar Reform'd."

In 1708 Jacob Tonson published *Fontenelle's Dialogues of the Dead. . . . Translated from the French. With a Reply to some Remarks in a Critique, call'd The Judgment of Pluto, &c. And Two Original Dialogues* by John Hughes (1677–1720), later the editor of Spenser and a contributor to the *Tatler, Spectator,* and *Guardian.* The preface is interesting as the first place in which a writer of English dialogues of the dead expresses a preference for Fontenelle over Lucian. Fontenelle, Hughes writes, "has a Wit which gives to every Subject the most agreeable and surprizing Turns in the World. The Edge of his Satyr is fine; he always preserves his good Humour; his Mirth has ever something solid, and his most judicious Reflections are mix'd with Pleasantry." Fontenelle, moreover, "has refin'd upon his

---

[1] Benjamin Boyce, *Tom Brown of Facetious Memory: Grub Street in the Age of Dryden,* Harvard Studies in English, XXI (Cambridge, 1939), 81, 38. Gildon's dialogue was reprinted in Vol. IV of Brown's *Works* (1711). Brown's *Letters from the Dead to the Living* (London, 1702), a collaborative effort, contains one dialogue, anonymous and translated from the French: "The Mitred Hog: A Dialogue between Abbot Furetiere and Scarron." The preface, by Brown, is worth noting because of its preference for Lucian over Fontenelle: ". . . with all due submission to Monsieur Fontenelle, . . . I look upon him to be as much inferior to the Grecian Dialoguist, both in the poignancy of his Satyr, and force of his Expression, as the Language of Paris is to that of Athens" (sigs. A2-A2ᵛ).

Predecessor. Lucian laughs too loud, is often licentious, and sometimes course in his Raillery: He has not thought it sufficient to make his Dead reason, but they scold too." Hughes's description of Fontenelle's manner is a good one, as is the translation; the description of Lucian's practice, unaccountably illustrated by a reference to that author's *Dialogues of the Gods,* seems no more than what one might expect in a preface to Fontenelle.[2] Hughes did not know that Fontenelle had composed the ironic *Jugement de Pluton:* ". . . 'tis every where a principal Beauty of the Dialogues, what this Writer is so gross as to mistake for a Fault."

Of his own two pieces Hughes writes very humbly, saying that they were written in imitation of Fontenelle's and that "tho' I have now suffer'd 'em to be printed, I can make no Apology for 'em, but only, that the shortest Errors are the most likely to be pardon'd, and that is the Reason why I added no more." The dialogues are short —also as short of Fontenelle's in merit as Hughes implied, the second a plain humorless exchange between Empedocles and Lucilio Vanini, types of the imposter. But the first has at least some historical significance, hinting the existence of a tenuous thread of causality joining several authors. Hughes's colloquy between "Lucius Junius Brutus the first Consul, and Augustus Caesar" recalls a piece in the *Dialogues of the Living and the Dead* of 1701, the collection described as a second part to King's. The earlier dialogue brought together Lucius Junius Brutus and an unidentified Englishman (it is called a "Dialogue of the Living" on the title page, though it might with as much accuracy have been called a dialogue of the dead).

The Englishman inquires about Brutus' "Receit" for turning "Blockheads into Wits." Brutus had been thought a fool by his contemporaries until, declaring himself against Lucretia's ravisher, he revealed himself to be quite otherwise. But Brutus argues that he was never a fool, that only real fools called him such, and that many

---

[2] That Hughes could appreciate Lucian, and imitate him more successfully than he could Fontenelle, is shown by a satirical narrative written, Hughes says, after he had read one of Lucian's dialogues of the dead: "Charon: or, The Ferry-Boat. A Vision," *Poems on Several Occasions with Some Select Essays in Prose* (London, 1735), II, 351–64.

judge others without sufficient understanding. Then the Englishman objects that Brutus showed his "Barbarity" in being able to look on while his sons were executed; and Brutus replies:

> How canst thou judge of things at this distance? How canst thou tell, but that finding that I had made the Commonwealth too strong for me, I knew there was no saving them, unless my appearing in publick should move the People in pity to rescue them; and that when I saw they would not, the extremity of my Grief stupified me, and made me look like that which Philosophers may admire if they please, but all People, that are not worse than Beasts, must abhor.

The same subjects recur in Hughes's dialogue. Augustus commences the conversation by admiring Brutus' "Masque of Folly," and Brutus tacitly admits that he was guilty of dissimulation. Later, Augustus criticizes Brutus for staying to watch his sons' execution—a deed Brutus refuses to explain, remarking only that all historical events permit "doubtful Interpretation." This skeptical comment recalls the other Brutus' remark about the difficulty of judging "things at this distance," and indeed, Hughes's very employment of Brutus, a comparatively rare figure in dialogues of the dead (not to be found in Fontenelle), reinforces the likelihood of some connection between the two colloquies. In the preface, Hughes says he wrote his dialogues "several Years ago" and made his translation "above six Years" before its publication, suggesting that he was engaged in this project shortly after the *Dialogues of the Living and the Dead* appeared.

The line of causality would seem to stretch farther, from Hughes's piece to one published in 1723 among the *Works* of John Sheffield, Duke of Buckingham and Normanby (1648–1721). Sheffield—a poet, a soldier, and a favorite of James and of Anne—wrote two dialogues of the dead, probably after the appearance of Hughes's volume. Sheffield's first dialogue, between Augustus and Cardinal Richelieu, bears several resemblances to Hughes's between Augustus and Brutus; Richelieu, in fact, plays so small a part that almost any other person, including Brutus, would have served as well. However, although both dialogues concern Augustus and raise the same issues, a large and basic difference separates them: whereas Hughes adheres to accepted historical facts, Sheffield distorts and fabricates history to an extent unmatched by any other British dialogue-writer. (It is not at all to Alexander Pope's credit that he prepared Sheffield's *Works* for publication.)

I strongly suspect that Sheffield wrote with Hughes's dialogue in mind. Augustus, in Hughes, reflects that even the best men "are not disinterested; they have a great many By-ends and conceal'd Designs. Their boasted Services to their Country are often but a Sacrifice to their own Pleasures and Passions." Comparably, Sheffield's Augustus observes, "Every thing which succeeds, is attributed to prudence. But believe me, there is a great deal more of luck than skill, in our game of policy; and the worst players sometimes have the better success." Thus, in both dialogues Augustus owns that his countrymen misunderstood him, but whereas Hughes's character simply confesses that he was guilty of politic dissimulation, Sheffield's character incredibly admits that his reputation rested entirely upon the imprudence of his enemies, the extraordinary skill of his ministers, and the natural tranquillity of Rome in his time. When the subject of Cicero's execution arises, Hughes again writes responsibly, making Augustus explain that Antony overruled his attempt to prevent Cicero's proscription. But Sheffield's Augustus claims that Antony tricked him, giving

all the assurances imaginable that he would spare [Cicero] for my sake, if I would set him down in the roll for his: and so at once cunningly satisfied his revenge, and blacken'd me to all posterity. But I think I was even with him.

Richelieu. Was this your quarrel? I thought it was about your Sister. Why did not you let the world know this story, to justify yourself?

Augustus. I was really asham'd of being us'd so like a child; and my friends told me it would never be believ'd, since Lepidus (who was the only person present) durst not disoblige Mark Antony with declaring the truth.

Revelations indeed! Further analysis is pointless, but it may be observed that Brutus, in Hughes's dialogue, says all men may be used like children.

An appropriate motto for Sheffield's dialogues would be *de mortuis nihil nisi malum.* It seems that, perhaps intoxicated by Fontenelle's radical view of the past, Sheffield tried to write as sensationally as possible, heedless of subtlety and even of the rudiments of composition. Sheffield's Augustus agrees to expose himself on the condition that Richelieu "will confess as ingenuously how you came by all your greatness; for among friends, you and I know 'tis not to be gotten honestly." Richelieu accepts, but when Augustus' disclosures are finished, the dialogue ends, incomplete. Its companion dialogue, in which Mahomet and the Duke of Guise agree to laugh together over "those tricks you and I have put upon the world," has a greater degree of completeness but is no less sensational and irresponsible.

I may mention one other work before turning to Prior's, a long pamphlet of 1715 in which Signior Glibertini (Gilbert Burnet) and Count Thomaso (the first Marquis of Wharton) describe their vices. The Romance names recall King's, though none of King's salt flavors this raucous ephemeron, the setting a Hellish Hades where Loyola is Lucifer's "First Secretary." [3] The dialogue belongs in the preceding century. In comparison with what his countrymen had achieved in the genre since King's *Dialogues,* Matthew Prior's accomplishment must seem thoroughly extraordinary.

Probably in or about 1721, at the end of his life, Prior amused himself by composing four dialogues of the dead which Alexander Pope pronounced "very good," a judgment echoed by everyone who has commented on them since their belated publication in 1907. [4]

---

[3] Another, comparable piece (*ca.* 1716), "A Dialogue between Sir William Handcock and Thady Fitzpatrick, in the Devil's Ante-Chamber," a poem, was first printed by John Barrett in *An Essay on the Earlier Part of the Life of Swift* (London, 1808), pp. 99–102. Barrett's conjecture that Swift was the author is rejected by Harold Williams in *The Poems of Jonathan Swift,* 2d ed. (Oxford, 1958), III, 1074.

[4] Joseph Spence recorded Pope's appraisal in *Observations, Anecdotes, and Characters of Books and Men Collected from Conversation,* ed. James M. Osborn (Oxford, 1966), I, 92. The dialogues' probable date of composition, *ca.* 1721, is given by H. Bunker Wright and Monroe K. Spears, eds., *The Literary Works of Matthew Prior,* 2d ed. (Oxford, 1971), II, 1011; my quotations are from the dialogues as printed in this edition (I, 599–663). The dialogues were first printed in Matthew Prior, *Dialogues of the Dead and Other Works in Prose and Verse,* ed. A. R.

Everyone, however, is not many people in this case. So little attention has been given to the dialogues that they remain insufficiently known and appreciated, yet they do not pale when set beside acknowledged masterpieces of eighteenth-century literature, and they tower above most other works in their genre. That the dialogues are good is not strange, for readers would expect something worthwhile from the witty Horatian poet. Nor is it odd that Prior set his hand to this somewhat out-of-the-way form, which could hardly have been so to the mind of a man who, in 1699, had supped with Boileau and Fontenelle,[5] a man who knew Fleetwood Sheppard well enough to make him the subject or recipient of four poems composed in 1688–89, a man who, together with William King, had been associated with the *Examiner* in its earliest days. Most important, perhaps, Prior not only knew Fénelon personally but drew praise from him for his fluency in French.[6]

There are signs that Prior profited from the work of his acquaintances, especially the French—the skeptical Englishman must have found Fontenelle particularly invigorating—but the signs are few and Prior's dialogues ample.[7] His head was full of history, as befitted

Waller (Cambridge, 1907), together with Waller's endorsement (p. v). Enthusiastic praise, but little detailed criticism, may also be found in Francis Bickley, *The Life of Matthew Prior* (London, 1914), p. 259; K. N. Colvile, "Dialogues of the Dead," *Quarterly Review*, CCLXVII (1936), 312; R. W. Ketton-Cremer, *Matthew Prior* (Cambridge, 1957), p. 23; L. G. Wickham Legg, *Matthew Prior: A Study of His Public Career and Correspondence* (Cambridge, 1921), p. 276; George Saintsbury, *The Peace of the Augustans* (London, 1946), p. 55n; and Thomas Seccombe, "Lesser Verse Writers," *The Cambridge History of English Literature,* ed. A. W. Ward and A. R. Waller (Cambridge, 1919–31), IX, 179. A. C. Guthkelch severely criticized Bickley for dealing with the dialogues in but a few sentences (*MLR,* X [1915], 234). The one published essay on the subject, Richard Morton's "Matthew Prior's *Dialogues of the Dead,*" *Ball State University Forum,* VIII (1967), 73–78, is casual but suggestive.

[5] Matthew Prior, Letter to the Earl of Jersey (June 17, 1699), in L. G. Wickham Legg, *Matthew Prior: A Study of His Public Career and Correspondence* (Cambridge, 1921), pp. 292–93.

[6] Charles Kenneth Eves, *Matthew Prior, Poet and Diplomatist* (New York, 1939), pp. 14–15, 223, 297.

[7] Wright and Spears (II, 1014) note that Clenard's rebuke to Charles for troubling a monastery after he tired of troubling the world echoes a portion of Fénelon's dialogue between the same Charles and a young monk. Prior also cared

an experienced diplomat, his brain effervescent, and his creative power more comprehensive than might be supposed by those who know only his lyrics well. The incidental wittiness of at least three of the dialogues lies along extensive, firm lines of dramatic development, which are found to be comparably ingenious when traced to their ends. Two of the pieces, for instance, the first and the last, are quite similar in construction, at the outset appearing to be clear-cut examples of the *eiron-alazon* pattern. In "A Dialogue between Charles the Emperor and Clenard the Grammarian," the scholar Nicolas Kleynaerts roundly defeats Charles V; in "A Dialogue between Oliver Cromwell, and his Porter," the mad porter is equally successful. Besides the general likeness of the dialogues, they display some particular similarities, the most conspicuous being a device that appears in each, a mock-heroic mimicry such as William King's butcher spoke when confronted with blustering Hercules. Charles opens the first dialogue thus:

> Burgundy with Brabant and Flanders, Castile, Arragon, Germany Possessed: Italy, France, Africa, Greece Attempted.
> *Clenard.* Noun Substantive and Adjective, Pronoun, Verb, Participle Declined: Adverb, Conjonction, preposition Interjection undeclined.
> *Charles.* Into this Model I had cast Europe, how Glorious was the Design?
> *Clenard.* How happy was the Division I made of all Greece into five Dialects.

And near the beginning of the last dialogue:

> *Oliver.* . . . . I raised my Self from a Private Person to the Dignity of a Prince.
> *Porter.* And from being Your Porter I made my Self a Prophet.

---

enough for Lucian to acquire editions in Greek, Latin, French, and English (*ibid.*, II, 1012). Engelbert Frey remarks that Fontenelle and Prior both set Charles against a renowned scholar, Erasmus and Clenard respectively, and also pair Montaigne with famous philosophers, Socrates and Locke (*Der Einfluss der englischen, französischen, italienischen, und lateinischen Literatur auf die Dichtungen Matthew Priors* [Strassburg, 1915], pp. 117–18). But Prior's dialogues are generally much longer than Fontenelle's, and in Prior it is Montaigne, not the philosopher, who has all the best lines.

Oliver. I was General of the Army, Head of the Parliament, and Supreme
Master of Three Kingdoms.
Porter. I was Senior Inhabitant of Old Bethlem, Prince of the Planets, and
absolute Disposer of every thing I saw or thought of.

Pleasant mimicry such as this, a forte of the Prior who "transvers'd"
The Hind and the Panther and travestied Boileau's *Ode sur la prise
de Namur,* was a staple of Prior's dialogue method; as shall be seen,
parody informs the most glitteringly inventive passage in these dialogues.

The presuppositions of the reader are fortified by Prior's use of another device, borrowed from the stage and rare in dialogues of the
dead, the "aside." Charles confides, "There is too much truth in what
this pert Philosopher says, but I must bear up to Him for the sake of
my Honor, that Dear Honor which makes us too often Commit a Second mistake in defence of the first—Well, friend Clenard You are
stil harping at a Comparison between your way of Living and mine."
Such asides occur regularly in the dialogues, four times in Charles-
Clenard alone, temporarily diminishing suspense. The reader feels no
doubt about what the outcome will be, and in the first dialogue Clenard himself becomes so confident that, near the end, he calls the Emperor "a Silly Combatant, to Fight me at my own Weapon. Every
Man to his Trade, Charles, You should have Challenged me at Long
Pike or broad Sword: In a Tilt or Tournament you might probably
have had the better of Me, But at Syllogism or Paradox—"

Riddled with parody, conceding defeat in asides, Charles falls, as
the reader knew he would, yet there is more to the dialogue than that.
Clenard's comments seem to signal an awareness that his conquest
owes more to rhetoric than to truth, that his victory rests upon a paradox. Winning, he clearly exaggerates his own importance, as when
he boasts of the power enjoyed by grammarians: "Two Latin preposi-
tions *Trans* and *Cum* joined with *Substantiation* a word invented by
us Scholemen were the Cause of all your troubles in Germany, and
the same Contention is stil on foot." This is no *eiron* speaking, not
any more; this is a man in his own sphere as megalomaniacal as
Charles. Clenard's words have become ironical in effect only, not in

intention, like those of the porter in the last dialogue, a wretch admittedly mad whose self-aggrandizement is sincerely spoken. During the conversation with Cromwell, Prior's artistry emerges as the porter's madness becomes a touchstone disclosing the greater, unacknowledged madness of the Protector. The porter's derangement, he confesses, began when he saw Charles I beheaded. That the event had no effect upon Cromwell's brain suggests he was mad all the time, so much so that he could kill his king without remorse. Moreover, Cromwell's insanity persists: even in death he is willing to argue with a man recognizably addled. And there is mania in Clenard too, though it does not amount to outright insanity; near the end of the first dialogue, the vanquished emperor cries out, "Whither in Gods Name art Thou running on?" to which Clenard replies, "Only to finish my Story and Comparison." The rhetorician, obsessed with words, must bring his discourse to its conclusion whether or not anyone is still listening. "I love Method extremly," he confessed earlier in the conversation.

A final parallel between these dialogues appears when the reader finds that the porter, like Clenard, is not simply attacking a megalomaniac but also claiming great prominence himself. The porter too can attack eloquently and justly, as when he criticizes Cromwell's desire to win peace through aggression: "You would have had what never happened to any even from the Result of his own Thought: Peace with Ambition and Tranquility founded upon Injustice." But the porter's description of the contentment madhouse life affords, while a good foil to Cromwell's uneasy career, hardly seems attractive in itself, and his own boasting is as much beyond Clenard's as madness is removed from sanity. Not content to criticize, the porter makes great claims: "The Pope dreaded your Fleets at Loretto and Civita Vechia did You say? No No, it was I that humbled that high Priest of Baal, I Bombarded his Spiritual Strong holds with my Anathamas, I confounded the Whore of Babylon." Thus the porter proves a Diogenes with more than a touch of Alexander, and neither madman yields an inch throughout the dialogue. The other disputants part amicably, Charles pleading that their conversation be kept secret, Clenard agreeing that it shall—for reasons the reader, unlike Charles, understands.

Rich as these dialogues are, the two others are richer, less conventional, having much of the man Prior in them. The third piece, "A Dialogue between the Vicar of Bray, and Sir Thomas More," sets the martyred chancellor against a legendary Berkshire cleric who, Prior supposes, received his living from More and held it fifty-seven years, despite the vicissitudes of Henry, Edward, Mary, and Elizabeth. Although the mythology of Hades has almost no part in Prior's dialogues, this conversation includes a genuine Lucianic touch, a hint of ghastly incongruity. The hardy vicar greets More thus: "Oh that ugly Seam, Sir; that remains stil about your Neck. O Sir a Head Sewed on again never sits well. I pittyed You Sir, I prayed for you." Already the lines of battle are drawn, an *eiron-alazon* pattern established; how astonishingly presumptuous, for one such as the vicar to *pray* for More! The reader will recall that on one occasion Swift named More as the greatest of Englishmen: apparently without irony, Gulliver includes him in that "Sextumvirate to which all the Ages of the World cannot add a Seventh" (III, vii). Addison too had accorded him the highest praise, building *Spectator* 349 about this man who, to the last, had preserved the "Beauty of his Character." "His Death," the genial observer explained, "was of a piece with his Life. There was nothing in it new, forced or affected. He did not look upon the severing of his Head from his Body as a Circumstance that ought to produce any Change in the Disposition of his Mind; and as he died under a fix'd and settled hope of Immortality, he thought any unusual degree of Sorrow and Concern improper on such an occasion as had nothing in it which could deject or terrifie him." [8] But Prior was not Addison. The saintly chancellor makes all the virtuous statements expected of him. Speaking forthrightly, eruditely, he overmasters the vicar again and again, but when the smoke clears after every exchange, the vicar is still there clinging to More as tenaciously as he clung to his vicarage. At one point, for example, More asks what religion the vicar really professed:

[8] *The Spectator,* ed. Donald F. Bond (Oxford, 1965), III, 299, 300–1.

Vicar. . . . Sometimes the Ancient Roman Catholic, sometimes that of the Reformed Church of England.

More. How came You to teach . . . the First?

Vicar. Why my Canonical Obedience, the Order of my Diocessan Bishop, the Missal and Breviary all injoyned it.

More. How happened it then that You taught the t'other?

Vicar. Why New Acts of Parliament were made for the Reformation of Popery. My Bishop was put into the Tower for Disobeying them, and our Missals and Breviarys were Burnt. You are not going to Catachise me, Are You?

More. And You continued Stil in Your Vicarage of Bray.

Vicar. Where would You have had me been? in Foxes Book of Martyrs?

Plainly, the vicar has no principles, has only an uncommonly vigorous instinct for self-preservation; yet he is appealing, so candid about his failings that their gravity seems lessened, so ready at repartee that, though dead, he seems still replete with the life he craved, as if he tasted more of its sweetness than other men can. The chancellor, on the other hand, speaks decorously, sententiously, regimenting his pronouncements with anaphora and other formal devices, balancing his phrases and clauses, turning the vicar's rude jibes into cadences stately enough to sound true regardless of their content.

Vicar. . . . We of the low Church thought it very Strange that with all your Law and Learning you should not have had Wit enough to keep your head upon your Shoulders.

More. It was that very Law and Learning that made me lay my head down patiently on the Block. My knowledge in Divine and Human Law gave me to understand I was born a Subject to Both. That I was placed upon a Bench not only to expound those Laws to others, but obliged to Observe them my Self with an Inviolable Sanction. That in some cases the King Himself could not change them. That I was commanded to Render to God the things that were of God, before I gave to Cæsar the things that are Cæsars, And when I was Accused upon a point, which I thought Strictly just, My Philosophy taught me to Dispise my Sufferings, and furnished me upon the Scaffold with the same Serenity of Mind and pleasantness of Speech with which I was used to Decide Causes at Westminster-Hall, or Converse with my Friends in my Gardens at Chelsea.

The vicar's is another style, more various and vulgar, occasionally rude but often obsequious. He constantly addresses his companion as "Sir," his manner suggesting that, as he says, "There are as many Common Rules by which We Ordinary People are Directed which You Wise Men (as You think your selves) either do not know, or at least never Practice." Again, "We were not all Born to be Martyrs any more than Lord Mayors." Somewhat like Eliza Doolittle's father, the vicar is too lowly to be good, and his rules, like Sancho Panza's, are a string of proverbs: "never Strive against the Stream, always drive the Nail that will go. . . ." He can quote Latin verse, self-consciously, but his literature trots in Hudibrastics, which he insists upon taking at face value. Because his every reply is *ad hoc,* made without reference to any settled notion of virtue, he contradicts himself— boldly: when his opponent, the humanist, has recourse to Plato and Cicero on the brave acceptance of death, the vicar objects that they were heathens. And he can parody if all else fails, for when More begins to speak of saints the vicar gives him back a calendar of grotesque examples, making the martyrs seem like so many exhibits in a wax museum: "Aye, Sir, and St Laurence was broil'd on a Gridiron, and St. Protatius had his head cut off; and a great many more of them: Lord, there were Females too St: Ursula was Stabbed with a Poynard, and St: Catharine broke upon the Wheel." Or he can strike a pathetic pose after More has spoken with particular effectiveness: "Aye, Sir Thomas but it is a sad thing to Dye." Infinitely, anarchically inventive, his wit continues to possess the protean power it had when he was alive, when if Henry VIII "went to the Seige of Bologne It was David that went out against the Jebusites or the Moabites. When he would be Divorced from Old Kate, and had a mind to Nanny Bullen; Why Vasthi was put away, and Esther was taken unto Ahasuerus into his House Royal. Little Edward was Josiah, who Destroyed the High Places. Then Mary again was Deborah or Judith, who Restored the Ancient Laws and Customs of the People of Israel. Elizabeth . . . had right to the same Texts, only with New Applications and with this difference that to Exalt her Praise I always clapt a little of the Jesabell or Athalia upon her Predecessor." Surely, to argue with anyone so unscrupulous is to preach honor to Falstaff.

How could two such different men come to any sort of agreement? Of course, they cannot, but they do communicate with each other, improbable as it seems, before the dialogue is finished. More begins to weaken his position by recurrently stepping back to muse aloud upon the astonishing replies of the vicar, relating them to the general failings of mankind. "But why Should I blame him," he apostrophizes on one of these occasions, more than halfway through the dialogue, "of an Error common to us all," in this case the vicar's senseless fear that his curate would outlive him and inherit the parish. Lucian had ridiculed a comparable obliviousness of death's meaning in his sixth dialogue of the dead, where Pluto paradoxically comforts Terpsion by telling him that old Thucritus will outlive all his other would-be heirs, Terpsion's rivals. But Prior, through More, proves tolerant of a folly so prevalent as to be an ineradicable element of human nature. As the dialogue nears its conclusion, More ceases to ask questions, his comments increasingly taking the form of general observations addressed to no one in particular—not asides; there are none in this conversation. (As illustrated by the other dialogues, an aside customarily entails a pause in which a character privately, for the benefit of himself and the reader only, assesses the strength of his position and reveals the strategy he will employ when debate resumes.)

The result is that More's opinions seem less and less pertinent to the situation of men other than himself. When a particularly relativistic argument of the vicar's demands a personal reply, More shows he is losing patience: "Once for all Vicar every Man is obliged to suffer for what is right as to oppose what is unjust." At last, climactically, as the reward of his obstinacy rather than the end of any deliberate line of questioning, the vicar has harried his opponent into an inconsiderate, intemperate, inapplicably broad pronouncement. The vicar presses his advantage, puts More on the defensive for the first time in the dialogue, and extracts an apology which makes More seem as much a victim of his scrupulous conscience as the vicar was the pawn of his own passion for survival:

Vicar. Ay, but a Man may be mistaken in what he thinks Right, as I
fancy you were in the point of the Popes Supremacy. Od Zooks Sir, to
venture ones head in a doubtful cause—

More. Suppose the Cause to be false; when I had done my best to inform
my self that what I did was Legal, and could not be convinced to the
Contrary, I had nothing more to do but to Submit my Self to the Severity of the New made Law, and leave the Event to the Creator and Disposer of the World, So I tell Thee again that an Upright and unprejudiced Conscience is our Plea before any Human Tribunal, Nay, more
that it is at once the Law and Judge that must Convict or Absolve Us
in all we do or think thô We stand accused by no Man. The Basis of
all Religion and the Bond of all Society is founded upon this Strict adherence to Truth, and constancy of Mind in the Defence of it.

"Suppose the Cause to be false"—a remarkable, disastrous conces-
sion which opens the way for the vicar, two pages later, to drive
home his point: "In honest Prose I must tell You, Sir Thomas, that in
difficult cases there must be some Allowances made; if we cannot
bring the thing to our Conscience, we must e'en Strive as much as we
can to bring our Conscience to the thing. Mahomet and the Mountain seems to me not so unreasonable as some Strait laced Christians
think it." More is thus provoked to authoritarian recrimination: "Go
to, I contemn You now." And he adds the petulant remark that were
he again chancellor he would not give the vicar a place.

Neither the vicar nor More is Prior's hero. There is none, though
the vicar has such a vibrant character that the reader may tend to
favor him, especially after More waxes self-righteous. Prior's own
"suppleness of spirit (not to give it a worse name)," in the words of a
distinguished commentator,[9] may seem to add weight to such an in-

[9] Maynard Mack, "Matthew Prior: *et Multa Prior Arte . . . ,*" *Sewanee Review,*
LXVIII (1960), 169–70. Monroe K. Spears remarks, "As usual, Prior sees both
sides of the question; his sympathy for the Vicar is at least as strong as his admiration for More" ("Matthew Prior's Religion," *PQ,* XXVII [1948], 162). In an
essay Prior was writing at about the time of the dialogues, he explained, "I did not
launch much out into Satyr; which however agreeable for the present to the Writers or Incouragers of it does in time do neither of them good, considering the un-
certainty of Fortune, and the various change of Ministry, where every Man as he
resents may punish in his turn of Greatness" ("Heads for a Treatise upon Learning," in Wright and Spears, I, 583).

terpretation, but the dialogue will not sustain it. The vicar, it is true, alludes at the end to Gilbert Burnet's adverse judgment on More, which, according to R. W. Chambers, became standard opinion in England through the eighteenth and nineteenth centuries. In the *History of the Reformation* (1679–1714) Burnet described More as a man who thought freely during his early years, the period of *Utopia,* but later became a slave and instrument of priestly repression.[10] This is not the More who speaks in Prior, however. Perhaps the key to Prior's attitude is best drawn from Addison, in the paragraph succeeding the lines already quoted above. "There is no great danger of Imitation from [More's] Example. Mens natural fears will be a sufficient guard against it. I shall only observe that what was Philosophy in this extraordinary Man, would be Frenzy in one who does not resemble him as well in the cheerfulness of his Temper, as in the sanctity of his Life and Manners." [11] The vicar's triumph is to have strained the patience of a saint, goading him into intolerance, into an attempt to impose his own exalted standards upon an ordinary man, and into divorcing his sanctity from the cheerfulness which Addison singled out. But it must be borne in mind that while More goes to excess, the vicar never, on his side, departs from it, never adopts any moral standard whatsoever, and in the final pages he too forsakes his cheerful insouciance, resorts to grave accusations, and finds refuge in sarcasm. That a bond of sympathy joins him to his creator cannot be doubted (*Noli contradicere Priori,* says the vicar; Don't argue with your master, or Prior), but there is no evidence that Prior admires *him* in any unreserved way. Yet the dialogue, ending more solemnly than it began, promotes an indulgent rather than a thoroughgoing skepticism, reflecting a world of disconcerting yet vital complexity in which an energetic scoundrel may stumble upon truth and a good, candid, eloquent, forbearing man be tripped into error.

Skepticism is written larger in the second and longest of Prior's dialogues. Whereas Pope, imitating the first epistle of Horace's first book, had confessed ambivalence on the subject—"As drives the

[10] R. W. Chambers, *Thomas More* (London, 1935), p. 353.
[11] *The Spectator,* III, 301.

storm, at any door I knock,/ And house with Montagne now, or now with Lock"—Prior's intellectual home was a tower near Bordeaux, as he shows decisively in this conversation "between Mr: John Lock and Seigneur de Montaigne," where contraries clash head on: the methodical philosopher versus a man professedly without and opposed to method; the dignified commoner, an unceremonious nobleman; the theorist, a man devoted to practice; the analytical thinker, a synthesizer; the systematizer, an eclectic; the innovator, a reader steeped in old authors; and the spider, a bee—a comparison Montaigne himself draws in the course of the dialogue. Here, as in the other pieces, one character immediately seems favored, Montaigne, whose essays provided the basic idea for Prior's "Alma"; [12] at one point in the dialogue, Montaigne even refers to "Friend Prior," making Prior's favoritism explicit. But this dialogue, unlike the others, sustains its apparent hero throughout, proving his merit in the fire of debate.

It is hardly a fair debate, however, for from the opening speech, which Locke utters before discovering his companion's identity, it is clear that Prior has created his characters unequal. "Is it not wonderfull," Locke asks, "that after what Plato and Aristotle, Descartes and Malbranch have written of Human understanding, it should be reserved to Me to give the most clear, and Distinct Account of it?" A little later, Locke describes how he proceeded "O, most happily, in proving that we have no Innate Speculative or Practical Principles." The character of Locke, in short, is meant to be broadly comical and to that extent unreal, but the character of Montaigne constitutes a triumph on Prior's part and may be the most delightful example of characterization in all the eighteenth-century English dialogues of the dead. Years later Richard Hurd would caution dialogue-writers not to depend upon close imitation of characters' known styles. "The studied imitation of such peculiarities would be what we call *mimickry;* and

---

[12] W. P. Barrett, "Matthew Prior's *Alma*," *MLR,* XXVII (1932), 455. In an essay entitled "Opinion" Prior supplied a useful gloss for this dialogue: "I DONT pretend to Examine the Nature and Essence of this Mind of Ours, This *Divinae particula auræ* as a Divine or a Philosopher, but as a Stander by to take a little Notice of some of its Motions" (Wright and Spears, I, 587).

would therefore border upon *ridicule,* the thing of all others which
the genius of this Dialogue most abhors. In Comedy itself, the most
exact writers do not condescend to this minute imitation." [13] Although Hurd had in mind serious dialogues, his remark regarding
comedy would seem to make his statement universal. However,
Prior's Montaigne proves a pleasing exception to the truth of Hurd's
observation, a character supremely fitted, like the real Montaigne, to
border upon the ridiculous and yet survive. It may be doubted
whether Montaigne in life was ever more himself than is his representation in this dialogue. Nearly all the man seems here: his volubility,
his miscellaneous learning, his earthy observations of ordinary life, his
humility, his audacity, his verve. Indeed there is some of the real
Montaigne, for Prior draws liberally upon the *Essays.* Like James Boswell, whose mind became so "strongly impregnated with the John-
sonian aether" that he "could, with much . . . facility and exactness,
carry in my memory and commit to paper the exuberant variety of
his wisdom and wit," [14] Prior's devotion to Montaigne resulted in a
wonderful representation of the Frenchman's personality and manner.
Unlike Boswell, Prior could legitimately invent sayings for his subject, and some of these sayings seem worthy of inclusion in the *Essays;* for example, "I have observed that there is Abcedarian Ignorance that precedes Knowledge, and a Doctoral Ignorance that comes
after it."

Poor Locke, to find himself in such a contest. Yet he gains strength
as he goes, soon leaving rodomontade for argument and, at one point
well into the dialogue, drawing blood. "Faith," Montaigne confides, "I
think he has me a little upon the hipp, with his Logic, where one
cannot perfectly Excuse, all one can do is to recriminate. You know,
Sir, I never was a great admirer of Logic." Somewhat like the vicar,
Montaigne has a reply for Locke's every statement and speaks with
unfailing assurance, if not with perfect congruency, soon driving

[13] *Moral and Political Dialogues with Letters on Chivalry and Romance,* 6th ed.
(London, 1788), I, 1.
[14] *Life of Johnson,* ed. George Birkbeck Hill, rev. by L. F. Powell (Oxford,
1934–50), I, 421.

Locke from logic to ridicule. Mockingly, Locke describes Montaigne
at home listening to a French peasant as he tries to read the *Essays*
aloud, floundering in a bog of hard names. Until Locke stops speaking, he seems to have the advantage, but his superiority is illusory because now Montaigne has Locke where he wants him, on shifting
ground, all formal logic out of reach. Montaigne retaliates in kind,
his rebuttal amazingly witty—a high point not just in the dialogues of the dead but in eighteenth-century writing. For more than
three pages Montaigne revels in parody, imagining that the philosopher, likewise at home, has just told his servant, "John, . . . You may
go down and Sup, Shut the door." Here is John's human understanding in action:

The vibration of the Air and it's Undulation Strike the Tympanum of my
Ear, and these Modifications being thus Conveyed to my Sensorium, certain words in the English Language, (for no other do I understand)
produce a determined Conception. John You may go down and Sup; Shut
the door. Now *John* has been a common Appellative to Millions of Men,
thrô many Ages, from Apostles, Emperors, Doctors and Philosophers,
down to Butlers and Valets de Chambre and Persons of my Quality; some
of whom however Christened John, are commonly called Jack, but pass
for that; Now to none of these could my Master Speak, for they are either
Dead or Absent; it must therefore be to me; doubtful again: for my Masters own Name is John, and being a Whimsical Person, he may probably
talk to himself. No, that cant be neither, for if he had Commanded himself, why did he not obey himself: If he would go down why does he sit
stil in the Elbow-chair, 'twas certainly therefore meant to me *John,* not to
him *John.* Well then, go down and Sup, go down. Whither? To the
Centre of the Earth, there I may Sup with Fiends upon Brimstone broth,
to the bottom of the Thames, there I may Sup with Cod and Mackerell,
and as Hamlet says not Eat but be Eaten, To the Coal hole or the Wood-
house, there indeed I may find what will dress a Supper, but nothing else
to the present purpose of my own Supping. It must therefore be to the
Kitching, and in this determined Sense I will receive my Masters kind
Admonition. Now again . . .

John does finally get to the kitchen, after threading his way through
the bewildering flow-chart of associations, but having extricated himself from one of Locke's webs he immediately finds himself in an-

other, a semantic dispute with the cook and the butler. Not until *Tristram Shandy* did Locke suffer a comparable manhandling.

Cromwell in the last dialogue complains of being jostled by hostile shades, and Clenard in the first offers to submit his dispute with Charles to be judged by Dionysus the Younger, but the two middle dialogues make no mention of other shades. Montaigne and Locke, More and the Vicar sit in isolation like Descartes within the little room of himself at the beginning of the *Meditations,* seeking stability, a base upon which to fix truth. There are no infernal judges like those in Fénelon, fulcrums with respect to which the reader may perceive whether a character's scale is rising or falling. The scales of More and the Vicar plunge through space—their dialogue, like Fontenelle's thirty-six pieces, exposing the bottomlessness of human reasoning— while those of Charles and Clenard, Cromwell and his porter, spin in parodic circles. These three dialogues are predominantly critical; construction is the business of Locke and Montaigne, or at least Montaigne. Straw Locke has merely intensified his isolation by delving into only himself, distracting himself with imaginings—or so Montaigne says and nothing in the dialogue contradicts it. Locke has concentrated upon method to the utter exclusion of substance. All Locke says against Montaigne, however, is that the essays draw too much from other authors and lack systematic order. Of the substance, the considered opinions to be found in Montaigne's writing, Locke says nothing, while Montaigne claims to have attained a comfortable degree of stability by looking beyond his own thoughts to the thoughts of others (the vulgar as well as the learned), to have ordered his thoughts according to his experience, and to have pondered upon proper living, not mere behavior. "Mr: Lock, Your Mind was given You for the Conduct of your Life, not meerly for Your own Speculation; nor should it be imployed only upon it self, but upon other things. I think we Should take our Understanding as Providence hath given it to us, upon Content, As we would do a handsom Summ of Money, sent us by a good Friend; and spend our time rather in making use of it than in counting it. A Man should live with his Alma (as Friend Prior calls her) as he would do with his Wife, having taken her for Better and for Worse. He should be civil to her, keep her in good humor." Instead of the inaccessible, absolute stability, the empiricist seeks buoyancy, and Montaigne proves that he has found it, to his friend Prior's satisfaction, by maintaining his wit and good humor to the end of the dialogue. His pusillanimous counterpart the vicar was not so successful. The blend of philosophy and cheerfulness which Addison attributed to More, Prior found in Montaigne.

Because this dialogue, unlike the others, is longer than it need have been, the dramatic action so uncomplicated and Montaigne so loquacious, it is reasonable to think that Prior dwelt lovingly upon it. The work became not simply a dialogue but also a compendium, such as a man banished from public life might record in his journal, of tried and heartening wisdom drawn from a favorite author. Montaigne had spoken in Fontenelle, Charles in Fénelon, Cromwell in several primitive English dialogues; here they speak anew, their voices counterpointed by Prior's distinctive blend of skepticism and energy, disillusionment and generosity. Had Prior lived longer, he would have written more dialogues of the dead, at least six. He recorded a few fragments of additional dialogues and listed some intended participants: Cardinals Ximenes and Wolsey (who later met in Lyttelton's twenty-first dialogue), Wolsey and Cranmer, Luther and Loyola, Spenser and Camden, Jane Shore and the wife of Edward IV, Virgil and Spenser.[15] Had all these conversations been completed, and published in Prior's time, the history of the genre in England might well have been much longer, richer, and more compelling. Given those he did write, however, the time is past due for readers to discover them and take them to their hearts.

In the years after Prior's death, the dialogue of the dead was put to a variety of uses. When Jack Sheppard and Jonathan Wild were executed, they could be shown meeting in Hades, as they were in a rude pamphlet entitled *News from the Dead,* or Sheppard could speak his mind to a Great Man like Julius Caesar, as he did in the *British Jour-*

[15] Wright and Spears, II, 1012.

nal for December 4, 1725: "Is it more a Crime to pick a Lock, than unhinge a Constitution? Are a Pair of Fetters more sacred than the Liberty of the People?" We are but a step away from *The Beggar's Opera* in this simple, lively colloquy, perhaps the first but not the last to appear in a British periodical. Royalty could be as interesting as roguery: Ulrica Eleanora of Sweden and Anna I of Russia discuss the incompatibility of love and ambition in the *Gentleman's Magazine* (1738), a little prematurely, since both the ladies were still alive; several monarchs convene to bewail the tribulations of sovereignty in the *Museum* (1747); and, as Mrs. Morley and Mrs. Freeman, Queen Anne and Sarah, Duchess of Marlborough, speak at length in a framed dialogue of 1745, before the Queen is conveyed to Elysium and the Duchess to Erebus. Or departed experts might be conjured up to pass judgment on matters of topical concern, as was Dr. Samuel Garth, the author of *The Dispensary,* who in a dialogue of 1744 questioned the efficacy of tar water, the nostrum which Bishop Berkeley had promoted earlier that year with his *Siris.* In a dialogue of 1753, Jonathan Swift returned to the aisles of St. Patrick's in order to say a few additional words about the economic condition of Ireland, during a long and lively conversation with Thomas Prior, a founder of the Dublin Society. It is not hard to imagine what posthumous conversations one might read today if the genre were still popular.

Playwrights too felt the attractions of the underworld. First produced in 1740, subsequently revised and expanded, David Garrick's *Lethe* became one of the century's most popular afterpieces, with its gouty lord (a part Garrick usually played) who complains to Aesop that the Elysian Fields are "laid out most detestably," that Styx wants a "Serpentine Sweep." [16] As if in a series of dialogues, Aesop speaks to a number of colorful characters, but they are still alive, only visitors

[16] *Lethe, a Dramatic Satire . . . ,* 6th ed. (London, 1767), p. 24. Based on similar works by William Walsh and James Miller, *Lethe* was first published in 1749, though an unauthorized version had appeared in Dublin in 1745 (Elizabeth P. Stein, *David Garrick, Dramatist* [New York, 1938], pp. 25–26). Mary E. Knapp traces the play's popularity in "Garrick's Last Command Performance," *The Age of Johnson: Essays Presented to Chauncey Brewster Tinker,* ed. Frederick W. Hilles (New Haven, 1949), pp. 61–71.

to Hades. There are also scenes below in two of Fielding's plays, *The Author's Farce* (1730) and *Eurydice,* the second of which accompanied *A Journey from This World to the Next* in his *Miscellanies* (1743). Indeed, it is strange that Fielding, whose admiration for Lucian led him to contemplate a translation of Lucian's works [17] and to write a Lucianic dream vision in the *Champion* (May 24, 1740), never managed to write a true dialogue of the dead. His "Dialogue Between Alexander the Great and Diogenes the Cynic," which first appeared in the *Miscellanies,* would be a fine dialogue of the dead if the characters were not supposed to be alive.

Toward mid-century, there emerged a new reason to fear death: what would one's shade be made to say immediately afterward? Immunity might not be granted even if a person uncooperatively kept living. In 1748, Letitia Pilkington's *Memoirs* was published, containing some unflattering reminiscences of Swift, and there appeared also Teresia Constantia Phillips' *Apology* for her amorous adventures. The women continued to live and breathe, but their doing so did not prevent the publication, in 1749, of *A Dialogue in the Shades Below,* where Mrs. Pilkington, to her great embarrassment, finds herself speaking with Swift, and both women are futilely defended before the infernal judges by the courtesan Lais. The sentence befits persons not really dead: the women are condemned to resume their bodies, return to the world, and "wear out the Tediousness of Time, in a continual Round of Gallantry and Apologizing." And in 1752 appeared another dialogue anticipating the death of its subject, *The Inspector in the Shades. A New Dialogue in the Manner of Lucian,* in which John Hill—who wrote as the "Inspector" for the *London Advertiser,* carried on a newspaper war with Fielding, and drew forth Christopher Smart's *Hilliad*—is introduced to celebrated authors of the early eighteenth century. Portrayed as a boastful incompetent, Hill meets

---

[17] Wilbur L. Cross, *The History of Henry Fielding* (New Haven, 1918), III, 324. Fielding's *Dialogue between the Devil, the Pope, and the Pretender* (London, 1745), set in Rome, is not a dialogue of the dead. For Fielding's relationship to Lucian, see Henry Knight Miller, *Essays on Fielding's Miscellanies: A Commentary on Volume One* (Princeton, 1961), pp. 365–419.

and antagonizes Prior, Pope, Swift, Steele, and Addison, greeting the last with the words "Jo, my buck" and finally incurring much scurrilous abuse, like the two ladies of the earlier dialogue.

No trace of such scurrility taints a more important work, the largest collection in the genre to appear in England before Lyttelton's, the twelve "Dialogues of the Dead" in an obscure volume called *Various Essays* (1752), by Sylviana Sola.[18] "Who is Sylviana?" it will be asked, but the question seems unanswerable. The book, evidently her only publication, created no stir whatsoever; what autobiography it contains is scanty, its "Epistles" telling only that she is middle-aged, was once addicted to "Free-thinking," and has become a devout, orthodox Christian. Indeed, her devotion and orthodoxy burgeon on nearly every page of *Various Essays,* as does her enthusiasm for literature—not all literature, however. Homer appeals to her, largely as an inculpable foil to Christianity, but she has few kind words for the likes of Virgil, Milton, and Ovid. In the "Dialogues of the Dead," Sylviana's obsessive religiosity dispels dialectic almost completely, as the ninth dialogue vividly shows. It juxtaposes Plato and a woman unfortunately called "Blandina"—"juxtaposes" being exactly the word to describe the dialogue's structure. There are but two speeches; as far as suspense is concerned, there need only have been one. Plato appears, proclaiming his regret that he corrupted Socrates' "pure and simple Morals" with "the Aegyptian Mysteries" of Pythagoras and particularly regretting that he thought the human soul "no other (in my foolish Opinion, and the Pythagoreans) than a Particle discerpted from the divine Nature." In turn, Blandina belies her name, waxing tart as she rebukes Plato and affirms some appropriate Christian teachings.

[18] The place of publication, not given, was apparently London, for the *Gentleman's Magazine* gives the publisher's name as Owen (XXII [1752], 587), which could mean either of two men, both based in London according to H. R. Plomer and others, *A Dictionary of the Printers and Booksellers . . . from 1726 to 1775* (Oxford, 1932), pp. 187–88. There were, to the best of my knowledge, no reviews, but there seems to have been a second edition in 1767, when *Select Essays, on Various Subjects,* by Sylviana Sola, was described in the *Monthly Review:* "We take this to be some old publication, vamp'd with a new title; yet we do not remember to have met with the book before: and if it had not fallen in our way now, . . . we had sustained no loss" (XXXVI [1767], 156).

In a similar manner, although at greater length, another fictitious woman subdues Alcibiades (Dial. I); Queen Elizabeth, Tiberius (Dial. IV); "Moderna," Virgil (Dial. V); Homer, Milton (Dial. VI); Aesop, Ovid and a coquette (Dial. VII); Edward VI, Aristotle (Dial. VIII); and the martyr Theodora, Pythagoras (Dial. X). Women defeat men in five of the colloquies, advertising Sylviana's feminism and suggesting—especially when the victory of the boy Edward VI over Aristotle is considered—that the meek have inherited the underworld. Furthermore, the victories are neither doubtful nor Pyrrhic; Sylviana's heroes and heroines trample their enemies. The hero or heroine speaks the final words in all but one of the dialogues and almost always takes more than a page to do so. Why, then, did Sylviana choose the dialogue form? Especially, why did she choose the dialogue of the dead? In a postscript to her "Epistles," she explains that she wished "to communicate . . . what I imagine, a few of the Ancients would say to each other, or to the Moderns, on the Fiction of their meeting after Death, in the Shades below, according to the Pagan Stile, but which we may with Greater Propriety, call the Region of Truth." Accordingly, Sylviana employs no mythological characters, says nothing about the place in which her shades converse, and neither refers nor alludes to Lucian or any of his followers. Her "Lucian," so to speak, was perhaps Mrs. Elizabeth Rowe, author of *Friendship in Death: in Twenty Letters from the Dead to the Living* (1728) and other pious fictions.[19]

In the "Region of Truth," where Homer knows the Scriptures as well as anyone, it would be foolish to expect argument, the soul of the dialogue. Still, disagreement occurs in the "Dialogues," making three of them bearable. All three set a venerable ancient against a modern who goes unnamed—unlike other dialogue-writers of her time, Sylviana seems to have thought the naming of anyone later than Milton an impropriety. So, in Dialogue II Cato of Utica opposes and defeats a "Modern Senator," and in Dialogue III Cicero does the same with a "Modern Orator," but Sylviana's best effort is Dialogue

---

[19] For an account of Mrs. Rowe's productions, see John J. Richetti, *Popular Fiction before Richardson: Narrative Patterns, 1700–1739* (Oxford, 1969), pp. 239–59.

XI, between Socrates and a "Modern Moralist" who is identifiable as the third Earl of Shaftesbury. Drawing on passages in the *Characteristics,* she gives Shaftesbury some temporarily effective arguments, though of course Socrates has the last, crushing words.[20] Against her well-intentioned failure, however, and against Sheffield's perverse use of history (matched, it may be said, by that of a dialogue between Wolfe and Montcalm published in 1759), Lyttelton's *Dialogues of the Dead* will be seen to best advantage. Lyttelton could, on occasion, enliven morality with wit, and if he had a muse she was certainly Clio.

[20] The Moralist remembers praising Socrates for laughing when satirized in the theater; the passage is in "A Letter Concerning Enthusiasm," *Characteristics,* ed. John M. Robertson (London, 1900), I, 23–24. Sola's dialogue also draws on "Sensus Communis . . ." (*ibid.,* I, 43–49).

Chapter IV

Lord Lyttelton and Mrs. Montagu

> Gentle to me and affable hath been
> Thy condescension. . . .
>
> —*Paradise Lost,* VIII. 648–49

Ready-made terms like "classical" and "neoclassical" cannot be made to cover a Pope or a Johnson, but they hang well on some of the eighteenth century's lesser men of letters, George, Lord Lyttelton for one. He was nothing if not conventional; all his graces lay within the reach of art, sometimes with room to spare, and much the same may be said of Elizabeth Montagu, who contributed three pieces to the collection of twenty-eight dialogues which Lyttelton published, anonymously, in 1760. Very successful in its time, the volume attained a third edition in four months,[1] was succeeded by *Four New Dialogues of the Dead* of Lyttelton's in 1765 (added the same year to the rest in a fourth edition), and attracted flattering notices, imitations, and replies in kind, even a long pamphlet of criticism, the

---

[1] Actually a fourth edition; an unidentified second edition appeared right after the first, according to William B. Todd, "Patterns in Press Figures: A Study of Lyttelton's *Dialogues of the Dead*," *Studies in Bibliography: Papers of the Bibliographical Society of the University of Virginia,* ed. Fredson Bowers, VIII (Charlottesville, 1956), 232. The first edition is reputed to have sold out the day it was published (Rose Mary Davis, *The Good Lord Lyttelton: A Study in Eighteenth Century Politics and Culture* [Bethlehem, Pa., 1939], p. 322). For the record, it was published on May 17 (*The Daily Advertiser,* May 17, 1760, p. 1), not in April as Davis says (p. 310).

anonymous *Candid and Critical Remarks on the Dialogues of the Dead: in a Letter from a Gentleman in London to his Friend in the Country.*[2] Periodicals reprinted a good many of the dialogues, French and German translators set to work on them; anthologists would appropriate them, and in 1771, creating a library for one of his countrymen, Thomas Jefferson did not overlook the *Dialogues of the Dead.*[3] Owen Ruffhead's representative review in the *Monthly Review* concludes like a seal of approval from the Enlightenment's consumer-protection agency: "There are few truths which men of sense and discernment are not convinced of; . . . is it no satisfaction to such, to find their opinion confirmed by an able, elegant, and judicious Writer, to see their sentiments illustrated by a pleasing variety of apposite and striking remarks; and to converse with the Worthies of Antiquity

[2] Published London, 1760. The author found the *Dialogues* disappointing, earning a hot bath of scorn from the *Critical Review,* IX (June, 1760), 494, and the *Monthly Review,* XXIII (July, 1760), 79–81, both of which had warmly greeted the collection.

[3] Reprinted: Dial. XIX, *Gentleman's Magazine,* XXX (May, 1760), 221–24; Dial. XIV, *London Chronicle,* May 20–22, 1760, pp. 490–93; Dial. II, *London Magazine,* XXIX (May, 1760), 227–28; Dial. XVII and XXVII (latter by Montagu), *Annual Register,* III (1760), 256–63; Dial. XXVI (by Montagu), *Universal Magazine,* XXV (May, 1760), 270–72; Dial. XXX, *Universal Museum,* I (June, 1765), 287–89; Dial. VI and XX, *Journal encyclopédique,* IV, Part i (May, 1760), 53–80; Dial. XXXII, *ibid.,* V, Part iii (August, 1765), 76–87. Egilsrud (*Le "Dialogue des morts" dans les littératures française, allemande et anglaise (1644–1789)* [Paris, 1934], p. 105) says that Dial. XVIII appeared in the *Imperial Magazine,* I (June, 1760), 299, and Dial. III and VI in *Nouveaux Dialogues des morts recueillis dans divers journaux et choisis avec soin* (Bouillon, 1775), but I have been unable to examine them. Translations: the *Catalogue général des livres imprimés de la Bibliothèque Nationale: Auteurs,* CII (Paris, 1930), 406–7 lists two editions of Elie de Joncourt's translation (The Hague, 1760); another translation, by Jean Des Champs (London, 1760); and an anonymous translation of the fourth edition (Amsterdam, 1767). Christian Gottlob Kayser's *Vollständiges Bücher-Lexikon, 1750–1910,* III (Leipzig, 1835), 616, lists a translation by J. Oelrichs (Berlin, 1761) and another, anonymous translation (Hamburg, 1767). Des Champs' work seems to have been supervised by Lyttelton; see Lyttelton's letter to Voltaire printed in the *Annual Register,* IV (1761), 34–35. Anthologies: *Harrison's British Classicks,* Vol. VII (London, 1795); *Cassell's National Library,* Vol. CXC (London, 1889). Jefferson's recommendation of Lyttelton is in a letter to Robert Skipwith (August 3, 1771), *Papers,* ed. Julian P. Boyd, I (Princeton, 1950), 80.

in that genuine cast of character, which they have always supposed them to bear when alive?" [4]

As satisfying, it may seem, as seeing oneself in a suit with a vest; the combined complacency and defensiveness of Ruffhead's remarks bespeak the limitations of Lyttelton's work. Stolid as Blenheim Palace, correct as St. Paul's, predictable as the other end of a formal garden, Lyttelton's collection offers few opportunities to the adventurous intellect, an abundance to the captious. *"Dead* dialogues," said Horace Walpole, and twenty years after their publication Samuel Johnson expressed himself only a little less severely in his life of Lyttelton: "the production, rather, as it seems, of leisure than of study, rather effusions than compositions," [5] a verdict not at odds with those of later critics. Johan S. Egilsrud found the work's distinctive quality to be *solidité;* Lyttelton's biographer, Rose Mary Davis, accepted an eighteenth-century pronouncement, that the nobleman was "rather too grave to be quite Lucianic, too polite to be merry, and too wise to be very entertaining." [6] Even someone so devoted to Augustan literature as Austin Dobson, though he insisted the dialogues might still give pleasure, conceded it was of a "faded" sort.[7] The trouble is, few of the past two hundred years' generalizations about the merits of these dialogues have been accompanied by much in the way of evidence or argument or, above all, qualification. Can so many separate dialogues be driven into one category? Hardly, yet even critics fond of Lyttelton's writing have been content to try. John Wilson Croker, for ex-

[4] *Monthly Review,* XXIII (July, 1760), 80.

[5] Walpole, Letter to Sir Horace Mann (May 24, 1760), *Correspondence,* XXI, ed. W. S. Lewis, Warren Hunting Smith, and George L. Lam (New Haven, 1960), 407. Johnson, "Lyttelton," *Lives of the English Poets,* ed. George Birkbeck Hill (Oxford, 1905), III, 451.

[6] Egilsrud, pp. 162, 168. Davis, p. 325.

[7] "Titled Authors of the Eighteenth Century," *Side-Walk Studies* (London, 1902), p. 200. Oliver Elton thought the *Dialogues* "dreary" (*A Survey of English Literature, 1730–1780* [London, 1928], I, 81); A. Hamilton Thompson, deplorably unoriginal ("Thomson and Natural Description in Poetry," *The Cambridge History of English Literature,* ed. A. W. Ward and A. R. Waller [Cambridge, 1919–31], X, 115).

ample, found most of the dialogues "the production of a well-stored and well-regulated mind—conceived with judgment, and executed with taste"; [8] which of the dialogues, or why he thought so, he did not say. The case is otherwise with earlier critics, the contemporaries of Lyttelton and Mrs. Montagu, who bent themselves to detailed observation and interpretation but whose comments often enough seem arbitrary or inaccurate—and suggest a degree of subtlety and tough-mindedness in some of the dialogues which criticism, on the whole, has overlooked. The dialogues pleased many but did not please long, in part because the assumptions on which the authors (and a critic like Ruffhead) operated are not immediately available to the modern reader, demand a conscious effort of imaginative sympathy; in part because of the collection's unevenness. No need to exalt the valleys or make the rough places plain; it is enough to see the collection whole in its parts if one seeks to understand what was vital about it and what may remain so.

Lyttelton's earliest readers might have found it hard to imagine that he would someday require introduction. A prominent Whig politician (1709–73), a cousin of the Grenvilles and related by marriage to William Pitt, Lyttelton sat in Parliament from 1735 on and proved an ardent "patriot" in opposition to Walpole. Beginning in 1744, he enjoyed about twelve years of political prosperity, becoming a Lord of the Treasury in the Broad Bottom administration and later attaining the positions of Privy Councillor and Chancellor of the Exchequer under the Duke of Newcastle, but his performance in these positions fell short of remarkable success, and he was unfortunately at odds with Pitt during the Great Commoner's years of glory; [9] poor Lyttelton (as Johnson called him),[10] a frail, ungainly man without

---

[8] Review of Robert Phillimore's edition of Lyttelton's *Memoirs and Correspondence, Quarterly Review,* LXXVIII (1846), 259. Ananda Vital Rao says almost nothing to support his favorable judgment (*A Minor Augustan: Being the Life and Works of George, Lord Lyttelton, 1709–1773* [Calcutta, 1943], p. 289).

[9] Walpole identified Pericles (Dial. XXIII) as Pitt (p. 409). So did Ruffhead (*Monthly Review,* XXII [May 1760], 410) and the author of *Candid and Critical Remarks* (p. 53), though without naming him.

[10] *Lives of the English Poets,* III, 452.

talent for debate, acquired more fame for his rectitude than for his abilities. As first Baron Lyttelton, a rank he attained in 1756, he brightened his remaining years with moderate political activity, scholarship, the cultivation of his renowned gardens at Hagley, Worcestershire, and the edification of his bluestocking admirers. These activities lent some measure of light to a melancholy old age, made so by successive political, marital, and paternal disappointments.

Though Lyttelton the statesman enjoyed no overwhelming success, there can be small doubt of his quality as a man; indeed, he was in many respects the pattern of an eighteenth-century gentleman. At Eton and Oxford, he excelled in scholarship, and later earned esteem for his enlightened patronage of such authors as Pope, Thomson, and Fielding (who dedicated *Tom Jones* to him). Esteemed too were his own writings, which range from satire in the "Persian Letters" tradition to a laborious history of Henry II, from poetry to political periodical essays to an apologetic work on St. Paul. His formal parliamentary speeches (as opposed to his impromptu efforts) often drew praise on all sides. Sad to say, the appellation "Good Lord Lyttelton" was originally employed to distinguish him from his rakish son Thomas, "the wicked Lord Lyttelton," but the elder Lyttelton probably deserved the honorific. As Thomson wrote of him in "The Castle of Indolence,"

> every worth he had;
> Serene yet warm, humane yet firm his mind,
> As little touched as any man's with bad. . . .[11]

The reader who opens the *Dialogues of the Dead* may soon think its poor reputation justified: the first five colloquies are among the

[11] I, lxv, 2–4, *The Complete Poetical Works,* ed. J. Logie Robertson (London, 1908), p. 274. Never published and now perhaps lost are the dialogues of the dead written by the "wicked" Lord Lyttelton, according to William Combe, "to ridicule those of his father and Mrs. Montagu. I remember three of them . . . if I recollect right replete with wit, Spirit and Blasphemy and Patriotism. —The parties were, King David of Israel and Caesar Borgia, —the Saviour of the World and Socrates, —Epaminondas and General Wolfe" (from a manuscript in the Huntington Library quoted by Harlan W. Hamilton, *Doctor Syntax: A Silhouette of William Combe, Esq. (1742–1823)* [London, 1969], p. 127).

least appealing in the collection, perhaps the most dismal moment occurring in the course of Dialogue IV, at the outset a promising piece. Addison and Swift begin to argue about who was the other's superior in wit. As Addison sets about defending himself, Mercury enters and Addison hails him. It is shocking, what the god does then; here is Addison speaking:

> Hail, divine Hermes! a question of Precedence in the Class of Wit and Humour, over which you preside, having arisen between me and my countryman, Dr. Swift, we beg leave—
> *Mercury.* Dr. Swift, I rejoice to see you—How does my old Lad? how does honest Lemuel Gulliver? Have you been in Lilliput lately, or in the flying Island, or with your good nurse Glumdalclitch? Pray when did you eat a crust with Lord Peter? Is Jack as mad still as ever? I hear that, since you published the history of his case, the poor fellow, by more gentle Usage, is almost got well. If he had but more Food he would be as much in his Senses as Brother Martin himself. But Martin, they tell me, has lately spawned a strange brood of Methodists, Moravians, Hutchinsonians, who are madder than ever Jack was in his worst days. It is a great pity you are not alive again, to make a new edition of your Tale of the Tub for the use of these fellows. —Mr. Addison, I beg your pardon, I should have spoken to you sooner; but I was so struck with the sight of my old friend the Doctor, that I forgot for a time the respects due to you.[12]

Unhappy Addison! Mercury's rude but spontaneous behavior, with the heartfelt preference for Swift it implies, is lively enough to seem visible. How amusing to see the First Victorian snubbed, his absolute construction left hanging, by the Fontenelle in Lyttelton.

But Lyttelton will not let us enjoy such spontaneity; the Whig statesman cared too much for order, truth, and decency to permit such mischief to be sustained (especially against another Whig). Mercury apologizes, then, a few lines further, begins to explain what caused his rudeness. "I am a Wit, and a Rogue, and a Foe to all Dignity. Swift and I naturally like one another. He worships me more than Jupiter, and I honour him more than Homer." The preference for Swift, Mer-

---

[12] Quotations in this chapter are drawn from *Dialogues of the Dead. The Fifth Edition, Corrected* (London, 1768).

cury confesses, rests on a fault in the god's nature; upon sober consideration he must prefer the wit of Addison: "Your's is divine. It tends to exalt human nature." Lyttelton's spark of drama sputters in the damp of Whig righteousness, and the reader who esteems Addison but prizes Swift, and who responds to dramatic momentum, feels let down. He may also feel that Mercury has not read Swift very attentively.

The event just described implies what Lyttelton thought of satire, an attitude which becomes explicit as the dialogue continues. Swift, upset by this late turn of affairs, asks whether his harsh satire was completely worthless, as Mercury claims. "Is Whipping of no use to mend naughty Boys?" Swift demands, and Mercury replies, "Men are generally not so patient of Whipping as Boys: and a rough Satirist is seldom known to mend them." The reply, probably true, epitomizes Lyttelton's view of satire. The question of how wit is to be employed comes up in numerous places throughout the dialogues, and moderation is inevitably recommended; the conventional, Horatian weapons have their place but savage indignation, like an ultimate bomb, must be reserved for only the most dire situations. Lucian, for example, terminates Dialogue XXII by telling Rabelais how much they must regret that they did not exert "all the Sharpness of our Wit, to combat the flippancy and Pertness of Those, who argue only by Jests against Reason and Evidence, in Points of the highest and most serious Concern."

This is not the Lucian met in Chapter I, or if he is he has suffered brainwashing, a hostage in Lyttelton's Elysium (it is never called Hades). In most of the dialogues, Lyttelton's cold-war attitude toward satire—comparable, Johnson thought, to Fénelon's,[13] so unlike Prior's and Fontenelle's—and a full bag of pieties set him far apart from Lucian; how far, the dialogue right after Addison-Swift reveals, a conversation between Ulysses and Circe. Not a dialogue of the dead, it was included, as Lyttelton explains in a footnote, in accordance with the precedent of Fénelon, who put a dozen dialogues of the living in

[13] *Lives of the English Poets,* III, 452.

his collection, one of them an encounter between Ulysses and a crew-man content to wallow among Circe's swine. In Lyttelton, Ulysses pleads homesickness, then responds to coaxing with the admission that he longs to rejoin Penelope. Clearly, Lyttelton had in mind not so much the Circe episode of the *Odyssey* as the Calypso episode; only the beasts he mentions recall the enchantress. Ulysses' requiring Circe to promise him a safe voyage home, and the comparison of her im-mortal beauty with Penelope's vulnerability to age come straight from the original Ulysses' debate with Calypso.[14] What is more, Lyt-telton departs radically from the pattern Homer set regarding Ulysses and Circe: although the hero falls homesick during the seven years spent with Calypso, he revels so in the hospitality of Circe that he consents to leave her, a full year after his arrival, only because his men demand to go.[15] So much for Penelope! Ulysses, in Homer, never so much as mentions her to Circe, and though he proves a cold lover to Calypso there is no indication that his amours with Circe were anything but satisfying to both parties.

Lyttelton's Ulysses, then, is more scrupulous than Homer's—still more so than Lucian's. Ulysses and Calypso, the former now a shade, have parts in Lucian's *True History,* where the hero gives the narra-tor a letter for Calypso (Calypso, whom even Homer's Ulysses dis-dained). In the letter Ulysses laments that he ever left her and prom-ises he will return, furtively, the first chance he gets. Here Ulysses has become Don Juan. In Homer, though Ulysses speaks with Calypso much as he does with Circe in Lyttelton, the pair nevertheless retire together for a night of love, a pattern of behavior that apparently does not change until Ulysses departs five days later. But the moment the eighteenth-century dialogue nears completion, it is good-by to Circe, and Ulysses off on his raft, the five nights deleted or at least scarcely implied. He has become Sir Charles Grandison, and not even the claims of the "young Gentry," for "whose Service" (Lyttelton's pref-ace has it) the volume "is more particularly intended," can excuse such an utterly bowdlerized reconstruction of Homer's protagonist.

[14] *Odyssey* 5. 177–79, 211–13.   [15] *Ibid.,* 7. 259–63; 10. 467–74.

Bourgeois and dishonest, it must appall the reader, displaying Lyttelton's priggishness in its major phase. (The printer of the *Dialogues of the Dead,* it is worth noting, was none other than Samuel Richardson, whose fiction Mrs. Montagu roundly praises in Dialogue XXVIII.) A libertine Swift, an uxorious Ulysses, stand with assorted dullards like the brood of Cerberus at the portals of Lyttelton's collection, enough to turn the curious visitor away. But there is a sop, patience. Once the reader has passed the fifth dialogue, the worst is behind him, and some of the better dialogues seem sufficiently craftsmanlike to balance, if not redeem, the bad.

In general, however, Lyttelton's writing lacks pointedness on those subjects about which, either personally or professionally—the distinction is hardly worth making—he cared a great deal. He was candid when he could be, not often; so close was his attachment to dogmatic opinion in some matters of private morality and public policy that, more than just depriving him of dialectical freedom, it stayed his hand from giving his "villains" even temporary advantages. In attempting to woo Ulysses away from Penelope, Circe gets no help from her author, the socially prominent Christian statesman. The fair-minded reader, whatever his ethical convictions, may bask a moment in her offer of immortality, but that is her only positive argument. She quickly trades reasoning for invective: "I pity and despise you," she rants. "All you have said seems to me a Jargon of Sentiments fitter for a silly Woman than a great Man. Go, read, and spin too, if you please, with your Wife." Since this, of all approaches conceivable, is the least suitable to persuade Ulysses if he bears any likeness to his old Homeric self, Lyttelton, who liked himself to read the classics with his dear first wife,[16] easily makes Ulysses adhere to his plan. The reader feels cheated; surely the delights of Circe and her isle, which kept Homer's Ulysses in bliss a year, deserve more consideration than Lyttelton could dispose himself to give them.

In a short but acute study of Berkeley's dialogues, Donald Davie comments that at their best they exhibit an engaging degree of "can-

---

[16] Davis, p. 104.

dour," defining the term broadly to embrace not just frankness on the part of the characters but also an utterly disinterested attitude toward the subjects discussed and the opinions entertained, a desire to learn more than to triumph, a thoroughgoing courtesy which leads the characters to help each other in the task of definition, clarification, and deduction; in short, a generous civility.[17] This, the dialogues of Lyttelton already discussed here lack completely, and they are not alone in that respect. A stifling single-mindedness bridles Dialogue XXIV (to mention but one additional example), where Locke gives Bayle no respite as they discourse on what Lyttelton considered a pernicious philosophy, skepticism. "You are very severe upon me," Bayle complains, justifiably; Sylviana Sola might have written the piece. But it is in those dialogues dealing with central matters of statecraft that Lyttelton's self-righteousness comes most to the fore, since the majority of the dialogues are political. The shamefulness of a monarch's abdicating is the burden of Dialogue X, where the Swedish Chancellor Oxenstiern scolds Queen Christina. She offers some meager defense but confesses her error as soon as he departs.

And when Lyttelton enters the realm of British politics he steps with unfailing caution. The Duke of Argyll, who supported the union of England and Scotland, in Dialogue XXV thoroughly convinces the rebel Earl of Douglas that the marriage was made in Heaven. "What God has joined let no Man put asunder," exclaims the enlightened Douglas. In a few of the political conversations there is a semblance of candor, but only because each character comes equipped with a supply of concessions and repudiations. The first dialogue brings together Hampden and Lord Faulkland, sterling figures, a parliamentarian and a royalist of civil war days. They speak cordially in Elysium, freely admitting their respective limitations and finding agreement in the most capacious of commonplaces. The issues remain so unparticularized that there is little merit in the openness of the speakers, no achievement wrought in the course of the conversation—though to

[17] Donald Davie, "Berkeley and the Style of Dialogue," *The English Mind: Studies in the English Moralists Presented to Basil Willey,* ed. Hugh Sykes Davies and George Watson (Cambridge, 1964), p. 92.

be fair, there is some poignancy in this confrontation of moderate men whose times required them to choose between excesses, and in the rueful relief they found when they met their premature deaths.

What accounts for such blandness? Lyttelton's defective understanding of drama, among other things. He explained in his preface that he thought the form of dialogue "perhaps, one of the most agreeable Methods, that can be employed, of conveying to the Mind any Critical, Moral, or Political Observations; because the *Dramatic Spirit,* which may be thrown into them, gives them more Life, than they could have in Dissertations, however well written. And sometimes a new Dress may render an old Truth more pleasing to those, whom the mere Love of Novelty betrays into error." Too often, Lyttelton tried to inject a dramatic spirit into his conversations instead of conjuring it from animate combinations of characters and points of view.

Not always, however, and hence a case may be made for the enduring respectability, or rather, beauty, of some of the dialogues. When writing about the people of ages and nations removed from his own, he found occasions of productive liberty, opportunities for candor and dramatic development. But one must look closely to perceive the results, something his critics, blinded by the glare of their general impressions, have infrequently accomplished. Tobias Smollett, who seems to have appraised the book for the *Critical Review,* mistook the direction of Dialogue XVII, which represents an admirable tempering of Lyttelton's moral and political allegiances and thus provides a useful text for transition to the better pieces in the collection. Here Marcus Brutus confronts Atticus, accusing him of venality. Atticus, though, turns out to be steel more than straw, defending himself with vigor for two thirds of the dialogue and giving Smollett the impression that he was Lyttelton's favorite.[18] The parties of his time, Atticus

---

[18] *Criticial Review,* IX (May, 1760), 392–93. Davis (p. 323) attributes authorship to Smollett on Johnson's authority. An odd review, it is favorable to Lyttelton most of the way, then turns incoherently antagonistic. Smollett had ridiculed Lyttelton as Sir Gosling Scragg in *Peregrine Pickle* nearly ten years before the publication of the *Dialogues.*

asserts, deserved no support; Brutus' action was ill-timed and useless. The reasons have weight, but Brutus, as the reader would expect (especially if he has not forgotten the conversation between Hampden and Faulkland), comes off the better at the end. Still, to make him win, Lyttelton is forced—cornered by the fairness with which he impersonates Atticus—to unsheathe the full blade of his idealism. "The motives of our Actions," Brutus pontificates, "not the Success, give us here Renown," but he has paid full attention to Atticus' arguments and even shown some appreciation of Atticus' accomplishments. It is to the author's credit that, sustaining balance and suspense, he kept the blade sheathed so long.

Another Roman dialogue, the fifteenth, treats a theme that may cause the most receptive reader to shudder in memory of the Ulysses-Circe colloquy. Here Octavia argues against Portia and Arria (a variation not infrequent in the collection, the addition of a third speaker), on the subject of conjugal fidelity. Though Portia and Arria have died for their husbands, Minos has assigned a higher place in Elysium to Octavia, who not only suffered Antony's notorious infidelity but went so far as to care for his illegitimate children—and through it all continued to love him. Octavia has the last words, but Arria and Portia, contrary to what the reviewer in *Candid and Critical Remarks* says in scorning this dialogue,[19] do not approve of her actions, seeing them as laudable but setting a bad example. "Too good Subjects are apt to make bad Kings," observes Arria (in italics) with worldly insight, saving the piece from being simply an example of neoclassical hagiography. Lyttelton escapes the saccharine inanity of Dialogue V and resolves the problem with a nice discrimination of the levels and perils of self-sacrifice. It is extolled in Octavia, but not without dramatic deference to another point of view.

Characters from a much later time, Penn and Cortez, come to grips in Dialogue VIII, where the author's aversion to enthusiasm on the one hand and to imperialistic Catholicism on the other provided him with perspective; there was no risk in giving the characters full rein.

---

[19] *Candid and Critical Remarks*, pp. 48–49.

At first, as the reader might expect, Penn's righteousness glows against the shadow of Cortez' worldly ruthlessness as brotherly love seems to prevail over aggression and cautious self-defense. Then there occurs a distinct shift in tone; Penn suddenly becomes sharply derisive while his platitudes grow increasingly sanctimonious. Egilsrud, who has some good words for this dialogue, nevertheless complains of Lyttelton's intrusion of Christian terms and expressions into Elysium,[20] a just complaint about some of the other dialogues, perhaps, but not about this one, for the setting emphasizes quite forcibly the hollowness, to Lyttelton's mind, of Penn's piety. The last words are given to Cortez—an important advantage in Lyttelton's historical dialogues, so rarely are they ironical. Cortez questions both Penn's zeal and the purity of his motives, while judgment is left to the reader. According to the *Candid and Critical Remarks*, "The preference in point of moral virtue is bestowed on Penn; yet, on the whole, the argument, if there is any to this dialogue, appears to be left entirely unconcluded." [21] To me, however, Cortez comes off the better, despite the foregoing quotation, as Penn is exposed for his hypocrisy. Lyttelton champions neither, for he owed no fealty to either Quaker or conquistador, but unintentional error is preferred to sham. Treating the characters aloofly, Lyttelton approaches finesse.

The reviewer in *Candid and Critical Remarks* also misjudged the twentieth dialogue, which begins with an abrupt question put by Alexander the Great to Charles XII: "Your Majesty seems in great Wrath! Who has offended you?" A newcomer to Elysium, Charles answers, the poet Pope; he has called the two monarchs madmen. Charles suggests that they unite to throw all insolent scribblers into Tartarus, whether Pluto will permit it or not—whereupon Alexander demurs, observing that Charles did act madly often enough to justify Pope's opinion. They argue, Charles finding likenesses in his behavior and Alexander's, Alexander denying them, blood spilt on both sides, the controversy finally issuing in mutual accusations of cruelty. Alexander, who has held the position of strength, somewhat incon-

---

[20] Egilsrud, p. 170.   [21] *Candid and Critical Remarks*, p. 37.

stantly, throughout, speaks the final words, in which Lyttelton again discriminates deftly between the merits of his disputants. The Macedonian rises by lowering himself, to a point: "Upon the whole . . . from some Resemblance between us, I should naturally be inclined to decide in your favour, yet I must give the Priority in Renown to your Enemy, Peter Alexowitz. That great Monarch *raised* his Country; You *ruined* your's. He was a *Legislator,* you were a *Tyrant.*" Here the reviewer in *Candid and Critical Remarks* cried foul, disturbed that a "third point, intirely independent of the original question or answer, is tacked to the former, and given in the place of the latter" [22]—a myopic objection because the dialogue hinges on the question of greatness, not the original question of madness, and because in another of the dialogues, the second, Peter himself appears and, though treated approvingly on the whole, suffers a sharp rebuke for his inhumanity. There also, Peter is permitted to rank himself above Alexander. If the Alexander-Charles dialogue is seen as part of a series, Lyttelton's aim becomes clear. Charles, Alexander, and Peter, like Hannibal, Scipio, and Alexander in Lucian, are commendable in different degrees—though here none of the three is pronounced thoroughly admirable.

Disappointed that Lyttelton does not terminate "this dispute by an acknowledged inferiority on either side," the reviewer in *Candid and Critical Remarks* generalized to this effect some pages later. "Notwithstanding these dialogues are considerably longer than those of the archbishop of Cambray, [Lyttelton] has generally either found them still too short to wind up his intended decision of character, or has intentionally avoided determining on them himself, submitting a series of facts to the attention of his readers, reserving to them the right of judging for themselves with regard to them." [23] Johnson voiced a similar objection, that the characters "too often part without any conclusion"; yet he also thought "the names of persons too often enable the reader to anticipate their conversation" [24]—the dialogues, that is, are somehow both conventional and irresolute. John-

---

[22] *Ibid.,* p. 58.   [23] *Ibid.,* pp. 57, 62–63.
[24] *Lives of the English Poets,* III, 452, 451.

son was not a sympathetic reader of Lyttelton. Politically, personally, they had not seen eye to eye. Moreover, Johnson could have small appreciation for a genre purporting, even just as a formality, to reveal conditions in the afterlife, so awfully did he regard it, and his criticism disdained to pursue a schoolmaster, or a Whig, to his commonplaces. "Talk not of the Punick war," he advised Mrs. Thrale in July, 1775; his "dislike of that subject," R. W. Chambers comments, "was a standing joke. . . . He was provoked by the extravagant praise of Roman Republican institutions and virtues that was part of the Whigs' stock-in-trade." [25]

Johnson was a man for the ages, Lyttelton mainly for his own, writing to please others like himself, more or less grave and lettered gentlemen full of filial piety for the past. With what satisfaction Sir William Temple might have read the dialogues. History was a virtually self-contained compendium of reality timeless in its application to contemporary affairs: one age's Pericles was another age's Pitt, a George had the choice of ruling like Augustus, William of Orange, or Swedish Charles. Secular history became sacred to men who meditated on a Cato or a Cicero much as the Church contemplated its patron saints, who fused Heaven and Elysium and located them, as much as anywhere, in the minds of posterity or in more tangible habitations such as Stowe, the renowned Buckinghamshire estate of Lyttelton's uncle, Viscount Cobham.

"If any thing under Paradise could set me beyond all Earthly Cogitations; Stowe might do it," Alexander Pope wrote in a letter of 1731. [26] Terrestrial matters got much attention there in the subsequent decade, as Stowe became a meeting place for an Opposition faction, the "Boy Patriots," the "Cousinhood," or "Cobham's Cubs" as it was called, of which Lyttelton was a prominent member. In the same period, however, William Kent decked the grounds with an Elysian Fields, a Temple of Ancient Virtue, and a Temple of British Worthies (among them William III, Bacon, Milton, Hampden, and

---

[25] *The Letters of Samuel Johnson,* ed. R. W. Chapman (Oxford, 1952), II, 57*n*.
[26] *The Correspondence of Alexander Pope,* ed. George Sherburn (Oxford, 1956), III, 217.

Locke), creating an unworldly refuge which Thomas Whately, later in the century, described as follows:

The temple of friendship also is in sight just without the place; and within it, are the temples of antient virtue, and of the British worthies, the one in an elevated situation, the other low down in the valley, and near to the water: both are decorated with the effigies of those who have been most distinguished for military, civil, or literary merit; and near to the former stands a rostral column, sacred to the memory of captain Grenville, who fell in an action at sea: by placing here the meed of valour, and by filling these fields with the representations of those who have deserved best of mankind, the character intended to be given to the spot, is justly and poetically expressed; and the number of the images which are presented or excited, perfectly corresponds with it. Solitude was never reckoned among the charms of Elysium; it has been always pictured as the mansion of delight and of joy; and in this imitation, every circumstance accords with that established idea; the vivacity of the stream which flows through the vale; the glimpses of another approaching to join it; the sprightly verdure of the green-swerd, and every bust of the British worthies, reflected in the water; the variety of the trees; the lightness of their greens; their disposition; all of them distinct objects, and dispersed over gentle inequalities of the ground . . . give it a gaiety, which the imagination can hardly conceive, or the heart wish to be exceeded.[27]

Writing from Stowe in 1739, to Martha Blount, Pope found the improved garden "beyond all description [in] the New part of it; I am every hour in it," and bid her adieu with the explanation, "I'm going into the Elyzian Fields, where I shall meet your Idæa." [28]

There was also a fourteenth-century church on the grounds, that had served the village of Stowe until the villagers were removed to Dadford, a few miles away, to make room for landscaping. Although taste suffered the old building to remain, to be used for family serv-

[27] *Observations on Modern Gardening*, 2d ed. (London, 1770), pp. 220–21. For the chronology of Kent's improvements, see Margaret Jourdain, *The Work of William Kent* (London, 1948), pp. 49, 79. Peter Coats names the British Worthies and provides an evocative color photograph in *Great Gardens of Britain* (London, 1967), p. 49. More information may be found in *Stowe: A Guide to the Gardens*, by Laurence Whistler, Michael Gibbon, and George Clarke, rev. ed. ([Stowe], 1968), and, with numerous photographs, in Christopher Hussey's *English Gardens and Landscapes 1700–1750* (New York, 1967), pp. 89–113.

[28] *Correspondence*, IV, 185–86.

ices, its intolerable architecture had to be concealed with foliage, and the Temple of Ancient Virtue rose to terminate the prospect.[29] What Peter Gay has called "pagan Christianity"[30] might be invoked to describe the aesthetic as well as the political and historical thinking of Cobham's circle; in Cobham's case, the adjective should be stressed, in Lyttelton's the noun. Lyttelton's gardens at Hagley were more modest, "natural," and, with their ruined castle, less ostentatiously classical, though they contained a Doric temple and a statue, in Roman dress, of Frederick the Prince of Wales,[31] the young Marcellus of the Patriots' cause. For men who knew their Plutarch, recurrent exposure to the heroes, sages, and villains of history was as acceptable, practically as requisite, as natural, as hearing about the Nativity each Christmas. And one read the orthodox version. Plato tells Fénelon, in Lyttelton's third dialogue, "Your *Dialogues* breathe the pure spirit of Virtue, of unaffected Good Sense. . . . They are in general as superior to your Countryman Fontenelle's, as Reason is to false Wit, or Truth to Affectation." Revisionism was tantamount to heresy: Mrs. Montagu condemns it with harsh sarcasm through the mouth of an unprincipled bookseller in Dialogue XXVIII: "Or if even by tradition, but better still, if by papers in the Portian family, you could shew some Probability that Portia died of dram-drinking; you would oblige the world very much."

Holding such thoughts in mind, one can begin to understand Ruffhead's praise of Lyttelton, which must have warmed his stately heart. Put negatively, the dialogues were unexceptionable; positively, everything about them was right, as it should be. Reading them, the critic was transported to a region of truth beyond the confines of time and space where the subjects of his meditations, the exemplars of his values, seemed to speak once more, in new and sometimes more revealing encounters than life had provided or history had recorded—to speak as they ought, to be realized, to move in the mind instead of being moved by it. What a blissful privilege, to hear Titus and Scipio

[29] Dorothy Stroud, *Capability Brown* (London, 1950), p. 29.
[30] *The Enlightenment: An Interpretation,* I (New York, 1966), 256.
[31] Davis, p. 177.

discourse on continence (Dial. XI), Cato of Utica and Messalla Corvinus on the subordination of rampant ideals to political practicality (Dial. IX), Cardinals Wolsey and Ximenes—"In full-blown dignity see Wolsey stand"—on luxury and asceticism, ambition and patriotism (Dial. XXI), Scipio again and Caesar on the deference rulers owe to law (Dial. XXIX), Plato and Diogenes on the philosopher's relation to government (Dial. XXX), the widow of Sidney and the haughty Louise de Coligni on marriage and social advancement (Dial. XVI). Their conversations brought paradise before one's eyes. If the endings were foreseeable, as predictable as Heaven for the righteous, the middle portions were not. There Lyttelton could exercise invention. We know that neither Machiavelli nor the infamous Duke of Guise can emerge unscathed from the twelfth dialogue, realize it from the opening words, and we can guess too what accusations will be sustained. But it may be agreeably surprising to find that Lyttelton had read enough of Machiavelli to eschew facile or unqualified condemnation—in technique, after all, they were kindred spirits, devoted to discoursing upon historical examples—and it can be delectable to hear the Duke's conduct appraised according to Machiavelli's maxims.

Perhaps many men and women and some children could have written comparable dialogues, then. Lyttelton separates himself from the mere commonplace in the more discriminating, witty parallels and contrasts he draws (Plutarch is the author cited most frequently in his footnotes), like that at the end of Octavia's dialogue, already discussed, or that whereby Machiavelli rebukes his opponent in the very act of giving ground: "I was a Duke of Guise in the Republic of Letters." Again, Aristides, investigating the disagreement between Demosthenes and Phocion about taking part in the war against Philip, agrees with Demosthenes that war was necessary while reproving him for not employing the able general Phocion; turning to Phocion, he chides him for despairing of success (Dial. XXXI). In the ninth dialogue Messalla Corvinus, after enduring the scorn of Cato for his service to Augustus, the autocratic executioner of Cicero, observes that Cato himself would have accomplished nothing had he lived unless he had forsaken republican principles and consented to become "our Prince." Even a badly flawed dialogue can ring with perceptiveness, as the fourth does, at the beginning when Swift remarks, "Surely, Addison, Fortune was exceedingly inclined to play the Fool . . . when she made you a Minister of State, and me a Divine!"—at the end too, as Mercury assigns to each character a responsibility in Elysium:

When any Hero is brought hither, who wants to be humbled, let the task of lowering his arrogance be assigned to Swift. The same good Office may be done to a Philosopher vain of his wisdom and virtue, or to a Bigot puffed up with Spiritual Pride. The Doctor's discipline will soon convince the first, that with all his boasted Morality he is but a Yahoo; and the latter, that to be holy he must necessarily be humble. I would also have him apply his anticosmetic Wash to the painted face of female Vanity, and his Rod, which draws blood at every stroke, to the hard back of insolent Folly or petulant Wit. But Addison should be employed to comfort those, whose delicate minds are dejected with too painful a sense of some infirmities in their nature. To them he should hold his fair and charitable Mirrour, which would bring to their sight their hidden Excellencies, and put them in a temper fit for Elysium.

How reminiscent of Fénelon's disposal, through the same Mercury, of Cato and Scipio in the dialogue mentioned in Chapter I. Lyttelton knew the work of his predecessors just as he knew the biographies of his characters, taking hints from Fénelon and others but, as one might expect, resting this side of both derivativeness and conspicuous originality.[32] As judiciously, he selected the historical details that his

[32] Davis suggests that Lyttelton's subtler touches may owe something to Fontenelle (p. 311), but her evidence is scanty: that Hampden-Faulkland (Dial. I) has to do with moderation, as does Fontenelle's first dialogue, between Alexander and Phryne; that Lyttelton's anecdote about Apicius' African pilgrimage to taste a rare fish occurs in Fontenelle's dialogue between Apicius and Galileo. But Alexander and Phryne agree that it is immoderation which produces lasting fame, and Apicius and Galileo discuss astronomy as much as gastronomy, their conversation turning on a theme quite different from Lyttelton's. Egilsrud says Fénelon had compared Ximenes and Wolsey (p. 168), although Fénelon's one dialogue employing Ximenes shows him conversing with Richelieu. The reviewer in *Candid and Critical Remarks* noted that almost all the information in Ximenes-Wolsey (Dial. XXI) may be found in that dialogue of Fénelon's (p. 60). Lyttelton's dialogue, however, is nearly three times as long, much more fully developed, and different in theme (Fénelon's being that it is better to be born with ability than to be born to a high social station).

characters would bring into conversational play. Nobody has ever challenged his reliability, except one reviewer who found fault with the representation of Caesar in Dialogue XXIX but owned that Lyttelton had conformed to the prevailing opinion about him.[33] Lyttelton's Boileau tells Pope in Dialogue XIV, "The Study of History, both sacred and prophane, requires a Critical and laborious Investigation. The Composer of a Set of lively and witty Remarks on Facts ill examined, or incorrectly delivered, is not an Historian," and Lyttelton, who had composed a history of Henry II and contributed short biographies of great men to the 1744 edition of Thomson's *Seasons,* erred only by laboring too hard, telling more than the reader cares to know,[34] as in the long conversation between William III and DeWitt (Dial. XVIII), or at times by laboring the too readily available. Dialogue VIII has the elder Pliny telling Pliny the Younger a story Lyttelton knew only because the latter Roman recorded it; [35] in the underworld he and his uncle must have other matters to discuss. On just one occasion did Lyttelton glaringly distort history, honesty leading him to point out, in a note to the passage in which Titus calls Berenice "a virtuous foreign Princess" (Dial. XI), that the "Character of Berenice in this Dialogue is conformable to the Idea given of her by Racine, not by Josephus." That is, both the ancient historian's description of her several marriages and his suggestion that she was guilty of incest [36] go unmentioned, as they do in Racine's tragedy *Bérénice.* The modification requires small apology, for Lyttelton's purpose was to set Titus' renunciation of Berenice against Scipio's forbearance with respect to the captured Celtiberian maiden; the women had to be comparably fresh and enticing. Besides, the focus of the dialogue is on the two men, the falsely rosy view of Berenice was established before Lyttelton wrote, and of course, history provides only the raw material for the form Lyttelton had adopted (a statement he would have

[33] Review of Lyttelton's *Four New Dialogues of the Dead, Critical Review,* XIX (June, 1765), 461–65.

[34] Bernard Bock, *George Lord Lyttelton und seine Stellung in der englischen Literatur des 18. Jahrhunderts* (Göttingen, 1927), p. 53.

[35] *Epistles* 6. 16, 20.   [36] *The Jewish Antiquities* 19. 276; 20. 145.

thought permissive, however). He wrote less to inform his readers than to exercise them on the common.

Lyttelton's humorous and satirical dialogues are weaker than his best historical pieces, as befits the work of a man who once advised Alexander Pope not to write satire.[37] The good lord seems to have laughed in his collection mainly because doing so would be expected of a follower of Lucian. In Dialogue XIII the practical Horace discomfits dense and arrogant Julius Caesar Scaliger, who soon repents; the other laughing dialogues have more to recommend them. Like the Scaliger dialogue, Lyttelton's nineteenth bears on the Quarrel of the Ancients and the Moderns, bringing together two of history's most trivial figures, the epicures Apicius and Darteneuf. Was eating more rewarding in antiquity or in the eighteenth century?—a topic that recalls earlier dialogues of the dead: Apicius speaks in Fontenelle, and King had sported with ancient eating in the dialogue between Bellamira and Calphurnia, like Lyttelton buttressing his nonsense with formidably learned notes. An unaccustomed extravagance characterizes Lyttelton's manner throughout. Apicius chagrins Darteneuf with accounts of delicacies the world has forgotten, astounds him by divulging that he spent nearly a million pounds, calculated down to the pence, in his Roman kitchen. Darteneuf counters like a modern-day Ozymandias: "What a new World of good Things for eating and drinking has Columbus opened to Us! Think of *That,* and despair." Yet Darteneuf has never tasted turtle, the marvel of the Americas, and he wonders, like Lucian's poor bridegroom Protesilaus, whether he might be allowed to revisit the earth for one day, not for love (earlier he exclaims, "And what is a Wench to a Barrel of exquisite Oysters?"), but for turtle. "I would promise to kill myself by the Quantity of it I would eat before next Morning."

Such vigorous playfulness is appealing, especially because so rare in the dialogues. The ingenuity of Darteneuf reveals that the author is momentarily thinking with him, not just of him. Then Mercury en-

[37] "An Epistle to Mr. Pope, from Rome, 1730," ll. 51–60, *Works* (Dublin, 1774), II, 613.

ters, that moralistic Mercury Lyttelton was wont to invoke. The god scornfully tells the pair that he knows of two men who ate better than either of them, a Spartan soldier and an English farmer whose plain fare was seasoned with toil and hunger, pangs the effete controversialists have never felt. "Thus is a pleasantly frivolous dialogue reduced, in the end, to the level of a cautionary tale," Sir Sydney Roberts comments.[38] True, and yet also somewhat harsh. Apicius does have the final words, in which he accepts Mercury's censure, but Darteneuf speaks before him, shedding brightness on the otherwise bleak ending. "This, Apicius, is more mortifying than not to have shared a Turtle Feast." The monomaniac remains unregenerate even in eternity, and the humorous consistency of his character makes the dialogue—an exceptionally deft performance most of the way through—palatable to the end.

More Lucianic, and Swiftian, than any of the other dialogues, the tenth pits an English duelist against an American savage, and might be used to demonstrate the longevity of Montaigne's "Of Cannibals." About to enter Charon's boat, the savage recoils from the notion of sharing his passage with so loathsome a creature as Tom Pushwell, while Lyttelton compares their former lives. The duelist ate the best foods, sang, danced with grace; in all the savage can claim to have excelled him. For instance, the savage ate *Frenchmen.* Yet he killed only enemies whereas Tom Pushwell killed a friend. Was it unwise, diffusive, to load the duelist with vices? a point debated by reviewers.[39] Something may be said on both sides; the important point about the dialogue is that Lyttelton's fury here took him beyond the prudent use of satire typical of his work. Dueling, as much as any vice, could provoke the most Grandisonian Whig to indignation, as a prominent scene in Richardson's novel shows, and savage indignation provoked Lyttelton to exploit the underworld in this dialogue more than he does elsewhere—Charon, the river, the boat. There is even

---

[38] "An Eighteenth-Century Gentleman," *An Eighteenth-Century Gentleman and Other Essays* (Cambridge, 1930), p. 20.

[39] *Candid and Critical Remarks,* pp. 31–33. Review of *Candid and Critical Remarks, Monthly Review,* XXIII (July, 1760), 80.

a sharp echo of Lucian, for the savage, rather than accompany the treacherous Englishman, offers (like the Micyllus of Lucian's *Voyage to the Lower World*) to swim across the Styx instead. Lyttelton, however, could write pertly only so long. Though no Mercury intervenes, the dialogue comes to an unsubtle end when the savage is permitted to kick his antagonist.

Sprightliness came more readily to Elizabeth Montagu, née Robinson (1720–1800), Lyttelton's companion in dialogue-writing. Indeed she seems in some respects like a prototype of Sheridan's Lady Teazle. A shrewd, country-bred aristocrat with powerful social ambitions, she married Edward Montagu, twenty-nine years her senior, in 1742, and their London home served as a kind of school throughout the entire second half of the eighteenth century. But here the parallel with *The School for Scandal* ends; the Montagu assemblies were for convivial literary conversation. Lyttelton became a prominent mentor there, so much so that at his death Mrs. Montagu lamented the loss of her "best Instructor, the noblest Example, the Director of my Studies, the Companion & Guide of all my Litterary Amusements . . . : My House, when he appeared in it was a School of Knowledge & Virtue to the Young." [40] Burke, Horace Walpole, Garrick, Reynolds graced her rooms; the erudite Elizabeth Carter, the translator of Epictetus, became her close friend; and Johnson too was a visitor, though his reception cooled after he disparaged "poor Lyttelton" in 1781. [41]

It seems no wonder that Mrs. Montagu, living in such company, wrote much herself. She had strengthened her style, and no doubt her arm, by transcribing the entire *Spectator* series before she was nine, [42] and the volume of her correspondence eclipses that of a Richardson heroine. But she published little—in addition to her celebrated defense of Shakespeare against the criticism of Voltaire, only the three

[40] From an unpublished letter in Lyttelton's Hagley MSS., III, 327, quoted by Davis (p. 390).

[41] R. Huchon, *Mrs. Montagu (1720–1800)* (London, 1906), pp. 258–62.

[42] J. Doran, *A Lady of the Last Century (Mrs. Elizabeth Montagu)* (London, 1873), p. 13.

dialogues of the dead in Lyttelton's book. Could Lyttelton have read posterity's remarks on the collection, and had he been less magnanimous a man, we might suppose that he came to regret opening his pages to his friend, for critics have generally shown themselves more cordial to Dialogues XXVI, XXVII, and XXVIII than to the rest. The reviewer in *Candid and Critical Remarks,* for instance, who could write so severely about Lyttelton, recognized Mrs. Montagu as "a very great master of the pen." Dialogue XXVII, between Mercury and a lady of fashion, he considered "the best in the book," "so intirely free from the fault I have pointed out in the generality of these discourses, of wanting character and dramatic expression, that I even think it might very safely stand the test of the stage." [43] Two of the dialogues reprinted in periodicals as specimens of the collection were Mrs. Montagu's.[44] Poor Lyttelton indeed, but the preference for her dialogues is just: all are rather appealing, none compares with Lyttelton's worst. Perhaps he felt so too, for his preface contains a generous acknowledgment: "Three of these Dialogues were written by a different hand; as I am afraid would have appeared but too plainly to the Reader, without my having told it."

In Dialogue XXVI Cadmus talks with a Hercules like the one whom William King set against the London butcher: both dialogues begin as the blustering hero invidiously rehearses his exploits— here, however, Cadmus proceeds sensibly but solemnly to argue the importance of intellect against his brawny companion. The tone of Dialogue XXVII is lighter. In this polite eighteenth-century *Everyman,* Mercury calls to escort a general, comedy-of-manners character named Mrs. Modish down to Hades. Though dead, she is most reluctant to go. "Indeed, Mr. Mercury, I cannot have the pleasure of wait-

---

[43] *Candid and Critical Remarks,* pp. 88–91. Reviewing the first edition, Edmund Burke noted deficiencies in Lyttelton's dialogues which were not to be found in Mrs. Montagu's, hers being "truly dramatic, and not inferior to the best comic dialogue" (*Annual Register,* III [1760], 257). Ruffhead thought them as good as Lyttelton's (*Monthly Review,* XXII [May, 1760], 421). Egilsrud (p. 177), Elton (I, 81), and Huchon (p. 74) express a preference for Mrs. Montagu's work; others have agreed with them, only Elie Fréron giving the contrary verdict (review of *Dialogues of the Dead, L'Année littéraire,* II [1761], 95).

[44] See note 3, above.

ing upon you now. I am engaged, absolutely engaged." These are the opening words and she soon explains herself, after a frank admission that she has neglected all her family responsibilities. "Look on my Chimney-piece, and you will see I was engaged to the Play on Mondays, Balls on Tuesdays, the Opera on Saturdays, and to Card-assemblies the rest of the week, for two months to come; and it would be the rudest thing in the world not to keep my appointments. If you will stay for me till the Summer-season, I will wait on you with all my heart. Perhaps the Elysian Fields will be less detestable than the country in our world. Pray have you a fine Vauxhall and Ranelagh? I think I should not dislike drinking the Lethe Waters when you have a full Season." Also set on the near side of the Styx, Dialogue XXVIII brings together Plutarch, Charon, and a "modern Bookseller"—an obstreperous fellow with no respect for authors, especially Plutarch, whose *Lives* attracted only dust while the Town cherished biographies of criminals. Mrs. Montagu's voice becomes shrill as she impersonates Mrs. Modish; the irony wears thin, Mrs. Modish grows so transparent in her definition of "the *Bon ton.*" But the character of the bookseller is maintained well throughout the lengthiest of Mrs. Montagu's dialogues.

The three pieces are written as if expressly for Lyttelton's approval. Like her companion and guide, Mrs. Montagu stresses the didactic function of literature, making Cadmus say, "Poetry . . . is of excellent Use, to enable the Memory to retain with more ease, and to imprint with more energy upon the heart, Precepts of Virtue and virtuous Actions." [45] Her Plutarch echoes this view when he says the correction of vice and folly should be "the first object of writers," and there is also insistence upon the indispensableness of historical exemplars as compared to merely fictive ones. "It has ever been my opinion," Plutarch observes, "that only the clear and steady Light of Truth can guide Men to Virtue, and that the Lesson which is impracticable must be unuseful." Mrs. Montagu's didacticism, too, is reinforced by the in-

[45] The drama existed, Mrs. Montagu thought, for "the effecting of certain moral purposes, by the representation of a Fable" (*An Essay on the Writings and Genius of Shakespear* . . . , 5th ed. [London, 1785], p. 12).

congruous presence of Christianity in Hades; much like the Brutus of Lyttelton's seventeenth dialogue, her Plutarch reminds man to consider that constant spectator, "the omniscient Being."

And as one might expect, she proves at least as energetic as Lyttelton in promoting feminine virtue, such as she saw it, scorning Mrs. Modish's marital and maternal irresponsibility and moving Plutarch, one of Lyttelton's favorite authors, to express regret that modern women give their time to vicious and absurd romances. "I wish for their sakes I had expatiated more on the character of Lucretia and some other Heroines." Yet "Examples of Domestic Virtue," he continues, "would be more particularly useful to Women than those of great Heroines." These remarks provide a clue as to why Lyttelton paid such extensive attention to the homely, unromantic virtues of Penelope, Octavia, and the modest widow of Sidney: he was supplementing Plutarch.

Indeed, there is little in the three dialogues to distinguish Mrs. Montagu's hand from Lyttelton's, unless it is her more constant vivacity and the fact that her dead feel a need to employ an occasional French word, a habit of the fashionable *bas bleus*. (One of her biographers expresses surprise that whereas Cadmus knows enough French to speak of *éclat,* Mercury must inquire about the meaning of *bon ton.*) [46] Mrs. Montagu's purpose would seem to have been as baldly propagandistic as Lyttelton's, yet she did manage to end her three colloquies with more grace than Lyttelton usually achieved. The preferred speaker has the last word in each, exploiting this advantage in different ways and degrees. Cadmus, after winning every exchange with Hercules, closes with the wish that authors "exert all their Powers in the service of Virtue, and celebrate the noble choice of those, who, like you, preferred her to Pleasure." Hercules says no more, but after this compliment we do not expect him to; cleverly, graciously, Cadmus has accorded him honorable defeat. In the next dialogue, when the time comes for Mercury to dispatch Mrs. Modish to Minos, he thinks the better of it. Sour Minos has no touch of the *bon ton,* Mrs. Modish had better wander forever among the futile, outside the

[46] Doran, p. 74.

underworld, lest Minos sink her in Tartarus. The softened ending makes its point with sufficient force, as Mrs. Montagu discovered when on account of it she felt the rancor of London ladies,[47] and her third dialogue (XXVIII) nearly ends the same way as Charon argues that the bookseller is "too frivolous an Animal to present to wise Minos." In a nice reversal, however, Mercury overrules him, rising to Popean indignation and predicting heavy vengeance against those who countenance the perversion of letters.

Here my remarks about Lyttelton's volume conclude, but there is more to be said about Mrs. Montagu, specifically about a *fourth* dialogue of the dead she composed, which remained unpublished until 1906.[48] Quite sternly purposeful in tone, without the witty lightheartedness the author displayed elsewhere, "Berenice & Cleopatra" has a startling point to it, stands in dramatic contrast to the dialogues Mrs. Montagu published. Berenice cannot understand how the gross Cleopatra could have been "by her Lover prefer'd to glory, to empire, to life," when she herself, despite her beauty, virtue, and complete fidelity, suffered Titus' renunciation. "Tell me Cleopatra, for 1700 years have not made me forget my love and my grief!" Cleopatra, the veteran, speaks sympathetically to the frustrated innocent ("I wish I could have assisted you with my counsels"), explaining, "Indeed Berenice you talk more like a sheperdess than a great queen. You might perhaps in the simplicity of pastoral life have engaged some humble swain, but there was too much of nature & too little of art in your conduct, to captivate a man used to flattery, to pleasures, to variety. I find you was but the mirror of Titus; you gave him back his own image, while I presented every hour a new Cleopatra to Anthony." The moral, if it may be called that, of the dialogue is clear: in Cleopatra's words, "Anthony was preserved by his doubt of my love, and Titus was lost by his confidence in yours." Love battens on artful deception; experience dispels the Arcadian dream.

Here is the same "virtuous" unhistorical Berenice mentioned in

---

[47] Emily J. Climenson, *Elizabeth Montagu, the Queen of the Blue Stockings: Her Correspondence from 1720 to 1761* (London, 1906), II, 183.

[48] *Ibid.,* pp. 238–40. Quotations here are from a photocopy of Mrs. Montagu's manuscript (HM MS. MO 2998), in the possession of the Huntington Library.

Lyttelton's eleventh dialogue, where Titus, the hero of the piece, praises her in words that must have caught Mrs. Montagu's eye: "She had all the Insinuation [that is, ingratiating qualities] and Wit of Cleopatra, without her Coquetry." Yet Mrs. Montagu's dialogue, with its ostensibly negative moral, is far different from Lyttelton's or even from those she contributed to his collection. Indeed, it seems to run counter to the general position on love taken in the *Dialogues of the Dead* as a whole; instead of a platitude, it presents a cynical dilemma. It echoes Lyttelton's fifteenth dialogue, which also concerns the Cleopatra triangle, but it does so in a dissonant way. There, among the blest in Lyttelton's heavenly Hades, Octavia could take comfort in the knowledge that while on earth, despite the loss of Antony, she had acted with unswerving generosity. Here Berenice, in a comparable position, draws only sorrow from her rectitude. The earthly Hades of this dialogue, like the Hades of Homer, shows a good person wishing she had been less so; Berenice resembles the lachrymose Achilles of the *Odyssey,* and of Lucian's fifteenth dialogue of the dead. Residence in the underworld has made Cleopatra candid enough to admit that art played a greater part than beauty in her conquests, but it has done nothing for Berenice, who encounters no sermonizing Mercury to console her with idealistic reassurance, no Minos to set her above Cleopatra in the Elysian Temple of Fame.

It is not known whether Lyttelton read this dialogue, or whether Mrs. Montagu composed it at the same time she did the other three. First mentioned in her published correspondence on April 28, 1761,[49] the dialogue may have been completed soon enough for inclusion in Lyttelton's earliest edition; if not, it surely might have been added to one of the subsequent editions, as were Lyttelton's four new dialogues of 1765. If Lyttelton did see it, he probably found it distasteful, and Mrs. Montagu herself may not have desired its publication, as unworthy of her public character. The dialogue is a product of the unpublicized, other Mrs. Montagu, the Mrs. Montagu upon whom Katherine G. Hornbeak cast "new light" some years ago: the Mrs. Montagu

---

[49] William Pulteney, Earl of Bath, Letter to Mrs. Montagu, in Climenson, II, 237.

who, if she was not a dram-drinker, was at least capable of considerable calculation, pettiness, and selfishness.[50] One of her biographers gently anticipated these charges when he contrasted her with the affectionate Mrs. Thrale, "Mrs. Montagu's opposite at all points." [51] It is tempting to think that nature, defenestrated while Mrs. Montagu was writing the three dialogues for Lyttelton's approval, roared through the door in her fourth dialogue.

Whatever the case, the dialogue grasps the reader's attention. Though in subject and paradoxical conclusion the conversation resembles the proceedings of some medieval court of love, the speakers probe an enduring question, in the process displaying the potentialities of the genre Mrs. Montagu employed. The conclusion of the piece is anything but heavy-handed. Yet, though Berenice does not see it, a resolution may be implied, namely, that her position and Cleopatra's are too exclusive as they stand. Aside from historical differences in the situation of the two women, perhaps Berenice ought to see that art, when joined to good nature, completes and does not necessarily pervert it: Tom Jones is better off with Sophia than without. Lyttelton would have said so in italics, but Mrs. Montagu does not, perhaps because she thought the reader ought to be trusted to find a solution himself, perhaps because she herself saw no solution. The question the dialogue poses might have occasioned a full evening of conversation in the Montagu *salon,* after the young gentry had been put to bed.

[50] "New Light on Mrs. Montagu," *The Age of Johnson: Essays Presented to Chauncey Brewster Tinker,* ed. Frederick W. Hilles (New Haven, 1949), pp. 349–61.
[51] Huchon, p. 41.

Chapter V

Lyttelton's Wake
1760-1800

O ho Said Doctor Johnson
To Scipio Africanus . . .

—Blake, *An Island in the Moon*

Lyttelton's success gave "dialogue of the dead" the status of a household word, like an apocalyptic trumpet calling up shades in numbers never seen before, in books and pamphlets, magazines and newspapers. There was no deluge, no torrent of such publications during the next forty years; but there was certainly a stream, the constancy of the genre's presence being revealed in the mechanical way writers put it to obituary purposes. To the four last things there was regularly added a fifth: the recorded meeting with some appropriate predecessor. Thus the death of John Rich, producer of *The Beggar's Opera,* provoked a dialogue (1762) showing his reunion with John Gay and—a common feature of the obituary dialogues—expressing the dismay both felt at the decay of their profession. In 1763 the Earl of Granville immediately, and much to his disadvantage, rejoined his one-time rival Robert Walpole, while the death of Susannah Cibber in 1766 as quickly brought her into a bawdy conversation with Peg Woffington, the actresses finding a common ground in scorn directed against contemporary audiences. Lyttelton himself died to reappear twice (1779, 1780), in the first dialogue scolding the present government, in the second conversing with Lucian, who had been summoned to recommend a new translation of his works. A more inviting object of recrimination, Lord Chesterfield bowed before Oliver Goldsmith (1775), Cicero (1779), and David Garrick (1785),[1] while Garrick, still alive, may have winced reading what the late actor Tom Weston had to say about him (1776) and, newly departed, comically entered Elysium in a farce of 1779 that is reminiscent of his own *Lethe*—unlike it, however, a dialogue of the dead in every respect. In due time, Samuel Johnson was welcomed to the underworld by a somewhat critical Goldsmith (1785).

More and more, in the closing years of the century, Elysium became a British colony, the likes of Alexander all but vanished. In his stead, among the most ubiquitous immigrants—or victims of transportation—there strutted David Hume, who almost deliberately incurred his prominence by reason of a deathbed joke in which he fancied himself expostulating with Charon: "Have a little patience, good Charon, I have been endeavouring to open the eyes of the Public. If I live a few years longer, I may have the satisfaction of seeing the downfall of some of the prevailing systems of superstition." Charon, though, would not be put off; Hume made him reply, "You loitering rogue, that will not happen these many hundred years. Do you fancy I will grant you a lease for so long a time? Get into the boat this instant, you lazy loitering rogue." [2] These facetious remarks, preserved by Adam Smith, ensured Hume's appearance in dialogues of the dead. In one, *A Philosophical and Religious Dialogue in the*

---

[1] *A Dialogue in the Shades between Lord Chesterfield and Dr. Johnson*, dated *ca.* 1780 and attributed to William Hayley, is listed by Samuel Halkett and John Laing, *Dictionary of Anonymous and Pseudonymous English Literature* (Edinburgh, 1926–62), II, 55. The title seems to be a "ghost," for the work is unmentioned in Hayley's *Memoirs* (London, 1823) and in N. J. Barker's bibliography, "Some Notes on the Bibliography of William Hayley," *Transactions of the Cambridge Bibliographical Society*, III (1959–63), 103–12, 167–76, 339–60. Hayley did compose *Two Dialogues* . . . comparing Johnson and Chesterfield (London, 1787), dialogues of the living.

[2] Adam Smith, Letter to William Strahan (November 9, 1776), in *The Life of David Hume, Esq., Written by Himself* (London, 1777), pp. 50–51.

Shades, between Mr. Hume and Dr. Dodd, a pamphlet of 1778, Hume swallows his words: "I amused myself somewhat inconsiderately before my death, with inventing ingenious and ludicrous reasons, why Charon ought to permit me a longer stay in the world. Now, to my no small vexation, I find a spirit of a severe countenance that is stationed here feigns several serious causes for retarding my passage into the Elysian abodes." Had Hume's last hours been more solemn, however, his writings alone would probably have brought him to Hades. Throughout this dialogue his speculations are held comparable to Dodd's forgery, and in another piece, of 1783, he must bear the animadversions of a companion in notoriety, the deist Lord Herbert of Cherbury, until finally a Mercury like Lyttelton's applies the caduceus and the beleaguered Scot recants. In 1777, on the other hand, an admiring dialogue-writer employed Hume, earnestly and at length, to promote a constructive end to the American war.

About several of the obituary dialogues something complimentary may be said (Chesterfield, especially, had a way of making satirists look good), but in them little happens to advance the history of the genre. There is extant just one dialogue written directly against Lyttelton, *An Additional Dialogue of the Dead, between Pericles and Aristides,* published within three weeks after the first appearance of his collection. The author, John Brown (1715–66)—or "Estimate" Brown, from the title of his celebrated *Estimate of the Manners and Principles of the Times* (1757)—wrote to vindicate Pitt, whom Lyttelton had criticized in the person of Pericles (Dial. XXIII), and also, according to John Nichols, to revenge himself upon the nobleman, who had slighted him "in a numerous and mixed company"; but Brown's onslaught came to nothing.[3] So too did the attempt by Samuel Pye, a physician who died in 1772,[4] to hoist himself

---

[3] John Nichols describes Brown's personal motive in *Literary Anecdotes of the Eighteenth Century* (London, 1812–15), II, 339; S. C. Roberts, his political motive in "Some Uncollected Authors XXIV: 'Estimate Brown,' 1715–1766," *The Book Collector,* IX (1960), 185. Advertised as published on June 3 (*London Chronicle,* May 31–June 3, 1760, p. 535), the dialogue displeased reviewers: *Critical Review,* IX (June, 1760), 465–67; [Owen Ruffhead], *Monthly Review,* XXIII (July, 1760), 22–30.

[4] *Gentleman's Magazine,* XLII (1772), 95.

by Lyttelton's coattails with a ludicrous dialogue between Moses and Bolingbroke claimed to be written "in The Manner of the Right Honourable . . . Author of Dialogues of the Dead" (1765), a learned, gravely fanciful performance unintentionally spiced by Moses' habit of calling Bolingbroke "Your Lordship" or "My Lord." Although two of the more ambitious and absorbing works following Lyttelton's, the anonymous *New Dialogues of the Dead* (1762) and a series in the *Sentimental Magazine* (1773–74), do depart sharply from his precedent, even here the genre reveals its essential conservatism. There were, indeed, several attempts, like that exemplified in the 1725 dialogue between Caesar and Jack Sheppard, to extend Elysian egalitarianism to the living: a pair of colloquies (1770) marked the suicide of Mungo Campbell, who while trespassing had shot the Earl of Eglinton rather than surrender his gun. In the more spirited of the pieces, attributed to John Langhorne (1735–79), Campbell claims that a commoner accused of murdering an aristocrat has no hope of a fair trial. Offered a new trial in Hell, he retorts, "It would be superfluous, my lord! I have already been tried in Scotland." And in a dialogue of 1798 Charles I brings some scraps of consolation to another beheaded monarch, Louis XVI: for a century and a half Charles has "had so much conversation with Hampden, Bradshaw, Milton, and the rest of their stamp, that I begin to enter into the grounds of their party."

Generally, however, the dead did not—could not—lend themselves to revolution; by nature they spoke for the past, and for authors like William Julius Mickle (1735–88), whose *Voltaire in the Shades* (1770) subjected the philosophe and Rousseau, eight years before their actual deaths, to a last judgment at the hands of Socrates, Julian, Porphyry, Augustine, Swift, and even Sterne. John Ferriar (1761–1815), Sterne's commentator, turned the dialogue of the dead against William Godwin in 1798, as it had earlier been used against Hume, and when so emancipated a thinker as Edward Gibbon approached it his purposes were, to say the least, uncharacteristic of the author of *The Decline and Fall.* In his memoirs Gibbon recalls that he once contemplated "writing a dialogue of the dead in which Lucian, Erasmus, and Voltaire should mutually acknowledge the danger of exposing an old superstition to the contempt of the blind and fanatic multitude." [5] He did not, apparently, pursue the project. The dialogue of the dead could deflate the importance of the past, as Fontenelle had demonstrated and as William Blake suggests in a passage, as if from such a dialogue, in "The Marriage of Heaven and Hell": "After dinner I ask'd Isaiah to favour the world with his lost works, he said none of equal value was lost. Ezekiel said the same of his." [6] Or the dialogue of the dead could hold up the past, including progressive elements to be found there, as a model for men to emulate; but, in the dramatis personae of the genre, children of the future time have no place. The body of this chapter concerns, first, two significant efforts to write dialogues different from Lyttelton's, and then, in the works of Thomas Tyers and James Hay Beattie, the consolidation of the genre's conservative tendencies, its dotage.

The most remarkable of the works called into print by Lyttelton's celebrity is a volume, *New Dialogues of the Dead* (1762), containing seventeen conversations, the third-longest English collection of the century. The anonymous author, according to John Nichols, was William Weston (1711?–1791), a clergyman, as might be suspected from the many religious personages who speak in the work— though not, perhaps, from the sort of things some of them say. And Weston, as he owns in the preface, was "assisted by some Friends, whose Names, if permitted, it would be an Honour for me to mention"—no overstatement: one was the Bishop of Lincoln, John Green (1706?–1779).[7] They were a formidable pair, Weston and Green, both having bared their spurs in the cockpits of controversy. A contributor to the satirical *Athenian Letters* of 1741–43, Green

---

[5] *Autobiography,* ed. Dero A. Saunders (New York, 1961), p. 203. The persons Gibbon names would meet nearly two hundred years later in a lively series of dialogues of the dead by Peter Gay: *The Bridge of Criticism* (New York, 1970).

[6] *The Poetry and Prose of William Blake,* ed. David V. Erdman, commentary by Harold Bloom (Garden City, N.Y., 1965), p. 38. Dialogues set in Hell rather than Elysium had become very rare in England by the end of the eighteenth century; two examples: John MacGowan's *Infernal Conference: or, Dialogues of Devils* (London, 1772); John Jamieson's *A Dialogue between the Devil and a Socinian Divine, On the Confines of the other World* (Edinburgh, 1791).

[7] *Literary Anecdotes,* IX, 668; VIII, 648.

had also published severe epistles against the Methodists in 1760 and 1761, the campaign cut short by archiepiscopal dissuasion. Weston, as early as 1739, had won notoriety in some quarters with sermons preferring atheism to papistry: the Cambridge antiquarian William Cole recalled him to be "a very warm man" who "for some very imprudent sermons . . . which I heard, was called before the Vice-Chancellor . . . but would make no submission." [8] A later theological work of Weston's incurred Richard Hurd's disdain and gave William Warburton occasion to call the author an "egregious coxcomb." [9] And the collaborators remained close enough, apart from literary affairs, for Weston, with Green's help, to become prebendary of Lincoln in 1771, a position he retained with two livings until death. Who wrote *which* of the conversations in the *New Dialogues,* it is generally impossible to say, though the preface indicates that Weston was responsible for the sixth, seventh, and fifteenth.

What a heap of oddments the book holds, including a few dusky pearls. Lyttelton's popularity, Weston maintains, encouraged him to print the dialogues (which had "lain by me several Years"), but not Lyttelton's example. "Of all those excellent Models of Composition delivered down to us by Antiquity, there seems not one to be more faintly imitated by the Moderns than Lucian's Dialogues of the Dead." It is impossible, Weston says, to revive "Pluto, Charon, and Cerberus, and all the amusing Mythology of antient Hell," yet in the face of such literalness he and his associates took Hades for their setting and thus invited some of the difficulties that beset Lyttelton—only the difficulties loom bigger here because of the more conspicuous religious orientation. Luther, for example, remarks in the second dialogue that the thought of the Reformation still pleases him, "even in these lower regions." Although Weston attempts to soften the impact of this and comparable incongruities, remarking that characters in modern dialogues of the dead "are allowed often to deliver themselves without strictly adhering either to the antient or modern No-

[8] Quoted by Robert Forsyth Scott, ed., *Admissions to the College of St. John the Evangelist in the University of Cambridge,* III (Cambridge, 1903), 416.
[9] Hurd, *Works* (London, 1811), VIII, 145–84; Warburton, Letter to Hurd (February 10, 1750), in Nichols, *Literary Anecdotes,* VI, Part I, 471.

tions of the State of departed Souls," he succeeds merely in revealing that the problem was not first discovered by the reader. Much of the time, however, the setting has a measure of plausibility and on occasion becomes vivid, as when the character Lucian remarks, "You see yonder, at a small distance, in as deep dispute as ourselves . . . the emperor Julian, and a zealous father of the Church" (Dial. XV). Similar references, populating the infernal plain, also color three of the other pieces.

Weston modestly set forth his aims: "Let it suffice now, in one word to declare, that my Intention in these Dialogues is to revere at a Great Distance the inimitable Lucian, and to steer directly between the unadorned gravity of Cambray, and the refined sprightliness of Fontenelle." There is no word of Lyttelton here, and so little (except a common use of Bayle and Lucian, for different purposes, as speakers) to connect the *New Dialogues* with Lyttelton's book that this collection may well have been compiled before the other was published. Yet, on the whole, the *New Dialogues* is so very mixed in content and quality that one might guess it the product of several hands, and, while in places the authors achieve sprightliness without much refinement, there is a good deal more of unadorned gravity than the preface would have one believe. About half the pieces offer nothing to recommend them, as Ann Boleyn compares her sufferings with those of Monimia, the wife of Mithridates (Dial. VII), or Mary Queen of Scots berates Elizabeth (Dial. XVI), or Popes Adrian VI and Sixtus V discuss the corruption of the papacy (Dial. XVII). Worse is the brutality of the eleventh conversation, in which a blasé St. Jerome scandalizes the pious Eustochium by revealing how he defrauded her into receiving baptism. For the most part, the simpler pieces, grouped toward the end of the volume, seem mere padding and justify a reviewer's lament that the *New Dialogues* "had not been reduced to half the number." [10]

An ineptness below dullness mars several conversations, for example the related Dialogues II and III. In the first Erasmus attacks Lu-

[10] *Critical Review*, XIII (May, 1762), 461.

ther for spawning so many sects, the names of which Luther (like Swift's Aristotle and Homer when asked about their commentators) does not even know, and when Erasmus inquires what right Luther had to break with the Pope, Luther can answer only, "I? because I —I was in such—I had so many—" Speaking with Calvin in Dialogue III, however, Erasmus seems disposed for a posthumous conversion as he hears his companion sing a paean to Calvinism ending in an ecstatic aposiopesis as awkward as Luther's: "I can say no more—the rest is rapture." Here the reader finds a grasp of history as weak as Sheffield's combined with evangelism comparable to Sylviana Sola's, and it is with relief that he encounters several of the more sensible, Lytteltonian colloquies, where the talk is lively, the progress reasonable, the plan neither too simple nor tortuous, the characters convincing and well paired—for example, Dialogue XII, between Cassius and Thomas Cranmer, who admits at the outset that history has been unjust to his companion. Yet when Cassius claims a life of consistent virtue, Cranmer seizes on one flaw, evident in the prayer mouthed by the otherwise consistent Epicurean before he killed Caesar. How predictable Cassius' reply, which Cranmer anticipates: "I see already my fatal recantation rising up against me!" But, Cranmer continues after several lines, "it is barbarous in you to forget how quickly I regained my former zeal, and how manfully I sustained the fire soon after; with what horror I looked back on the action of recantation; and with what firmness I consumed that hand first, that had any part in it."

Cassius relents: "Ay, there the Christian returned to himself in Cranmer, as the Epicurean did afterwards in Cassius at Philippi." Although the Roman persists in thinking himself the more virtuous, "as there is no one but must think that it was a great deal easier for you to stand firm against temptations, by the aid of the excellent system you professed, than for me to be free on every occasion from the vulgar superstition," he nevertheless concludes that, when human frailties are taken into account, "we cannot readily find a better Epicurean than Cassius, nor a better Christian than Cranmer." Neatly, graciously, the dialogue ends, a dialogue comparable to Lyttelton's best colloquies, so apt, if unstartling, are its parallelisms and contrasts. More or less comparable are Dialogue VI, between Otho and Margaret of Austria; VIII, between Philippe de Commines and Archbishop King; IX, between LeClerc and Bayle; and XIII, between Jeremy Collier and Congreve.

Weston's mirthless collection successfully maintains the intended "Great Distance" from Lucian, who makes a grave and sacerdotal appearance in Dialogue XVI to tell the controversialist Mellinus, famous for condemning Lucian as anti-Christian, that it was unchristian to do so. But Fontenelle, though disparaged in the preface for exploiting "Whim and Refinement," almost speaks anew in several of the dialogues. That between the Holy Roman Emperor Otho and Margaret of Austria (Dial. VI) supposedly occurs soon after the French conversation Margaret pursued with Hadrian, and the first and fourth pieces in Weston may unsettle a reader as effectively as some of the pieces in the *Nouveaux Dialogues.* Dialogue I bears on the abuse of spiritual power, a common topic here, with Louis XII accusing Pope Julius II "of debauchery, rage, ambition, faction, and perfidy." Louis is obviously a much better man than the evil Pope, but the dialogue seems a good, dramatic one nevertheless, for as it progresses the reader discovers that the Pope is just as obviously a more intelligent man than Louis. The King makes accusations; the Pope documents them, usually exceeding the knowledge or suspicions of his antagonist. Julius neither contests the accusations of evil nor retaliates, except by calmly maintaining intellectual supremacy. He admits that Louis, unlike himself, was "amiable," but then he capitalizes on the admission: "This excellent disposition that did you honour in the world, only exposed you more effectively to my plots and contrivances; and I made use of it as well in my prosperity to oppress you, as in my adversity to appease you."

In exposing his own crimes, he speaks without remorse; in enumerating his "contrivances," he speaks without gloating. His main contention is that people cannot separate the priest from the man, that in a Catholic nation the Pope has as many allies as the king, and that they cling more closely to the Pope. "Even the wife of your bosom

["Ann of Brittany," a footnote reads, "who constantly teized Lewis into peace with the pope"] co-operated here with the church, and frequently undid in bed all that you had done in the field." The dialogue is certainly one-sided, the Pope a prodigious gangster, but both are admirable creations. Particularly to the point seems the setting, for Julius becomes remarkably menacing in Hades—a calculating, thoroughly evil opportunist who in life gained the whole world, or at least much of its wealth, and who in death, far from suffering any loss whatsoever, has leisure to chat about his machinations. Complacent, unscathed, not headfirst in the smoky hole Dante reserved for evil popes, Julius seems supremely diabolical.

The fourth dialogue, much lighter in tone, is a flagrant yet arresting tour de force, displaying not just one unexpected reversal in the manner of Fontenelle but two, at least. Mary of Burgundy first manages to bewilder Montaigne (the naïf of Fontenelle, not Prior's shrewd Gascon) in a labyrinth of paradox; then, with artful candor, she reveals the clew and leads him out. Montaigne speaks first, his position apparently unassailable: "You may say what you please, but certainly your's was a very ridiculous death: because you had hurt yourself in a certain part, which it naturally gave you offense to name, you would hinder its being looked at, and so take pet and die"—notwithstanding Sterne's jokes about the right and wrong ends of a woman, an unusual subject for a vicar. From this moment Mary takes control, praising herself for delicacy, deflecting an innuendo of Montaigne's with the aid of a casuistical distinction between delicacy and chastity, and rebuffing him with the remark that sensitivity like hers must be lost upon a person of no delicacy whatsoever. In Fontenelle's dialogue between Hadrian and Margaret, the lady had claimed that her resolution in the face of death surpassed Cato's; here, Mary calls her own death a martyrdom excelling Cato's and Lucretia's. They necessarily chose death; Mary freely, and only for the sake of honor. No one, not even the worst scandalmonger, could suspect her of any base desire. Confounded, Montaigne shifts his ground, accusing his opponent of pride, but to no avail. Given the final words, Mary covers herself with humility, first observing that "a Lucrece could not live after a rape, nor I after my fall; yet it is possible, that Lucrece might have lived after my misfortune, and I after hers," and then swelling with bold submissiveness in the confession that had she lived longer she might have proved less heroic. (If Weston and his associates did not accuse Lucretia of tippling—to recall for a moment Mrs. Montagu's example of tampering with the historic springs of morality—it may have been simply because the thought did not occur to them.) Predictably, the reviews which had praised Lyttelton were cool to the *New Dialogues,* in one case censuring the indelicacy of the conversation just described, and though several of the dialogues appeared in periodicals, there was no second edition. The *Gentleman's Magazine* promised a specimen, then evidently thought the better of it.[11]

Although Lyttelton may have read some of the *New Dialogues* with satisfaction, had he lived a year longer (he died in 1773) he would have found almost nothing to his taste in the next significant English collection, six conversations published in the *Sentimental Magazine* early in 1774. The editors rewarded outstanding contributions with a newly minted prize medal, and before he was finished the anonymous author had accumulated a handful; I suppose all the pieces, except possibly the fifth, to be the work of one hand, so alike are they in every respect.[12] Whoever he was, the author loved novelty—more than truth, Lyttelton might add. Despite the title of the magazine, the dialogues are sensational rather than sentimental.

---

[11] *Ibid.,* p. 460 (where the authors' taste is questioned); [William Kenrick], *Monthly Review,* XXVII (July, 1762), 31. Reprinted: Dial. V, *London Magazine,* XXXI (May, 1762), 275–77; Dial. XIII, *ibid.* (June, 1762), 305–7, and also *London Chronicle,* May 20–22, 1762, pp. 484–85; Dial. X, *Universal Museum,* I (July, 1762), 377–79. A reprinting promised: *Gentleman's Magazine,* XXXII (May, 1762), 243. Egilsrud all but ignores the *New Dialogues,* attributing Philip Parsons' *Dialogues of the Dead with the Living* (London, 1779), which contains no dialogues of the dead, to William Weston (*Le "Dialogue des morts" dans les littératures française, allemande et anglaise (1644–1789)* [Paris, 1934] p. 209). Another work he lists, *A Dialogue between Two Great Ladies* (London, 1760), has only living speakers.

[12] The first five dialogues, unsigned, won medals; the sixth, signed "Candaliensis," did not—which may explain why the series ended (*Sentimental Magazine,* I [1773], 480; II [1774], 32, 88, 184, 232).

In the first, Eloise disputes with Lady Mary Wortley Montagu (a pairing based perhaps on the association of the two ladies established by Pope's "Eloisa to Abelard"). To Eloise's contention that marriage dispels true love, Lady Mary can summon no effective reply, a failing common to nearly all the spokesmen for conventional morality throughout the series. How Lyttelton would have writhed in the presence of the dialogue between Cervantes and Lord Herbert of Cherbury, the only English dialogue of the dead written to support the practice of dueling, or, for that matter, to support Lord Herbert. But the next dialogue is still more perverse: the topic, chastity; the argument, which of the characters possessed it "in the most eminent degree"; the characters, Messalina, the adulterous wife of the first Emperor Claudius, and Lord Rochester, most infamous of titled rakes. At this point, however, the author's nerve faltered, as well it might, for while triumphantly losing the contest Messalina musters enough pulpit virtue to exalt the double standard, condemning the lover who would take advantage of his beloved's sympathies.

Two of the three last dialogues deserve but a word here: the fifth rather tamely lets Zeno and asceticism prevail over Epicurus, in a style more flaccid than that of the other pieces, while the sixth proves that something commendatory may be said about Swedish Charles XII if one compares him with a Cromwell little different from the Protector of Restoration satire. More notable—even, within the *dona* of the form, revolutionary or counter-reactionary—is the fourth dialogue, between Scipio Africanus and Mahomet the Great, conqueror of Constantinople. As we have seen, in dialogues of the dead Scipio and sterling virtue were synonymous from Lucian onward, and the fierce tyrant Mahomet, an alien in Elysium even after it admitted Christians, as a rule drew little sympathy from eighteenth-century authors; Johnson's, in his tragedy *Irene,* is a representative view.[13] But here the tables turn: from the beginning of the conversation Mahomet belittles Scipio's proverbial magnanimity, particularly as it was manifested in the case of the fair Celtiberian

[13] Bertrand H. Bronson, "Johnson's 'Irene': Variations on a Tragic Theme," *Johnson and Boswell: Three Essays* (Berkeley, 1944), p. 442.

captive: "I dare swear she was heartily mortified, to find that her charms made so little impression on the youthful conqueror; and that she thought you an unfeeling cub for parting with what she considered as far more valuable than all your other conquests." Mincing no words, Mahomet enforces his argument with praise for the man who acts passionately, regardless of what his superiors or his public thinks, then, in response to Scipio's accusation of hedonism, tells of beheading his treasured Irene, in full view of the troops, to maintain their loyalty; he too could reconcile passion and concern for reputation, but did so out of need, not out of timid, abstract scrupulosity. Set against the dour and masterful Sultan, who speaks the last, bitter words, Scipio watches his own stature shrink, his traditional excellence effectively questioned, his aura turn monkish. Here, it must be noted (if doing so will not seem to confer undue importance upon an obscure work), Scipio speaks for the last time in an English dialogue of the dead. The tradition which kept alive the classical exemplars was expiring.

A reviewer commented in 1785, "Dialogues in the Shades have become so hackneyed, that we wonder how the poor ghosts find spirits to keep up the conferences," [14] the quality of the pun surpassing his literal statement as a testament to weariness. And Samuel Johnson, one of the speakers in the dialogue under review, in his lifetime did not content himself with registering contempt for Lyttelton's performance but also scorned the genre itself, his disparaging comment preserved by the only Englishman to write more such dialogues than Lyttelton, Thomas Tyers (1726–87). "When," Johnson asked, would Tyers "give over writing in the obsolete cast of dialogues of the dead?" In the preface to *Conversations Political and Familiar* (1784), where Johnson's question appears, Tyers omits his own reply but does explain why he chose to write in that cast. One day, with Fénelon's volume on the table before him, he was moved to attempt an imitation. "The composition was conveyed to the Public Advertiser, that it might be observed, how it looked in print. It had the

---

[14] *Town and Country Magazine*, XVII (May, 1785), 253.

stale denomination of a Dialogue of the Dead. The writer was found out, and became afterwards suspected of writing frequently and indeed almost all that appeared with that title. It was time to withdraw his pen and conceal his productions in the privacy of his desk." Upon reviewing them "several years later," he decided to risk publication. The dialogue sent to the *Public Advertiser* is evidently that between Milton and Pope, a conventional piece published July 3, 1779. Another, between Rockingham and Pitt, was printed in Tyers' *Dramatic Conversations* (1782).

A man little known except to students of Johnson's circle (and one of the oddest persons Johnson knew), Tyers needs, even deserves, some words of introduction; the work and the man are so at one as to be inseparable. His father the proprietor of the pleasure dome known as Vauxhall Gardens, Thomas was graduated B.A. from Johnson's own Pembroke College, Oxford, and M.A. from Exeter College. In 1757 he was admitted barrister-at-law of the Inner Temple and ten years later, with his father's death, became a joint manager of Vauxhall. But despite the pull of his education, his profession, and his inheritance, Thomas remained very much himself, an eccentric gadabout chiefly remembered for the friendship Johnson recorded in the *Idler*. There, in an essay appropriately devoted to the description of that "kind of idleness . . . which dignifies itself by the appearance of business," Johnson wrote of those "who fancy themselves always busy in acquiring [learning]. Of these ambulatory students, one of the most busy is my friend Tom Restless." [15] Although Tom, Johnson wrote, had a distaste for books and reading, he actively made the rounds of London gathering places, listening to the conversations of men of wit but carrying little wit away, preserving less. Tyers' literary work, the bulk of it in dialogue form, seems to corroborate Johnson's description.

Tyers, in turn, wrote about Johnson, was in fact the author of the first biographical account of Johnson to appear after the great man's

[15] No. 48 (March 17, 1759), *The Idler and The Adventurer*, ed. W. J. Bate and others, *Works*, II (New Haven, 1963), 150–51. Nichols identifies Restless as Tyers (*Literary Anecdotes*, VIII, 81*n*).

death, a "sketch" in the *Gentleman's Magazine* (December, 1784) that Tyers subsequently published by itself in a revised form.[16] Boswell characterized Tyers as "exceedingly obliging to me" but not entirely admirable: "Having a handsome fortune, vivacity of temper, and eccentricity of mind, he could not confine himself to the regularity of practice. He therefore ran about the world with a pleasant carelessness, amusing every body by his desultory conversation. He abounded in anecdote, but was not sufficiently attentive to accuracy."[17] Like one of the "Blanks of Society" described in the tenth number of the *Spectator,* Tyers seemingly gleaned in the morning what he gave forth in the afternoon—yet Johnson accorded him enviable praise, saying he never met Tyers without learning something.[18]

Boswell was right about Tyers' love of anecdote, and perhaps it was Tyers' anecdotes that Johnson relished. The manager of Vauxhall, fittingly a raconteur more than anything else, acknowledged that character freely, calling himself a "dealer in Anecdotes; the small ware of history," and again, a "collector of fugitive Anecdotes."[19] In his anecdotal biographies, *An Historical Rhapsody on Mr. Pope, An Historical Essay on Mr. Addison,* and the piece on Johnson, he progressed with Shandean indirectness, thinking "a green lane and a verdant track, no matter how much out of the way, . . . better than the turnpike road."[20] He tells the reader, close to the end of his justly entitled *Rhapsody,* that he would have terminated it sooner, were the day not "rainy," and midway through the life of Johnson, he digresses momentarily to say his fingers are numb: "It is cold within, even by the fire-side, and a white world abroad."[21] Truly, this small person

---

[16] *A Biographical Sketch of Dr. Samuel Johnson* (1785), intro. Gerald Dennis Meyer, Augustan Reprint Society, Pub. No. 34 (Los Angeles, 1952), p. ii.

[17] *Life of Johnson,* ed. George Birkbeck Hill, rev. by L. F. Powell (Oxford, 1934–50), III, 308. Meyer, in the introduction to *A Biographical Sketch* (p. v), argues that Boswell exaggerated Tyers' inaccuracy.

[18] Nichols, *Literary Anecdotes,* VIII, 88*n.*

[19] *An Historical Essay on Mr. Addison,* 2d ed. (London, 1783), p. viii; *Political Conferences between Several Great Men, in the Last and Present Century,* 2d ed. (London, 1781), p. 192.

[20] *An Historical Rhapsody on Mr. Pope,* 2d, rev. ed. (London, 1782), p. vii.

[21] *Ibid.,* p. 136. *A Biographical Sketch,* p. 16.

was a memorable fellow (surprising that Virginia Woolf did not describe him in the *Common Readers*), so cheerful, garrulous but unprepossessing, generous in his writings, carefree.

Yet he did have at least one care: he dreaded the critic rapacious. "What composition," he wrote, "can stand before the porcupine pen of criticism?" [22] Fearful, he published his works sometimes anonymously, always in the most limited of limited editions; only twenty-five copies of his dialogues of the dead were published, a number just slightly less than what was usual for his books.[23] If his friends like the dialogues, he may publish, he says in the preface. He adds, however,

Preserve this little volume to yourself, gentle reader, and keep it as a manuscript, from the fault-finding critic (who will criticise every thing away from you) or from the person who knows too much to be pleased with what he reads. If, notwithstanding . . . , it should be insisted upon there is nothing new, the author will confess he has lost his labour. After all, what security can he have, that it may not be said of the very best anecdote, and therefore of the rest, collected to amuse the reader, in the words of Horatio in Hamlet,
"There needs no Ghost to tell us this!"

The reader of Tyers' dialogues may feel ashamed, like an eavesdropper; primed by reading such an apology, who could bring himself to criticize severely? Severity, though, seems uncalled for, as does any great amount of applause.

Quite representative of Tyers' performance is his title, *Conversations Political and Familiar.* Perhaps because of Johnson's disparagement of the genre, Tyers almost invariably called dialogues "conversations," a significant trait: if the word "dialogue" implies some sort of conflict, "conversation" is milder, indicating amenity, by far the dominant attitude of the speakers in this collection of twenty-eight pieces.[24] Like the shades employed by Lyttelton and Sylviana Sola, Tyers' converse in a region where, ostensibly, "nothing but truth is

---

[22] *A Biographical Sketch,* p. 20.   [23] Nichols, *Literary Anecdotes,* VIII, 80*n*.
[24] In referring to the pieces in the *Conversations,* which are misnumbered, I use the numbers they ought to bear.

spoken." Yet the reader does encounter some disagreement, some actual dialectic in the *Conversations*. Typically, one character describes himself and then his companion does likewise; along the way there is a measure of disputation. When a conversation contains disagreement, however, it usually ends in concord or, if the participants were rivals or enemies in life, reconciliation, and sometimes Tyers' efforts to preserve cordiality between his speakers become amusing. Charles V, for example, is heard speaking to Henry VIII in Conversation XVII: "It was marvellous the hand of violence was not raised against you for what you committed. It was said of you, 'that you never spared a man in your anger, nor a woman in your lust.' Excuse my warmth on this occasion." Less incredibly, Bulstrode Whitelock abates his harsh criticism of Henry Ireton's republicanism with the words "But our conversation ought not to be so rigorous in these regions" (Conv. XXV). Among Tyers' asphodels, argument seems as unwelcome as it was at Vauxhall Gardens, and sentiment as welcome.

Though no Charon, no Mercury, make their appearance, the setting is nevertheless Hades. References to Styx abound; the presence of other, nearby shades is suggested in several of the conversations; and the reality of mythological denizens of the nether world seems certified by Voltaire in Conversation XXIII: "After having treated as a fable, in my writings and conversation, the story of Charon, of Minos, and the Elisian fields (and knew of no other than the Elisian fields near Paris, where I was walking a few days ago) my satisfaction is to find myself at full liberty to wander in these delightful groves." Yet despite the presence of Lucian's props, Tyers displays little Lucianic comedy or satire; the Elysian Vauxhall has no room for a Diogenes or a Menippus.

Some conversations approach wittiness: the seventh, in which Samuel Foote, the actor, in Hades the equal of his proud antagonist, Condé Olivares, roundly criticizes the latter's arrogance; the ninth, between the beauteous Duchess of Mazarine and the deformed impresario Heidegger, in which Heidegger suggests he might make a suitable Vulcan for the Duchess' Venus; and the twenty-first, which displays Queen Elizabeth in conversation with Sixtus V:

How can you expect I should be desirous of your conversation, when you put me under deposition, my dominions under excommunication, and granted a crusade against Scotland and Ireland?

Sixtus. That was a matter of course, and a mere formality. It was copied from the interdict of my predecessor Pope Pius; of which, to tell you the truth, I had the drawing up. But I wished you no harm at the same time. Though the thunder of the Vatican was launched against England, I did not expect to gain anything by it.

Yet only the Foote-Olivares dialogue remains comical throughout, a simple *eiron-alazon* performance.

Most of the conversations are serious and historical in nature, employing real persons, only two of whom are ancients. These sober pieces, too, have diverting moments. It is amusing, for example, to hear Sir Thomas More attempting in Conversation III to explain *Utopia* to the hardened, world-weary Sir Francis Drake. But the conclusion of the dialogue, very much in Drake's favor, cannot please much. There Drake attacks the notion that Utopian principles might successfully have been applied to American colonization: "The indolence of the human species would prevail, and industry would be deprived of motives. No man could keep his own for an hour (nay indeed, according to your book, it would not be his own to keep) and a throat would be cut in the new world, in a moment, for a cocoanut." Drake's expression is colorful, but his opinion tells more about Tyers than about Drake, Sir Thomas, or *Utopia.*

It is amusing also, in Conversation XII, to learn from Swift that he did indeed marry Stella but "did not think the daughter of Sir William Temple's steward good enough to be the acknowledged wife of the Dean of St. Patrick's." And interest is held by the conversation of Garrick and Shakespeare (Conv. XVI), in which the actor-dramatist endures stern criticism for adapting Shakespeare's plays to please eighteenth-century taste. Particularly, Shakespeare abhors Garrick's deletion of the gravediggers' scene in *Hamlet.* "The characters were low," crestfallen Garrick protests, perhaps not ingenuously; they turned the attention of the audience away from "the principal persons." But Shakespeare holds his ground: "Novelty is of higher value than regularity." Though the conversation grows hot, the two participants take leave of each other with mutual congratulations—the way most of Tyers' pieces end.

There are some exceptions. Charles V and Henry VIII, although Charles attempts to remain dispassionate, nevertheless part in an unfriendly manner, accusing each other of extravagance. The reader, despite his knowledge of Charles's typical role—the braggart of Fontenelle, Fénelon, and Prior—agrees with Charles that Henry's extravagance was more sordid and outrageous. And in Conversation XIX, Charles II and the first Earl of Shaftesbury exchange blunt remarks, ending up about even. A really conspicuous exception to Tyers' usual practice occurs in Conversation XXVI, in which Raleigh confronts Addison. The adventurer ridicules Addison's shyness in Parliament, whereupon Addison closes the dialogue with an acerbity unusual here: at least, Addison retorts, "I always had wit and sense enough to keep my head upon my shoulders." This conversation, perhaps the most dramatic of Tyers' collection, recalls Lyttelton's better dialogues; judgment is left to the reader, not simply pronounced by a Charles V and accepted. Lyttelton is recalled earlier in the dialogue too, when Addison remarks that "Fortune, who sometimes makes a laughing-stock of mankind, may be supposed, in a frolic, to have made Addison a secretary of state, when he could have discharged the function of a bishop with applause"—a statement almost identical with Swift's opening remark, to Addison, in Lyttelton's fourth dialogue, a dialogue Tyers singled out for special praise in the course of another work, where he compares Lyttelton to Plutarch.[25]

Although Tyers rather comprehensively remarks in the preface that while composing his conversations he did not lose "sight of Lucian, Fontenelle, Fenelon, or Lyttelton," Lyttelton was his dominant model, despite initial indebtedness to Fénelon. The second piece in *Conversations Political and Familiar,* which accords Elizabeth preeminence as a queen, Mary Queen of Scots preeminence as a woman, recalls the pleasant Plutarchian discrimination of several of Lyttelton's collo-

[25] *An Historical Essay on Mr. Addison,* p. 72.

quies. Compared with Tyers, Lyttelton wrote both better and worse, though Lyttelton's best work is better than Tyers', more dramatic, more ironical, more frequently satirical and comical. Far more than Lyttelton's, Tyers' conversations deserve Johnson's stricture: "the production rather, as it seems, of leisure than of study, rather effusions than compositions." [26] The modest author of *Conversations Political and Familiar,* even when writing dialogues, remained primarily a retailer of anecdotes. What the quibble was to Shakespeare, the anecdote was to Tyers, a "fatal Cleopatra"—not entirely fatal but certainly debilitating and distracting. In the first of his books, *Political Conferences between Several Great Men, in the Last and Present Century* (1780), a collection of dialogues of the living, Tyers added anecdotal supplements to each conference. One of these supplements ends with Waller's clever explanation, to Charles II, of why he wrote so well in praise of Cromwell: "We poets, Sir, succeed best in Fiction." Tyers apologetically adds: "This anecdote has been told an hundred times. Excuse it, Reader: the Note is not much the longer for it." [27] Tyers' dialogues of the dead, however, contain their own notes, and amble along their anecdotal way. In Conversation XIX, Shaftesbury quotes from Rochester's well-known epigram upon the same Charles II, who "never said a silly thing, and never did a wise one," whereupon Charles, for the hundredth time, replies, "That, I hope, was perfectly true; and it was much to my credit: for my wit was my own, but my actions were my minister's." There needs no ghost to tell us this; the reader of dialogues cannot be pleased about the way such material swells and burdens the *Conversations.* Yet he remains an eavesdropper. Tyers sought, after all, merely to provide "enough for three hours reading," stipulating in the preface that he would publish this private collection only if his friends liked it; and he never did. A reader may wonder, though without hope of resolving the question, whether Tyers' absorption in nostalgic small talk was the result merely of his personal inadequacies or whether it was also imposed to

---

[26] "Lyttelton," *Lives of the English Poets,* ed. George Birkbeck Hill (Oxford, 1905), III, 451.

[27] *Political Conferences,* p. 64.

some extent by a new intellectual environment in which history had virtually ceased to be regarded as philosophy teaching by examples. Were there less evidence for the former explanation, it might be reasonable to put forward the latter.

Garrulous old age gave way to prattling youth: the century's last collection of Lucianic dialogues was the work of James Hay Beattie (1768–90), son of James Beattie, author of *The Minstrel*. The precocious boy had been appointed at the age of eighteen to an assistant professorship in Marischal College, Aberdeen, and but for his early death would have succeeded his father in the chair of logic and moral philosophy. In 1794, four years after young James's death, the heartbroken father privately published his son's literary remains, a volume entitled *Essays and Fragments in Prose and Verse* that contains four dialogues of the dead. The next year they were printed in magazines, and in 1799 Dr. Beattie allowed the commemorative volume to be republished commercially.[28] He may have polished the dialogues as well, for shortly after James's death he wrote that his son had "left many things in writing" but "it will be a long time before I shall be able to harden my heart so far as to revise them." [29] Father and son were so close that such revision would have accorded with James's own wishes: Dr. Beattie's thinking informed the dialogues and may even account for their genesis. Not only was he an enthusiastic admirer of Lyttelton [30] and friendly enough with the nobleman's collaborator to name his second son "Montagu"; he also was one of the few eighteenth-century readers privileged to see Prior's dialogues. In a let-

[28] All four dialogues were reprinted in the *Universal Magazine*, XCVI (February, 1795), 92–96, (March, 1795) 169–74, (April, 1795), 247–52; XCVII (July, 1795), 21–23. Three appeared in the *Scots Magazine*, LVII (March and April, 1795), 158–60, 221–22 (Dial. I); (May, 1795), 289–93 (Dial. IV); (June, 1795), 357–61 (Dial. III). Dr. Beattie published Dial. I, II, and IV in the second volume of *The Minstrel . . . with Some Other Poems. . . . To Which Are Now Added, Miscellanies. By J. H. Beattie* (London, 1799), doing so because an unauthorized edition had been published (according to Margaret Forbes, *Beattie and His Friends* [Westminster, 1904], p. 253n).

[29] Letter to the Duchess of Gordon (December 1, 1790), in Sir William Forbes, *An Account of the Life and Writings of James Beattie*, 2d ed. (London, 1824), II, 248.

[30] Margaret Forbes, p. 145. Rose Mary Davis describes Lyttelton and Beattie's mutual esteem in *The Good Lord Lyttelton* (Bethlehem, Pa., 1939), pp. 307–9.

ter to Mrs. Montagu (November 15, 1785), Dr. Beattie says the Duchess of Portsmouth has permitted him to read "some prose-treatises in manuscript of the poet Prior. . . . I read them with great pleasure. One of them, a dialogue between Locke and Montaigne, is an admirable piece of ridicule on the subject of Locke's philosophy; and seemed to me, when I read it, to be, in wit and humour, not inferior even to the Alma itself." [31] (Another friend of Mrs. Montagu's, the essayist and poet Anna Laetitia Barbauld, was also moved to write dialogues of the dead, two of them published in 1825–26. In one, Clio deletes names from the rolls of history; in the other, resembling Mrs. Montagu's "Berenice & Cleopatra," Madame de Maintenon and Helen of Troy lament their secret disappointments in love.)

Although the fourth of young James's dialogues, between "Swift, a Book-seller, and Mercury," recalls Mrs. Montagu's between Plutarch, Charon, and "a modern Bookseller," the influence of his father (or the contribution) is more conspicuous, for whereas Mrs. Montagu had ridiculed the tradesman's debased valuation of masterpieces, James attacks his taste for newfangled language. The bookseller scatters words such as "incivism," "substantiate," "sported"—words like and including some of those which Dr. Beattie, under the pseudonym Jonathan Jogtrot, had attacked in a 1787 letter to the *Northern Gazette*.[32] James's third dialogue, between "Mercury, Socrates, and a Modern Philosopher" (the philosopher, of course, being Hume), carries forward the offensive against skepticism and its chief Scottish exponent which Dr. Beattie had undertaken in the *Essay on the Nature and Immutability of Truth* (1770). And the first two dialogues also bear signs of Dr. Beattie's involvement. Johnson, whom father and son had visited in 1781, speaks in both, not entirely to his advantage. The second questions the virtue of those who, immediately after Johnson's death, circulated intimate biographical details. The first, more directly adverse to Johnson, pairs him with Addison and subjects the Rambler to sharp criticism for the heaviness of his style and the gloominess of his thinking. The Johnson portrayed here, familiar to readers acquainted with nineteenth-century biography, is the Johnson

[31] Sir William Forbes, II, 160.
[32] Reproduced from his MS. by Margaret Forbes, pp. 309–12.

who defends such things as a style "close without obtenebration" and can accuse Addison (whose prose he called the "model of the middle style") [33] of "colloquial imbecility." With the death of Cato the Elder in the popular imagination, a new Cato had to be invented, but of this matter I shall say something in my Epilogue.

Of James Hay Beattie's dialogues, nothing more need be said. The product of a conservative scholar's conservative pupil, they are likely to entertain only someone who knows nothing about the history of the genre in England. Exercises, in their academic subject matter as well as their triteness, they stand as a memorial to an exhausted literary fashion and also as a small, diverting milestone in the development of taste. James's Socrates, Addison, and Swift rise like Leonidas, temporarily blocking the gap against superior forces—most strikingly, perhaps, when the jargon-spouting, parvenu bookseller heartily recommends the *"Passions of Werter"* to Swift:

Werter is a true hero, and in his *line of conduct,* as a person of the highest honour and fashion, most *correct;* though a German by birth, he must have kept the best company in France; and so extraordinary a scholar, that he actually carried a Homer, a Greek Homer, Sir, in his pocket. But misfortune *ingurgitated* him in the very lowest *ebb* of distress. His affections were *captured* by a neighboring gentleman's lady, with whom he wished to have a *sentimental arrangement,* a little *flirtation*—(you understand me)—an *affair of gallantry,* I mean; and whose cruelty *fractured* the good young man's heart, and made him *temerariously* put a termination to his *existence.*

Here enters Lytteltonian Mercury, who has read Goethe's novel and can make its plot intelligible to Swift: "Werter tried to corrupt his neighbour's wife, and not wholly without success; but finding the lady not quite so forward as he wished, he left her in a rage, blew out his brains with a pistol, and (if we may believe some men of rhime . . .) went incontinently to heaven."

"Is it possible," Swift asks, "that so silly a tale can be popular?"

---

[33] "Addison," *Lives of the English Poets,* II, 149. James Gray enumerates the reservations that qualified Dr. Beattie's admiration for Johnson in "Beattie and the Johnson Circle," *Queen's Quarterly,* LVIII (1951), 519–32.

Epilogue

> The ghosts fled, gibbering, for their own dominions—
> (For 'tis not yet decided where they dwell
> And I leave every man to his own opinions)
>   —Byron, *The Vision of Judgment*

Whatever Romanticism was, the dialogue of the dead was not, for reasons entailing too much guesswork to be pursued very far. It is probably significant that conventional classical or Christian visualization of personal immortality rarely occurs in the foremost nineteenth-century authors: if they looked forward to the possibility of meeting Coriolanus or Sir Philip Sidney, they did not write about it. Those old stamped faces, moreover, had been handled to indistinctness, as Coleridge jauntily complained in the *Biographia Literaria:* "the example of Alexander and Clytus," he recalled from his schooldays, ". . . was equally good and apt, whatever might be the theme. Was it ambition? Alexander and Clytus!—Flattery? Alexander and Clytus!—Anger? Drunkenness? Pride? Friendship? Ingratitude? Late repentance? Still, still Alexander and Clytus! At length, the praises of agriculture having been exemplified in the sagacious observation, that, had Alexander been holding the plough, he would not have run his friend Clytus through with a spear, this tried and serviceable old friend was banished by public edict in secula seculorum." [1] After 1800, with the coming of much-increased rigor to his-

---

[1] *Biographia Literaria,* ed. J. Shawcross (London, 1907), I, 5.

torical investigations, the study of the past became too complicated
to serve the purposes of moralists [2]—people, as Thomas Tyers
might have observed, began to know too much to be pleased with
what they read—and morality itself, in the sense of the word illustrated by Pope's *Moral Essays* and Johnson's *Vanity of Human
Wishes,* had virtually expired. An anonymous, framed dialogue of
1822 has Johnson, Goldsmith, and Savage ruminating this very point,
Savage having just praised Scott's novels for constituting "a perfect
manual of true gentility."

Johnson. Hath this age produced any thing like Rasselas?
Savage. No, Doctor; the world is tired of allegory, of visions, apologues,
    and all the pretty little vehicles and go-carts of morality, so much in
    vogue during our time.
Johnson. I believe you, Sir: having no taste for the commodity itself, they
    can dispense with the vehicles.
Savage. The present is not an immoral age, Doctor, but it is a fastidious
    one; and if morality as a theme displeases it, it is that our worthy con-
    temporaries and their immediate predecessors converted it into an utter
    common-place.

But a genre never dies completely: bookish writers still rise on occasion to compose aubades. Dialogues of the dead continued to be
published, unobtrusively, into the present century. *American Dialogues of the Dead* came in 1814, introducing Washington to King
Alfred and William Tell in a manner clearly recalling Lyttelton's;
Franklin refutes Napoleon point by point in *The United States Literary Gazette* (1826). Sometimes an odd purpose retrieved the genre
from oblivion: one lachrymose series (1832), almost the only nineteenth-century dialogues with Charon, Mercury, and Minos in them,
attacks the practice of autopsies. Walter Savage Landor, whose initial
impetus to write the *Imaginary Conversations* owed something to
Lyttelton,[3] and whose conversations occasionally and briefly resem-
bled dialogues of the dead (because, for example, he sometimes paired

---

[2] George H. Nadel, "Philosophy of History Before Historicism," *Studies in the
Philosophy of History,* ed. George H. Nadel (New York, 1965), p. 73.

[3] Robert Southey's plan to write dialogues modeled on Lyttelton's and Richard
Hurd's (like most of Landor's conversations, Hurd's *Moral and Political Dialogues*
of 1759 comprised dialogues of the living set in past times), communicated to Lan-

characters from different ages), wrote one outright dialogue between shades, to do so imagining that Czar Nicholas I, whom he despised, had been assassinated. But that Landor's heart was not in Elysium seems evident even in this slight, vitriolic newspaper piece, for Nicholas simply plays Alexander to his adversary's Diogenes, according to a tradition distinct from that which I have been tracing (Fielding's dialogue of the living between Alexander and Diogenes is the readiest example). Much later, Salvador de Madariaga's *Elysian Fields* (London, 1937) permitted a passel of ghosts, prominently Goethe, to criticize American mores on the eve of World War II, and in the following years Eric Linklater marshaled Lincoln, Confucius, Lenin, and other eminences to rally the British with the kind of ringing sentiments that decline from pitch as soon as the shooting ends.[4] Still less memorably, and farther afield, the American Frederic Townsend had

---

dor, encouraged Landor to begin the *Imaginary Conversations,* according to Malcolm Elwin, *Savage Landor* (New York, 1941), p. 198. Southey's *Sir Thomas More, or Colloquies on the Progress and Prospects of Society* (1829), in which he supposes himself conversing with the ghost of More, has little connection with the tradition of dialogues of the dead. Later, remotely related philosophical pieces—closer to Plato than to Lucian or Lyttelton—are George Santayana's *Dialogues in Limbo* (London, 1925; expanded ed., New York, 1948), where a still-living Stranger converses with Democritus, Alcibiades, Socrates, and others, and G. Lowes Dickinson's *After Two Thousand Years: A Dialogue Between Plato and a Modern Young Man* (London, 1930), set without emphasis in the Elysian Fields. Many other works in some way contiguous to the dialogue of the dead might be mentioned—Bonamy Dobrée's *As Their Friends Saw Them* (London, [1933]), where five of the seven dialogues have historical figures chatting about a recently deceased acquaintance; John Kendrick Bangs's *A House-Boat on the Styx* (New York, 1896), its narrative full of conversation from below; and so forth. The myth of the underworld may be always with us; not the dialogue of the dead, however. How obscure the genre had become by the beginning of the present century is revealed in a series of so-called dialogues of the dead, really imaginary conversations of an odd sort, in the *Spectator,* CXI (1913), 130–32; CXII (1914), 1081–82; CXIII (1914), 882–84; CXIV (1915), 398–99. Never before in England or America had a work entitled "dialogue of the dead" been anything but just that.

[4] *The Cornerstones: A Conversation in Elysium* (London, 1941); *The Raft and Socrates Asks Why* (London, 1942); *The Great Ship and Rabelais Replies* (London, 1944). Graham Hough's *The Last Romantics* (London, 1949) closes with a "Conversation in Limbo" between W. B. Yeats and H. G. Wells; G. Norman Laidlaw's *Elysian Encounter: Diderot and Gide* (Syracuse, 1963), with a dialogue of the dead between the principals. *Musicians in Elysium,* by Ferruccio Bonavia (London, 1949), contains twenty brief, light, and generally charming dialogues in which Beethoven figures as a kind of musicological Dr. Johnson.

put together a dozen long, extremely bland *Ghostly Colloquies* (1856) where volant shades, such as Byron and Salvator Rosa, alight by such places as Niagara Falls to promote causes such as the conservation of natural resources. Only the existence of these and comparable works needs to be noted.

The most remarkable dialogues of the dead composed after the eighteenth century are those of Henry Duff Traill (1842–1900), a man of numerous talents invested in a full career of journalism, history, and criticism. *The New Lucian, Being a Series of Dialogues of the Dead,* with fourteen colloquies of ample size, was published in 1884, followed in 1900 by a second edition with fifteen, six of them new.[5] It is a work of its time, manifesting an attitude toward history significantly different from Lyttelton's; of Traill's twenty dialogues, approximately half combine characters who in life were, more or less, nineteenth-century contemporaries: Disraeli and Peel, Gladstone and General Gordon, and so forth. Three of the four speaking ancients are drawn into the work largely because the moderns they address attract them: Landor, Plato; Tennyson, Virgil; Darwin, Lucretius. Lucian is present himself by fief, conversing with Pascal in one of the merely two dialogues involving no nineteenth-century figures; in the other, Fielding engages Richardson. The rest bring together nineteenth- and eighteenth-century counterparts: Thackeray and Sterne, the dramatist and critic George Henry Lewes and Garrick, the M.P. Edward Horsman and Burke, Lord Sandwich and Wilkes.

Admirable as it is, *The New Lucian* seems distressingly dated, more so than some similar works of the preceding century, for Traill the journalist was profoundly concerned with topical affairs. Three of his dialogues (O'Connell and Butt, Parnell and Butt, and an earlier dialogue of the living and the dead between Parnell and Grattan) bear heavily upon the Irish Question. Several vehemently attack Gladstone. Persons as arcane as the first Lord Westbury, De Morny,

---

[5] Two of the six first appeared in magazines (1884, 1892). Traill also published a dialogue of the living and the dead, but did not include it in either edition of *The New Lucian:* "Parnell and Grattan: A Dialogue," *Contemporary Review,* XLIX (1886), 18–31.

Gambetta, Blanqui, the Compte de Chambord, and Philippe Egalité have major parts. In short, most of the dialogues employ history less than history employs them, illustrate past events rather than their enduring meaning. Almost oblivious of the universal—of topics like the maxims of private and public life which Lyttelton sought— Traill plunges into the details of his century's political relationships, supplying dates, places, the names of obscure collaborators, and presenting his characters' posthumous appraisals of current events as well as accounts of events in their lifetimes. Says Isaac Butt to Daniel O'Connell in a dialogue omitted from the second edition (where Traill attempted to decrease the ephemerality of his work): "I cannot say then that Mr. Parnell has . . . lost an inch of popular ground; for he has certainly not lost a fraction of his parliamentary importance. He is feared as much as ever by his political opponents: he is followed as obediently as ever by his party" (Dial. VI). In a conversation with Virgil introduced in the second edition, Tennyson argues that the empire of Britain surpasses Rome's, and the poets speculate about whether British domination will find an epic bard to sing it; in another, General Gordon, now at peace with the Mahdi in Elysium, as if with foreknowledge predicts that the reversal of Gladstone's policy in the Sudan "will spread peace and light and mercy throughout a land of darkness and cruel habitations" (Dial. I). The reader finds himself witnessing not just discussions of past events but conspicuously outdated discussions, deflated prophecies.

Yet Traill's dialogues do have substance because, on the whole, he knew much about what he chose to describe and he could write with energy. Passages glow; here O'Connell rhapsodizes on the powers he once possessed as an orator: "A million hearts, a million wills under the control of a single man! Roar and silence, tears and laughter, joy and fury—each of them obedient to his lifted hand. Thunder as of the ocean, and I its Neptune! Hush as of the desert, and I its Memnon at the hour of dawn! Now I flung laughter like a sudden burst of windy sunlight across their upturned faces; now I blanched them like aspens under the hurricane with the pallor of gathering tears. Ah! Isaac! What an hour was that, and worth what ages spent among the passionless shades!" Yet the dialogues have a discursiveness like Landor's. As whole dramatic actions, they bring few surprises, no intricate turns. The characters are broad; once launched, they keep to a predictable course. Thus Fielding, from the start of the conversation with Richardson, establishes himself as the generous and wise character, never suffering any discomfiture, and this observation, with a change of names, will hold for all the dialogues where conflict occurs. Numerous references sustain the fiction of the underworld, yet Traill's pieces seem designed, at least half the time, for nostalgic, historicist pilgrimage back to some vanished historical moment—a purpose of Landor's dialogues and Richard Hurd's—rather than for portrayal of a confrontation beyond time in the manner of Lyttelton and Lucian. The frequency of meetings between quondam contemporaries tends to support this impression.

Although the climax of Fielding-Richardson has to do with the neglect they suffer from Victorian readers, and the starting point is clearly occasional (the unveiling of a bust of Fielding in 1883), this and the other specifically literary dialogues survive with more freshness than those bearing on political history. All the literary dialogues are of the ancients-moderns variety, some "ancients" wearing periwigs not togas, and reflect Traill's sympathy with the classics of England as well as the classics of Rome and Greece. "The eighteenth century is undoubtedly much better understood and more justly appraised at this moment than was possible fifty years ago," wrote one of Traill's contemporaries, naming Traill together with W. E. H. Lecky, Leslie Stephen, W. J. Courthope, and Austin Dobson as a leader of the revaluation.[6] In addition to studies of the first Earl of Shaftesbury (1886) and William III (1888), Traill produced, with J. S. Mann, the six-volume historical compendium *Social England* (1893–97), and contributed a sympathetic and perceptive biography of Sterne to the English Men of Letters series (1882). The dialogues make his feelings fully apparent: virtually no eighteenth-century figure emerges from

[6] William Watson, *Excursions in Criticism: Being Some Prose Recreations of a Rhymer* (London, 1893), p. 121. Watson's dialogue, "Dr. Johnson on Modern Poetry," is reprinted here, pp. 140–66.

them without honor. Richardson, it is true, is at the disadvantage of being paired with a manly Fielding whom Traill preferred, yet Traill gives the antagonist some measure of his due. Only William Paley, the natural theologian of the later eighteenth century, sustains real abuse, and that because he is set against the indomitable Darwin, supported by Lucretius; Pascal too suffers, the butt of Lucian, whom Traill praised elsewhere in a loving essay,[7] but Peter the Great, the object of Lyttelton's highly qualified enthusiasm, comes off well. Most significantly, Samuel Johnson enters in the second edition to rout another English Man of Letters whose life Traill had written (1884), and written with feeling—Coleridge.

Nobody speaks more often than Johnson in later dialogues of the dead, confirming Macaulay's assertion that he was "better known to us than any other man in history." [8] Boswell's detailed biography, as Bertrand H. Bronson has shown,[9] made of Johnson a myth now discounted by scholars but, in nineteenth-century minds, potent and durable: the myth of the massive, colorful curmudgeon; *the* conversationalist, whose truculent speech excelled his ponderous writing; the acidulous literary despot; the disheveled moralist who, in another phrase of Macaulay's, famously represented "the union of great powers with low prejudices." [10] Here was an Elder Cato, magnificent in some respects, disreputable in others, who held a place in history proximate to the experience of a readership which, in a quantitative way, had outgrown the classics; Johnson was found to be the perfect, vital spokesman for an older, in some degree a severer age—"Brave

---

[7] "Lucian," *The New Fiction and Other Essays on Literary Subjects* (London, 1897), pp. 196–225. One significant excerpt: "Lucian's dramatic gift is assuredly conspicuous in all his dialogues. His *personae* are not, as Landor's in most cases almost avowedly and designedly were, mere mouthpieces for the exposition of his own views" (p. 216).

[8] Thomas Babington Macaulay, Review of John Wilson Croker's edition of Boswell's *Life of Johnson, Edinburgh Review,* LIV (1831), 20.

[9] "The Double Tradition of Dr. Johnson," *ELH,* XVIII (1951), 90–106. Professor Bronson's own expert, vigorous dialogue of the dead between Johnson and Prior, entitled "On Choosing Fit Subjects for Verse: or, Who Now Reads Prior?" is printed in his *Facets of the Enlightenment: Studies in English Literature and Its Contexts* (Berkeley, 1968), pp. 26–44.

[10] Macaulay, p. 27.

old Samuel," in Carlyle's words from *On Heroes and Hero-Worship,* *"ultimus Romanorum!"* As we have seen, Hades had awaited Johnson with impatience: Garrick and Shakespeare abandon Chesterfield to welcome him in a dialogue of 1785, and in another of the same year Goldsmith stands in the receiving line, tempering his cordiality with remarks against the *Lives of the Poets.* Within a decade, James Hay Beattie brought Johnson into two dialogues, sounding themes that would dominate comparable later pieces: a Fine Gentleman accuses Johnson of having been "more ready to punish than to praise," of having, Cato-like, "let fly his unmerciful lash upon the whole community of mankind"; and Addison ridicules what Macaulay later called "Johnsonese." Nor is Boswell ignored, the question of propriety in biographical revelations being raised as it would be many times in the years to follow—for example, in the several-times-reprinted dialogue, by J. B., wherein Johnson harshly reprimands his disciple for incontinence with respect to both speech and gin (1802–4). In a dialogue of 1798 Boswell and Johnson discuss post-Revolutionary France.

Johnson's conversation of 1822, with Savage, has already been noted here; in 1868 he made one, and not the least conspicuous, of a talkative company including Macaulay, Boswell, Goldsmith, Goethe, Thackeray, Richardson, Fielding, Sterne, Addison, Voltaire, and Bacon, in an overpopulated series swelling the periodical *Once a Week.* But more competent use of the myth may be found in the Elysian conversations written by Traill and William Watson (1858–1935). Watson's "Interview" (1889) discovers Johnson at ease in a little Ionic temple stocked with editions of nineteenth-century poets and, the reader is given to believe, often visited by Johnson's old clubmates, except unwelcome Boswell; the Censor's function, according to what had become his conventional duty, is to review what he died too soon to read [11]—for example, Wordsworth

[11] Or what was published too late; but history could be modified, as it was in a dialogue of the living, virtually a dialogue of the dead, wherein Boswell shows Johnson a copy of the Kilmarnock edition of Burns (published in 1786, two years after Johnson's death) and extracts the pronouncement: "a nine-days' wonder—a minor Macpherson" ("An Imaginary Conversation," *Hogg's Instructor,* V [1855], 89–99).

—A Poet who, before the society of wits and scholars, preferred that of clowns and hinds, and who found the cultivated shores of Thames less to his liking than the savage wilds of Westmoreland, where man is only less rude and forbidding than Nature. I have looked into the writings of this gentleman, and of other poets his contemporaries, and it seems to me that their range is as narrow as their subjects are unedifying. Shakespeare portrayed man in various action; Mr. Pope exhibited man in elegant society, but your modern poet can show nothing but man in presence of some huge comfortless mountain or inhospitable seashore. Your modern poet would appear to be a taciturn and unsocial person, who never opens his mouth until he comes where there are none but ravens and seamews to listen. I have sometimes wondered whether the art of conversation, as understood by my contemporaries, hath since my time perished altogether from amongst living men.

Before he has finished, Watson brings Johnson's literary reckonings further up to date, with harsh common-sense judgments against Shelley, Rossetti, and Browning, some of the comments in a recognizable style: "Yes, Sir, Browning could read men. The pity is, men cannot read Browning." Johnson in a grudging way respects Tennyson, despite his "multiflexuous anfractuosities"; admires Arnold without reservation.

Whereas Watson's Johnson embraces all the jostling aspects of the folk-image, a Johnson simultaneously formidable and ludicrous, Traill's is more of a piece, overbearingly formal without pedantry, precise without cumbrous language. The paragraph I have quoted from Watson begins sharply, then subsides into a languor uncharacteristic of Johnson; not so the speech of Traill's Censor. And while Watson's discursive purpose is to make Johnson survey several poets, Traill's focuses precisely on one circumscribed subject, *The Ancient Mariner* and its ill-at-ease perpetrator.

Johnson. Nay, sir, let us have no more on't. This sort of argument can never be anything but barren. Shall we examine the poem together? Recite it for me; for of course you have it by heart. . . . You hesitate. Come, my dear sir, be no more backward than your own mariner. You have, at any rate, a less unwilling hearer than his wedding guest.
Coleridge. Well, Dr. Johnson, if it will give you pleasure to hear it—
Johnson. Sir, I did not say that. It will give me pleasure to criticise it; and

as you, I doubt not, will find pleasure in reciting it, we shall mutually oblige each other.   (Dial. X, 2d ed.)

By eighteenth-century standards, at least by Johnson's, *The Ancient Mariner* is egregious nonsense. Turning upon it the artillery he once leveled at Gray's Pindarics, Johnson ridicules such things as the diaphanous ship's opaque ribs, underlining his dissatisfaction with analogies painful to contemplate. A little less waspishly, he inquires about the "concatenation of cause and effect" in such cases as the following: "It further appears, too, that [the Polar Spirit] was somewhat precipitate in slaying the whole crew as accessories after the fact to the murder of the albatross, since he has to raise them from the dead in order to navigate the ship; though why the navigation of a ship which is being propelled by a spirit under her keel should require the resurrection of anybody but the steersman, or why the mariners 'gan work the ropes' of a vessel with no wind to fill her sails, you have not told us."

Ironical, that Johnson would be pressed so regularly into the service of a genre he explicitly repudiated, even if a reader supposes that he posthumously changed his mind—as Eric Linklater imagined him changing it, in "Socrates Asks Why," on the subject of Americans and Whigs: finding no Whigs in Elysium, he detests them less.[12] At Johnson's house on Gough Square, London, visitors may or may not be surprised to see a cartoon by Max Beerbohm, "In the Shades. 1915," depicting Boswell in conversation with his massive mentor about the presentation of the house to the public. It is more ironical still that Johnson would be made to say some of the things put in his mouth by dialogue-writers on the order of Charles Erskine Scott Wood, who, in a series of a radical political stamp, had the insensitivity to make him bellow, "Show me patriotism and there I will show you trade exploitation hiding its bestial head"![13] How far fallen is such a travesty from even the playfully rancorous remarks in the dialogues of William King, not to mention the penetrating musings of

[12] *The Raft and Socrates Asks Why,* pp. 67–68.
[13] "A Pacifist Enters Heaven—in Bits," *Heavenly Discourse* (New York, 1942; first published, 1927), p. 106.

Prior and the nobly motivated, sometimes very apt sallies that salt Lyttelton's collection. Happily, the Elysium those dead authors knew, though generally lost to twentieth-century writers, remains within a reader's reach.

And still, occasionally, within a writer's—especially if, like Traill, he has a taste for scholarship and the eighteenth century, as did Lytton Strachey. With essays on Voltaire in *Books and Characters French and English* (London, 1922), Strachey published "A Dialogue between Moses, Diogenes, and Mr. Loke," in a note prefatory to the volume explaining that "The 'Dialogue' is now printed for the first time, from a manuscript, apparently in the handwriting of Voltaire and belonging to his English period." In the dialogue Locke voices distress at finding his companions so complacent about the deceptions perpetrated by otherwise good rulers. An economical, pointed piece, it might indeed have been written by Voltaire; he did write two dialogues of the dead, and this one looks enough like his work to have deceived a distinguished scholar (who employed it as a primary source for a study of Voltaire, then defended himself in a later edition by asserting its fidelity to Voltaire's mind).

But the manuscript, which I have seen, is in Strachey's handwriting: the first speech has several initial small letters superimposed with capitals, as if it occurred belatedly to the author that he might mimic eighteenth-century usage. And among Strachey's unpublished manuscripts lie several more such dialogues, some of the titles tantalizing: "Cleopatra and Mrs. Humphry Ward," "King Herod and the Rev. Mr. Malthus," "Sennacherib and Rupert Brooke," "Catullus and Lord Tennyson." [14] In addition there are "Julius Caesar and Lord Salisbury" (which is perhaps the best), "Boccaccio and General Lee," "Salter and Cleopatra," and, predictably, one employing the eighteenth-century Cato—"Gibbon, Johnson, and Adam Smith"; plus two fragments, less than a page of "Carrier and Sir Edmund Du Cane" and a three-page conversation between "Headmaster and Parent." The last, as well as the dialogue with Johnson in it, is set in this

[14] I am deeply grateful to Mrs. Alix Strachey, Mr. Michael Holroyd, and Mr. Paul Levy for permission to read and quote from the Strachey papers.

world, the latter taking place just before Smith assumed a professorship at Strachey's Cambridge. But the locale of the other pieces, explicit in some—Cleopatra tells Mrs. Ward that she reads away the "long Stygian evenings"—implicit in others because the characters come from different ages, is the Greek underworld. "Scene: The Infernal Regions" says a subheading of "Salter and Cleopatra," the longest of the pieces, seven pages. It is also subtitled "An Imaginary Conversation," but this and the other dialogues bear small resemblance to Landor. No, the fountainhead of Strachey's series is Lucian, though the tone, in general, is one of feline skepticism rather than canine cynicism.

As if acting in sketches for *Eminent Victorians,* Mrs. Ward, Malthus, Tennyson, and Salisbury all run blindly into difficulties. Mrs. Ward prattles about Oxford culture and her uncle Matthew Arnold; Malthus discovers that he and Herod agree, in principle at least, about the dangers of overpopulation and what should be done to remedy it; Tennyson ineffectively tries to chasten Catullus; Salisbury neatly explains Christianity to Caesar. If Victorian attitudes brought about World War I, there is further indictment of the last age in "Sennacherib and Rupert Brooke," where the young soldier insists that his war was fought for purposes of high nobility but his companion stands incredulous, defending his own war against Egypt in words perfectly applicable to other campaigns. Brooke claims he would be a conscientious objector rather than obey Sennacherib, inducing the reply: "Tut, tut, tut! You are quite mistaken. You know nothing of the facts. Our war with Egypt was undertaken purely for self-defence; it was also undertaken to preserve the rights of the smaller nationalities. Egypt was aiming at a world-empire. Every right-thinking person in Assyria would have told you that. It was a necessary war, a just war, and a glorious war." Something of the same kind appears in the conversation of indulgent Boccaccio, who behaves most respectfully with General Lee but expresses curiosity about what sustained the commander in defeat; his self-respect, his sense of having done his duty, Lee answers. But Boccaccio, though only an Italian in Lee's eyes, a trifler, has spoken so hauntingly of wine and poetry, love and women, that duty seems very cold indeed. Rather like Boccaccio, Catullus tells prudish Tennyson that man must be seen whole, and Herod, recognizing the force of passion, has doubts about the efficacy of Malthus' nostrum, common sense and self-restraint.

Two of the completed dialogues, by the peculiarities of their form and subject matter, seem disparate from the rest. The dialogue of the living between Johnson, Gibbon, and Smith has a unique title, "Essay," and meanders as the trio discusses the state of the universities. Johnson covets the leisure and disputation enjoyed by undergraduates; Gibbon would like to be a professor. The lexicographer could be the source of some peppery talk, and he does not speak blandly: when Gibbon asks whether Alma Mater may still be said—quoting Pope—to lie "dissolved in port," Johnson answers, "No, sir, pudding"; and to Gibbon's objection that Pope's line would no longer scan, Johnson thunders, "I didn't mean it to scan, sir; I meant it to make sense. And that is more than was ever done by a Fellow of a College. Sir, the Universities may have been seats of learning in the past; they may be seats of learning now; I do not deny that. What I deny is that they ever have been, or ever will be, seats of sense." But Strachey fails to provide as much fire as one would like. More different, still, from the rest of the dialogues is the little drama between W. H. Salter and Cleopatra, complete with brief stage directions unusual in the genre, a cruel, sniggering conversation in which the queen baits Salter into love-making, then rebuffs him at the critical moment.[15] If Salter is a fool, Cleopatra is a devil, to little purpose except the venting of Strachey's hostility. Shockingly, the subtitle says: "Time: The future. (It is hoped the near future)."

The other dialogues, more of a piece, are more admirable for their art, calculating but not cool, in fact sometimes affecting. Though a

---

[15] William Henry Salter was Strachey's approximate contemporary at Trinity College, Cambridge. *A Primer of General History, Part I: Ancient History* (London, 1904), by Salter, does not flatter Cleopatra: "Rome would not brook an open despot, but that the despot should be a woman and an Oriental, was the greatest degradation which could have been proposed" (p. 187); but Strachey may have had in mind some other, less public remark. (I am grateful to Mr. Thomas Treadwell for information about Salter.)

menacing figure, Sennacherib speaks not unkindly to poor Brooke. Cleopatra treats Mrs. Ward with generosity, even if mistakenly: she thinks Mrs. Ward is Marie Corelli, author of the popular *Sorrows of Satan.* Herod and Malthus get along together like old collaborators. Boccaccio proves extremely deferential to Lee, Caesar less so, but gentle, with Salisbury. Only Catullus approaches the acerbity of Cleopatra's behavior with Salter, threatening at the end to write something that will singe Tennyson's ears. But Tennyson's arrogance warrants such revenge, whereas Brooke seems a mere blasted flower, Mrs. Ward simply self-important and garrulous, Lee an example of military insensibility, and Salisbury a comparable politician. Sparks fly here and there, but not so much at the less favored characters as at the institutions they represent, and the tone is critical rather than hostile, more comical than cruel. Says Herod: "I saw the evil; I saw the cure; and I was possessed of absolute power. Supposing you, Mr. Malthus, had been King of Judaea, what would you have done?" To which Malthus replies: "As a clergyman of the Church of England, my position would have been so extremely anomalous that I hesitate to answer." Says Sennacherib at one point, referring to 2 Kings 19:35 and Isaiah 37:36: "I remember once I sent an army of 180,000 men into Palestine, where it was destroyed with quite extraordinary suddenness by some microbe or other. As the native chronicler put it, when they arose early in the morning, behold, they were all dead corpses." With just such spare imagination and wit did Lucian ridicule the claims of religion throughout his dialogues.

Perhaps most artful, and most characteristic of its author, is the conversation of Caesar and Salisbury, a soufflé confected of rationalism, elegance, and some tenderness—and a dialogue it is easy to imagine Lucian writing if he were Strachey's contemporary. What shall the speakers discuss?

Lord Salisbury. There is only one subject that is more important than politics. Let us talk about that.
Julius Caesar. Certainly; but what is it? Literature?
Lord Salisbury. No.
Julius Caesar. Philosophy?

Lord Salisbury. No.
Julius Caesar. Love?
Lord Salisbury. Oh, no.

The subject is religion, and Caesar, after first denying it any importance, agrees to consider its sociological and political effects. But Lord
Salisbury wants to maintain its truth, and when Caesar has described
his own beliefs, which his companion promptly recognizes as the Epicurean, he asks Salisbury to describe Christianity. Caesar seems genuinely curious, especially because Salisbury's is the religion of a man renowned for wisdom and practicality. "I will tell you," Salisbury
begins: "The world was created in seven days. . . ." Baldly, insensi-
tively, oblivious of what seems his present condition, Salisbury recites
a fundamentalist credo, soon concluding appropriately with the last
things:

> Then the evil, who will be in the majority, will go down to Hell, where
> they will suffer the greatest possible torment eternally, while the good
> will ascend to Heaven and be perfectly happy for ever after. That is my
> religion.
> *Julius Caesar.* And for many years you ruled over a great Empire, and
> under your government that Empire reached a height of power and
> prosperity it had never known before. So I am told. And that is your
> religion. Is it possible?
> *Lord Salisbury.* I assure you that during the whole course of my life I have
> never for one instant doubted it.
> *Julius Caesar.* My dear Lord Salisbury, let us talk about politics.

Almost two thousand years before, stern old Minos had stepped
back from an uncomfortable debate with Sostratus, that sly enquirer
into Elysian justice, when a comparable topic was becoming too troublesome; not, however, before the reader could feel the author's satirical, subversive point. How futile to admonish Sostratus not to "put it
into other people's heads to ask questions of this kind." People will always ask them, and authors (in some manner sustaining Socrates'
vision of a world "where they do not put a man to death for asking
questions") will continue to prompt them, from time to time in Elysian

conversations. Minos' words, the reader may remember, conclude the last conversation in Lucian's *Dialogues of the Dead,* that remarkable collection which introduced what would become an occasionally neglected but—as the works of Strachey and his English predecessors show—an enduring, rather homogeneous, sometimes engaging and even potent literary tradition.

Part II

ANTHOLOGY

The twenty dialogues collected here have been chosen to serve several purposes: to illustrate the history of the dialogue of the dead in English, to provide examples of works difficult to find except in a few great libraries, and to display each important author at what I take to be his best. Dialogues by Lucian, Erasmus, Fontenelle, and Fénelon, in seventeenth- and eighteenth-century translations, are included because of their impact upon English writers and because they seem too little known. For the latter reason, I have also reprinted one of Matthew Prior's dialogues, though they are readily available in a fine edition.

It has seemed best to retain nearly all peculiarities of spelling, capitalization, and punctuation, both because alterations would affect tone and also because oddnesses will remind the reader that he is walking upon old ground; to enter into the spirit of a bygone genre entails a constant exercise of historical imagination. Some customary changes have been made: *s* for long *s*, *w* for *vv,* etc. Quotation marks appear only at the beginning and the end of quoted passages, not at the beginning of each line. In a few places I have silently emended words obviously misprinted and have expanded abbreviations, and I have adopted a uniform system of italicizing and printing at full length the names at the beginning of speeches.

Lucian

Of the dialogues of the dead composed by Lucian in the second century, these are, traditionally, numbers II, VI, XII, and XXX. The first three are taken from Jasper Mayne's *Part of Lucian Made English* . . . (Oxford, 1663), pp. 49–52, 61–64; the last, which Mayne did not translate, from Thomas Francklin's *The Works of Lucian, from the Greek* (London, 1780), I, 153–55. Lucian's hero Menippus, who in the course of the collection harries Tantalus, Charon, Hermes, and others, is called a "Barker" because he is a Cynic (from the Greek for *dog*); in Dialogue XXI he addresses Cerberus as a relative. Sostratus has been tentatively identified as a pirate mentioned by Demosthenes (M. D. MacLeod, ed., *Lucian,* Loeb Classical Library, VII [Cambridge, Mass., 1961], 137*n*).

Pluto, or a Complaint against Menippus

The Speakers, Crœsus, Pluto, Menippus, Midas, Sardanapalus

Crœsus. Tis not possible for us to endure, Pluto, this insufferable Barker Menippus to be of our company. Therefore remove him hence, or we will depart some where else.

Pluto. What hurt can he do to you, being dead as you are?

Crœsus. When we howl, and sigh at the memory of our pleasures in the other world, Midas of his gold, Sardanapalus of his Luxury, I of my treasures; he laughs and upbraides us, calling us slaves, and base villains: sometimes he drowns our howlings with singing, and in a word he is very troublesome.

Pluto. What say you to this, Menippus?

Menippus. Tis all true. These men I hate as degenerous and lost; who think it not enough to have lived wickedly, but remember and dwell upon the thought of those things above. Therefore I delight to plague them with themselves.

Pluto. But you do ill; for they lament no small losses.

Menippus. Are you mad too, Pluto, that you approve their whinings?

Pluto. No, Sir. But I would not have you divide your selves.

Menippus. Know this, O ye worst of Lydians, Phrygians and Assyrians, that I will never leave you; but wheresoever you go I will follow, vexing you, and singing, and laughing.

Crœsus. Is not this plaine Contumelie?

Menippus. No. That was contumelie which you usually practiced, suffering your selves to be adored, and abusing free people; not at all remembering your mortalitie: wherefore howle, now you have lost all.

Crœsus. Where are my rich and Numerous possessions?

Midas. How much gold do I misse?

Sardanapalus. And I how much pleasure?

Menippus. So, this I like: weep on; Ile joyne with you, and sing the old sentence, *Know thy selfe.* A fit dittie to be mingled with your mournings.

A Dialogue between Terpsion, and Pluto

Terpsion. Is this Justice, Pluto, that I should die, who am but thirty yeers old, and that Thucritus, who is almost an hundred, should live?

Pluto. Great Justice, Terpsion; For though he lives, yet he wishes none of his friends dead; whereas you all the time you lived, laid nets for his estate.

Terpsion. Was't not fit, being an old man, and no longer able to use his riches, he should die, and leave them to those that are younger?

Pluto. You make new lawes, Terpsion, that when a man can no longer use his riches with pleasure, he ought to die. Fate and Nature decree otherwise.

Terpsion. I accuse them, therefore, of disorder. For the businesse ought to run in this succession: The most aged to die first, then those who are next in years; And not to be inverted, or he to live who is decrepit, hath but three teeth left, scarce sees, is supported by four servants, distills at nose, hath eyes filled with rheume, hath lost all sense of pleasure, and is laught at by boyes as a living sepulchre; and the most beautifull, and lustiest young men to die. This is to make rivers run backwards. At least 'twere fit we knew the date of old mens lives, that they might not cousen us as they do. But now the old Proverb is brought to passe, the Cart leads the Oxe.

Pluto. These things are wiselier carried, Terpsion, then you are aware of. For what ailes you, that you yawne after other mens fortunes, and enslave your selves to childlesse old men? You do, therefore, but make your selves ridiculous, and they bury you first; which to many is matter of great pleasure; for just as you pray'd for their deaths, so much delight is it to others to have you die first. For you have introduced a new Art, to make love to old women, and old men, especially to those who have no children, neglecting those that have; whilest many of those who are courted by you, well acquainted with your aimes, if they chance to have children, pretend to hate them, that they may have observers. At length those who had for a long time wasted themselves in gifts, are shut out of the will, and the sonne, as there is good reason, enjoyes all: the rest cheated of their hopes gnash their teeth.

Terpsion. You speak truth. Thucritus hath almost quite eaten my estate; still making me believe he would die. And as often as I came to visit him, he would groan, and sob inwardly, and counterfeit a noise like an abortive chick in the shell; wherefore by how much the neerer I thought him to his grave, so many gifts the more did I send him, least his other flatterers should exceed me in presents: many nights have my cares taken my sleep from me, numbring and disposing my fortunes. And indeed care, and watching were the causes of my death: whilest he having swallowed my bait, assisted at my funerall, and went before my beer laughing.

Pluto. Maist thou live eternally, Thucritus, to grow rich, and laugh at such men. And maist thou not die, till thou have sent hither all thy flatterers before thee.

Terpsion. It would be a pleasure to me too, Pluto, if Chariades should die before Thucritus.

Pluto. Take comfort, Terpsion; Phido, Melantus, and all the rest shall die before him of their Cares.

Terpsion. This I like. Live eternally Thucritus.

A Dialogue between Alexander, Hannibal, Minos, Scipio

Alexander. 'Tis fit I be prefer'd before you, Lybian, being the better man.

Hannibal. No, Sir, 'Tis fit I should be prefer'd.

Alexander. Let Minos judge.

Minos. Who are you?

Alexander. This is Hannibal, the Carthaginian; I am Alexander the Sonne of Philippe.

Minos. Afore Jove, both famous men. But about what is your contention?

Alexander. About taking place. He saies he was a greater Commander then I. I, as all the world knowes, not only excell'd this fellow, but all men els in Warres.

Minos. Both therefore speak for your selves as well as you can: and do you begin, Lybian.

Hannibal. I am glad Minos, that I have here learnt the Greek Tongue, that herein also Alexander may not excell me. I say, then, that those men are most worthy of renown, who from small Originals, have arrived to great Atchievements, and by their own power have made themselves worthy of Empire. With a small Troope I made an inrode into Spain at first, as Lieuetenant under my brother; where I was held fit for the greatest imployments and counted the best souldier. For there I conquered the Iberians, and overcame the Gaules, and Hesperians; and having march't over great mountaines neer the Po, I over ran and demolish't diverse cities, wasted all the Champion Countrey of Italy, and led my army to the suburbes of Rome; and slew so many Romans on one day,

that we measured their Rings by Bushels, and made Bridges over
rivers with dead bodies: And all this I did, neither call'd the sonne
of Ammon, nor faining my selfe a God, nor telling my mothers
dreams. But confessing my selfe to be a man, I fought against
tryed, experienced Captaines, and joyned battle with stout and warlike souldiers; not with Medes, or Armenians, who flie before they
are pursued, and yeeld the victory to any man of a bold spirit.
Whereas Alexander, succeding his Father in his Kingdome, enlarged it, indeed, but by the current of Fortune; who when he had
overcome, and taken the miserable Darius in the plaines of Arbela,
contrary to the custome of his Ancestors, would have been adored;
And corrupting himselfe with the Persian Luxury, he slew his
friends at Banquets, and assisted at their murthers. I had the rule of
my Countrey too; yet when they called me home, because a great
fleet of enemies sailed towards Lybia, I speedily obeyed, and render'd my selfe a private man: and when I was afterwards condemned, bore the sentence contentedly. And this I did, being but a
Barbarian, and not bred to the Greek Discipline: who never read
Homer, like him, nor was instructed by Aristotle; but was lead by
my own excellent Genius. And these are the things wherein I pronounce my selfe better then Alexander. But if he think himself my
superiour, because he hath encircled his head with a Crown: perchance such ornaments may seem venerable to his Macedonians; but
it followes not that therefore he should be preferred before a valiant and Warlike Captain, who still went more by Counsell then
Fortune.

Minos. He hath made a generous speech for himselfe, and not to be
expected from a Lybian. What say you to this, Alexander?

Alexander. 'Tis fit, Minos, I should make no reply to such a bold fellow: since fame can sufficiently instruct thee how great a Prince I
was, and how great a Thiefe he: Yet consider how farre I excell
him, who began my Atchievements, with my youth; when succeeding in a troubled and distracted State, I tooke revenge of my Fathers Murtherers. Afterwards, striking a terrour into all Greece by
my conquest of Thebes, they chose me their Generall: nor was I

content to straighten my selfe within the Kingdome of Macedonia left me by my Father, but projected the victory of all the world. Thinking it poor not to raigne over the Universe, with a small Army I entred into Asia, and in a great battle wonne Lydia, Ionia, and Phrygia. And conquering all as I march't, I came to Issus, where Darius with an Army consisting of Myriads expected me. After this, Minos, you may remember how many thousand shades I sent you in one day: The Ferry-man saies his Boat was not sufficient, but that he was faine to joyne boards together, and waft them over upon planks. And this I did, still exposing my selfe first to danger, and offering my selfe to wounds. And that I may not recount to you, what I did at Tyre, and in the fields of Arbela, I went as farre as India, and made the Ocean the period of my empire; tooke their Elephants; and brought away Porus Captive. Passing over Tanais, in a great horse fight I vanquish't the Scythians, a people not to be contemned: Rewarded my followers, and revenged my selfe of my foes. If men thought me a God, they are to be pardoned, being perswaded from the greatnesse of my Actions. After all, I died a King. Whereas Hanniball died Banish't in the Court of Prusias the Bythinian; A fit death for so deceitfull, and perjured a fellow. For I forbeare to tell how he overcame the Italians, not by valour, but by cousenage, perfidiousnesse, and stratagems. There being nothing just, or cleare in all that enterprize. But whereas he objects to me my Luxury, he forgets what he did at Capua; where he had his Mistresses, and like an admired souldier voluptuously squander'd away the opportunities of warre. Had not I, out of contempt of the Westerne parts, turned my march to the east, what great matter had I atchieved? Have taken Italy, perchance without bloud, or have subdued Lybia, to the utmost coasts of Africk. These were Countries below my Conquests, being already terrified by my fame, and acknowledging me for their Lord. I have said: give sentence, Minos. And let these few Atchievements pick't out of many suffice.

Scipio. Stay, Minos, till you have heard me too.

Minos. What are you, Brave Sir? or from whence come you?

Scipio. I am the Romane Scipio, who overthrew Carthage, and in many great Battles subdued Lybia.

Minos. What would you say more?

Scipio. Marry, that I am inferiour to Alexander, but greater then Hanniball, who conquered, and pursued him, and compelled him to a dishonorable flight. He is therefore very impudent to compare himselfe with Alexander, with whom I, who vanquisht him, presume not to rank my selfe in comparison.

Minos. Afore Jove thou speakest rightly, Scipio: wherefore I pronounce Alexander to be first, next to him you Scipio; and, if you please, let Hanniball be third, since he is not utterly to be despised.

Minos and Sostratus

Minos. Let this ruffian, Sostratus, be cast into Phlegethon: and that sacrilegious fellow torn in pieces by the Chimæra; and, do you hear, Mercury, chain down the tyrant along with Tityus, and let the vulturs gnaw his liver: but go ye good and virtuous into the Elysian Fields, inhabit the islands of the blessed, as a reward for your piety and virtue whilst upon earth.

Sostratus. Do but hear me first, Minos, whether I am right or not.

Minos. What! hear you again? do not you stand convicted already of being a villain, and killing so many people?

Sostratus. Granted: but consider whether my punishment is just, or not.

Minos. Most certainly; if every one should have the reward which they deserve.

Sostratus. But pray, Minos, answer me one short question.

Minos. Ask it; but be brief, that I may have time to try some other causes.

Sostratus. Whatever I did, whilst upon earth, did I do it of my own accord, or was I compelled to it by fate?

Minos. By fate: no doubt of it.

Sostratus. And, in obedience to that, do we not all act; those who are called good, and we who seem to do evil?

Minos. Most certainly; as Clotho enjoins them, who pre-ordains what every man shall do, from the moment of his birth.

Sostratus. If a man, therefore, kills another, being obliged to it by one whom he dare not disobey; a hangman, for instance, by command of the judge, or an officer, by order of the king, who is guilty of the murther?

Minos. The judge, or the king, undoubtedly: it cannot be the sword, which is no more than an instrument to fulfill the desire of him who directs the use of it.

Sostratus. Excellent Minos: thus, in support of my axiom, to add a corollary; again, if any one, sent by his master, brings me gold or silver, who am I to thank for it, to whom am I indebted for the favour?

Minos. To him who sent it: the man who brought was only agent to the other.

Sostratus. Do not you perceive, therefore, how unjust it is to punish me, who was only an instrument employed to do those things which Clotho had commanded, and to reward those who only administered the good imparted to them by others? you can never say it was possible to act in opposition to the dictates of necessity.

Minos. On a diligent enquiry, Sostratus, you will find out many things of this kind not easily to be accounted for; and all you can gain by your discoveries will be, to the title of thief, to add that of sophist also: however, let him go, Mercury, without any farther punishment; but take care you do not teach other ghosts to ask the same questions.

Erasmus

Charon had to make rafts, Lucian wrote, to accommodate all Alexander's victims, and in the fourth conversation of the *Dialogues of the Dead* the ferryman confesses he cannot pay for Hermes' chandlering, business is so slow—circumstances like those Erasmus exploits in the following dialogue, first published in 1529, from the *Colloquia*. The translation is by Sir Roger L'Estrange, in *Twenty Two Select Colloquies Out of Erasmus Roterodamus* . . . (London, 1689), pp. 265–72. Alastor, the avenging god of classical mythology, Beelzebub's royal executioner in medieval demonology (E. Johnson, ed., *Colloquies,* tr. N. Bailey [London, 1878], II, 452), seems mellow by comparison with the "Three great Potentates," Henry VIII, Francis I, and the Holy Roman Emperor Charles V. Erasmus' "Hue and Cry after Peace" is his *Querela pacis:* in the original Latin he refers to himself not by name but as Polygraphus, "Scribbler."

Col. XXI. Hell Broke Loose

The Divisions of Christian Princes are the Scandal of their Profession.
The Furies Strike the Fire, and the Monks blow the Cole.

Charon, Alastor

Charon. Why so Brisk Alastor, and whither so fast, I prethee?

Alastor. Why now I have met with You, Charon, I'm at my Journeys
end.

Charon. Well! And what News d'ye bring?

Alastor. That which you and your Mistress Proserpina will be glad to
hear.

Charon. Be Quick then, and out with it.

Alastor. In short the Furies have bestirr'd themselves, and gain'd their
Point. That is to say; what with Seditions, Wars, Robberies, and all
manner of Plagues, there's not one spot left upon the Face of the
Earth, that does not look like Hell Above-Ground. They have
spent their Snakes and their Poyson, till they are fain to Hunt for
more. Their Skulls are as Bald as so many Eggs: Not a Hair upon
their Heads; not one drop of Venom more in their Bodies. Wherefore be ready with your Boat, and your Oars, for you'll have more
work e're long than you can turn your Hand to.

Charon. I could have told you as much as this comes to my self.

Alastor. Well, and how came you by't?

Charon. I had it from Fame, some two days ago now.

Alastor. Nay Fame's a Nimble Gossip. But what make you here without your Boat?

Charon. Why I can neither Will nor Chuse: For mine is so Rotten a
Leaky Old Piece, that 'tis impossible, if Fame speak Truth, it
should ever hold out for such a Jobb: And I am now looking out
for a Titer Vessel. But true or false, I must get me another Barque
however; for I have suffer'd a Wrack already.

Alastor. Y'are all Dropping Wet, I perceive; but I thought you might have been new come out of a Bath.

Charon. Neither better nor worse, Alastor, then from Swimming out of the Stygian Lake.

Alastor. And where did you leave your Fare?

Charon. E'en Paddling among the Froggs.

Alastor. But what says Fame, upon the whole matter?

Charon. She speaks of Three great Potentates, that are Mortally bent upon the Ruine of One Another, insomuch, that they have possest every Part of Christendom, with this Fury of Rage, and Ambition. These Three are sufficient to Engage all the Lesser Princes and States in their Quarrel; and so Wilful, that they'l rather Perish then Yield. The Dane, the Pole, the Scot, nay, and the Turk Himself, are Dipt in the Broyl, and the Design. The Contagion is got into Spain, Britany, Italy, and France: Nay, besides these Feuds of Hostility, and Arms, there's a worse matter yet behind: That is to say; there is a Malignity that takes it's Rise from a Diversity of Opinions; which has Debauch'd Mens minds, and manners, to so Unnatural, and Insociable a Degree, that it has left neither Faith, nor Friendship in the World. It has broken all Confidence betwixt Brother and Brother; Husband and Wife: And it is to be hop'd that this Distraction will one day produce a glorious Confusion, to the very Desolation of Mankind: For these Controversies of the Tongue, and of the Pen, will come at last to be tried by the Swords Point.

Alastor. And Fame has said no more in All this, than what these very Ears and Eyes have heard and seen. For I have been a constant Companion, and Assistant to These Furies; and can speak upon Knowledge, that they have approv'd themselves worthy of their Name, and Office.

Charon. Right, but Mens minds are Variable; and what if some Devil should start up now to Negotiate a peace? There goes a Rumour, I can assure ye, of a certain Scribling Fellow, (one Erasmus they say) that has enter'd upon that Province.

Alastor. Ay, Ay: But He talks to the Deaf. There's no Body heeds

Him, now a days. He Writ a kind of a Hue and Cry after Peace, that he Phansy'd to be either Fled or Banish'd: And after that an Epitaph upon Peace Defunct, and all to no purpose. But then we have those on the other hand, that advance our cause as heartily as the very Furies Themselves.

Charon. And what are they, I prethee?

Alastor. You may observe, up and down, in the Courts of Princes, certain Animals; some of them Trick'd up with Feathers: Others, in White, Russet, Ash Colour'd Frocks, Gowns, Habits: Or call 'em what you will, These are the Instruments, you must know, that are still Irritating Kings to the Thirst of War, and Blood, under the splendid Notion of Empire, and Glory: And with the same Art, and Industry, they enflame the Spirits of the Nobility likewise, and of the Common-People. Their Sermons are only Harangues, in honour of the out-rages of Fire and Sword, under the Character of a Just, a Religious, or a Holy War. And, which is yet more Wonderful; they make it to be Gods Cause, on Both sides. God Fights for us, is the cry of the French Pulpits: And (what have they to fear, that have the Lord of Hosts for their Protector?) Acquit your selves like Men say the English, and the Spaniard, and the Victory is certain: For (This is Gods Cause, not Cæsars.) As for those that fall in the Battle, their Souls mount as directly to Heaven, as if they had Wings to carry 'em thither. (Arms and all.)

Charon. But do their Disciples believe all this?

Alastor. You cannot imagine the Power of a Well dissembled Religion; where there's Youth, Ignorance, Ambition, and a natural Animosity, to work upon. 'Tis an easie matter to impose, where there is a Previous Propension to be Deceiv'd!

Charon. Oh, that it did but lie in my Power to do these People a good Office!

Alastor. Give 'em a Magnificent Treat then; there's nothing they'l take better.

Charon. It must be of Mallows, Lupines, and Leeks, then, for we have nothing else you know.

Alastor. Pray let it be Patridge, Capons, Pheasant, they'l never think they'r welcome else.

Charon. But to the point, what should set these People so much a Gog upon Sedition, and Broyles? What can they get by't?

Alastor. Do not you know then, that they get more by the Dead, then by the Living? Why, there are Testaments, Funerals, Bulls, and Twenty other pretty Perquisites that are worth the looking after: Besides that a Camp-Life agrees much better with their Humour, then to lie droneing in their Cells. War breeds Bishops, and a very Block-Head, in a Time of Peace, comes many times to make an Excellent Military Prelate.

Charon. Well! They understand their business.

Alastor. Stay: But to the matter of a Boat; what necessity of having another?

Charon. Nay, 'tis but Swimming once again, instead of Rowing.

Alastor. Well, but now I think on't; how came the Boat to sink?

Charon. Under the weight of the Passengers.

Alastor. I thought you had carry'd Shadows only, not Bodies. What may be the Weight, I prethee, of a Cargo of Ghosts?

Charon. Why, let 'em be as Light as Water-Spiders, there may be enow of them to do a bodies Work. But then my Vessel is a kind of a Phantome too.

Alastor. I have seen the time, when you had as many Ghosts as you could Stow a-Bord; and Three or Four Thousand more hanging at the Stern, and your Barque me thought never so much as felt on't.

Charon. That is all according as the Ghosts are: For your Hectical, phthisical Souls, that go off in a Consumption, weigh little or nothing. But those that are Torn out of Bodies, in a Habit of Foul Humours; as in Apoplexyes, Quinzies, Fevers, and the like: But most of all, in the Chance of War: These, I must tell ye, carry a great deal of Corpulent, and gross matter, along with them.

Alastor. As for the Spaniards, and the French, methinks they should not be very Heavy.

Charon. No not comparatively with Others: And yet I do not find them altogether so Light as Feathers, neither. But for the Brittains, and the Germans, that are rank Feeders, I had only Ten of 'em a-Bord once, and if I had not Lighten'd my Boat of part of my Lading, we had all gone to the Bottom.

Alastor. You were hard put to't I find.

Charon. Ay, but what do ye think, when we are Pester'd with Great Lords, Hectors and Bullies?

Alastor. You were speaking of a Just War, e'en now. You have nothing to do, I presume with those that fall in such a War: These go to rights, all to Heaven, they say.

Charon. Whither they go, I know not; but this I'm sure of; Let the War be what it will, it sends us such sholes of Cripples, that a body would think there were not one Soul more left above ground; and they come over-charg'd, not only with Gut, and Surfeits, but with Patents, Pardons, Commissions, and I know not how much Lumber besides.

Alastor. Do they not come Naked to the Ferry then?

Charon. Yes, yes; but at their first coming they are strangely haunted with the Dreams of all these things.

Alastor. Are Dreams so Heavy then?

Charon. Heavy, d'ye say? Why they have Drown'd my Boat already: And then there's the Weight of so many Halfe-pence, over and above.

Alastor. That's somewhat I must confess, if they be Brass.

Charon. Well, well! It behoves me at a venture to get a stout Vessel.

Alastor. Without many Words; upon the main, thou'rt a happy Man.

Charon. Wherein, as thou lov'st me?

Alastor. Thou't get thee an Aldermans Estate, in the turning of a Hand.

Charon. There must be a World of Fares, at a Half-penny a Ghost, for a man to thrive upon't.

Alastor. You'l have enough I warrant ye, to do your business.

Charon. Ay, ay, 'Twould mount to somewhat indeed, if they'd bring their Wealth along with them. But they come to me, Weeping and Wailing, for the Kingdoms, the Dignities, the Abbies, and the

Treasure that they have left behind 'em; pay their bare Passage and that's all. So that what I have been these three Thousand years a scraping together, must go all away at a swoop, upon one Boat.

Alastor. He that would Get Mony, must Venture Mony.

Charon. Ay; but the People in the World have better Trading they say: Where a Man in three Years time shall make himself a Fortune.

Alastor. Yes, yes, and Squander't away again, perhaps in half the time. Your gain 'tis true, is less, but then 'tis steady and surer.

Charon. Not so steady neither, perchance. For what if some Providence should dispose the Hearts of Princes to a General Peace: My Work's at an end.

Alastor. My life for yours, there's no fear of that, for One-half-Score Year. The Pope is Labouring it, I know: But he had as good keep his Breath to Coole his Porridg. Not but that there is Notable Muttering and Grumbling every where? 'Tis an unreasonable thing they cry, that Christendom should be Torn to pieces thus, to gratifie a particular Picque, or the Ambition of two or three Swaggering pretenders. People, in fine, are grown Sick of these Hurly-Burlies: But when Men are bewitch'd once, there's no place left for better Counsels. Now to the business of the Boat. We have Workmen among our selves, without need to look any further. As Vulcan, for the purpose.

Charon. Right: If it were for an Iron, or a Brazen Vessel.

Alastor. Or 'twill Cost but a small matter, to send for a Carpenter.

Charon. Well! And where shall we have Materials?

Alastor. Why, certainly you have Timber enough.

Charon. The woods that were in Elyzium, are all destroy'd: Not so much as a stick left.

Alastor. How so, I beseech ye!

Charon. With burning Hereticks Ghosts. And now, for want of other Fewel, we are fain to Dig for Cole.

Alastor. But these Ghosts methinks might have been punish'd cheaper.

Charon. Rhadamanthus (the Judge) would have it so.

Alastor. And what will you do now, for your Wherry and Oars?

Charon. I'll look to the Helm my self, and if the Ghosts will not row, let 'em e'en stay behind.

Alastor. And what shall They do, that ne're serv'd to the Trade?

Charon. Serve or not serve: 'Tis all a case to me; For I make Monarchs Row, and Cardinals Row, as well as Porters, and Carmen. They all take their Turns, without any Priviledg or Exception.

Alastor. Well! I wish you a Boat to your mind, and so I'll away to Hell with my good News, and leave ye. But Hark ye first.

Charon. Speak then.

Alastor. Make what hast you can, or you'll be Smother'd in the Crow'd.

Charon. Nay, you will find at least two Hundred Thousand upon the Bank already, besides those that are Plung'd into the Lake. I'll make all the dispatch I can, and pray'e let them know I'm coming.

Fontenelle

Lucian, without utter severity, represents Socrates as inferior to Menippus in Dialogues XX and XXI: fearful of
death despite his pretenses, still insisting he knew nothing
at all, and still fond of comely students. Fontenelle more
indulgently pairs him with a presumptuous Montaigne in
this example of the *Nouveaux Dialogues des morts*
(1683), the third of the first group of dialogues between
dead ancients and dead moderns. It is reprinted from John
Hughes's *Fontenelle's Dialogues of the Dead* . . . (London,
1708), pp. 72–77.

Socrates and Montaigne

Montaigne. 'Tis you then, divine Socrates! How I'm transported to
see you! I am but newly come into these Parts, and immediately
upon my Arrival I made it my Business to find you out. In short,
after having fill'd my Book with your Name and Praises, I have
now the happy Opportunity of your Conversation, and of inform-
ing my self from you, by what Means you became possess'd of such
a native Virtue, the Motions of which were all so unaffected, and
which had no such Example before it, ev'n in that happy Age in
which you liv'd.

Socrates. I am very well pleas'd to meet with one of the Dead, that
seems to have been a Philosopher. But because you are lately come
from above, and 'tis a long time since I've seen any Person here
(for they leave me lonely enough, and I have no Crouds, I'll assure
you, that press for my Conversation) therefore give me leave to ask
you what News? How goes the World? Is it not mightily chang'd?

Montaigne. Extreamly; you wou'd not know it.

Socrates. I'm ravish'd to hear it; I was always of Opinion it must of
necessity grow better and wiser, than 'twas in my Days.

Montaigne. What d'ye mean? Why 'tis ten times more foolish and
corrupt than ever; that's the Change I speak of; and I expected to
hear from you the History of the Times which you have seen, in
which there reign'd so much Honesty and Integrity.

Socrates. On the contrary, I was prepar'd to hear Wonders of the Age,
in which you have just finish'd your Life. What! Have not Men by
this time shaken off the Follies of Antiquity?

Montaigne. You're an Antient your self, and for that Reason, I suppose, make so bold with Antiquity: But be assur'd that Men's Manners are at present a large Subject of Lamentation, and that all
things degenerate daily.

Socrates. Is't possible? I thought in my Time things went as perversly as cou'd be, and was in hopes that at last they wou'd fall into a more reasonable Train—and that Men wou'd have made their Advantage of so many Years Experience.

Montaigne. Alas! What Regard have they to Experience? Like silly Birds, they suffer themselves to be taken in the same Nets that have caught a hundred thousand of their Kind already. There's not one but enters a perfect Novice upon the Stage of Life; the Follies of the Fathers are all lost upon their Children, and do not serve to instruct 'em at all.

Socrates. But what's the Reason of this? I shou'd think that surely the World, in its old Age, ought to become wiser and more regular than 'twas in its Youth.

Montaigne. Mankind has, in all Ages, the same Inclinations, over which Reason has not the least Power. So that to the World's End there will be Follies, and the same Follies too, as long as there are Men.

Socrates. Then why wou'd you put a greater Value upon the Ages of Antiquity, than upon this present Age?

Montaigne. Ah! Socrates! I know you to have a particular Mastery in the Art of Reasoning, and to be able so ingeniously to beset those, with whom you dispute, with Arguments whose Consequences they do not foresee, that you can lead 'em whither you please. This is what may be call'd playing the Midwife to their Thoughts; I'm sure I find my self deliver'd of a Proposition directly opposite to what I had advanc'd, and yet I cannot give up the Controversie neither. 'Tis certain we find not now any of those robust and vigorous Souls of Antiquity: Shew me an Aristides, a Phocion, a Pericles, or to name one for all—a Socrates.

Socrates. Why what hinders? Is it because Nature's exhausted, and has not Spirits left to produce such great Souls—If so, why is she yet exhausted in nothing else, but in reasonable Men? None of her other Works are degenerated, and how comes it then to pass that Mankind is degenerated alone?

Montaigne. That they are degenerated is Matter of Fact: It appears to me as if Nature had sometimes shewn such great Men to the World, as Patterns of what she cou'd produce if she pleas'd, and after that form'd all the rest with Negligence enough.

Socrates. Take care you are not deceiv'd: Antiquity is an Object of a peculiar kind; its Distance magnifies it: Had you but known Aristides, Phocion, Pericles and my self, (since you are pleas'd to place me in the Number) you wou'd certainly have found some to match us in your own Age. That which commonly possesses People so in Favour of Antiquity, is their being out of Humour with their own Times, and Antiquity takes Advantage of their Spleen; they cry up the Antients in Spight to their Cotemporaries. Thus when we liv'd we esteem'd our Ancestors more than they deserv'd; and, in Requital, our Posterity esteem us at present more than we deserve. But yet our Ancestors, and we, and our Posterity, are all upon the Level; and, I believe, the Prospect of the World wou'd be very dull and tiresome to any one that shou'd view it in a true Light, because 'tis always the same.

Montaigne. I shou'd have thought the World was always in Motion, that every thing chang'd, and that Ages, like Men, had their different Characters: And, in Effect, do we not see that some Ages are learned, and others illiterate; some barbarous, others polite; some serious, others whimsical; some ingenious, and others stupid?

Socrates. True.

Montaigne. And consequently are not some more virtuous, and others more wicked?

Socrates. That does not follow. Men change their Habits, but not the Form of their Bodies. Politeness, Barbarism, Learning or Ignorance, more or less Plainness, the grave Genius or the Buffoon; all these are no more than the Dress, the Outside of Mankind; and these indeed are chang'd. But the Heart, which is the Man himself, does not change at all. People are ignorant in one Age, but Learning may come into Fashion in the next. People are interested, but Disinterest will never be the Mode. Among the prodigious Number of Men irrational enough, that are born in a hundred Years, Nature produces it may be thirty or forty rational; and these, like a prudent Administratrix, she's oblig'd to disperse thro' all the Earth; and I leave you to judge, if they are like to be found in any Place in Numbers sufficient to bring Virtue and Integrity into Fashion.

Montaigne. But is this Distribution of rational Men made with Equality? Some Ages, in all Probability, have been better us'd in the Dividend than others.

Socrates. Nature, without question, acts always with exact Regularity, but we have not the Skill to judge as she acts.

Fénelon

The earliest publication of *Dialogues des morts* by Fénelon occurred in 1700. Here the redoubtable Cato, author of a treatise on agriculture, continues to censure the extravagant family of splendid Scipio and its love of Greek arts and letters. The L. Scipio appointed to keep an eye on Cato at the end is the greater Scipio's brother Lucius, mentioned earlier in the dialogue, which is reprinted from James Elphinston's *Dialogues of the Dead; together with Some Fables, Composed for the Education of a Prince. By the Late M. de Fenelon* . . . (Glasgow, 1754), I, 193–204. Elphinston's quasi-classical use of small letters at the beginning of sentences has been regularized, as it was in a superficially reworked version of his translation published in London: *Dialogues of the Dead. By the Late M. de Fenelon. . . . A New Translation* (n.d.), II, 12–25.

Dialogue XXXV. Rhadamanthus, Cato the Censor, and Scipio Africanus

Avarice is a crabbed and censorious passion, which dishonours the greatest virtues.

Rhadamanthus. Who art thou, old Roman? Tell me thy name. Thou hast but an ominous physiognomy, a stern and snappish countenance. Thou lookest like an ugly, red-haired fellow; at least I suppose thou hast been such in thy youth. Thou hast been, if I mistake not, upwards of an hundred when thou diedst.

Cato. No; I was but fourscore and ten, and I thought my life very short: for I liked vastly to live, and enjoyed a course of perfect good health. My name is Cato; hast thou never heard of me, of my wisdom, of my courage against the wicked?

Rhadamanthus. O! I could easily know thee by the picture given me of thee. Ay, 'tis just thyself, the very same person, ever ready to extol himself and to snarl at others. But I have a difference to settle between thee and the great Scipio who vanquished Hannibal. So ho, Scipio, make haste and come hither: here is Cato come at last, I purpose to judge your old quarrel immediately. Stand forth then, and let each plead his own cause.

Scipio. As for me, I have to complain of the malicious jealousy of Cato; it was unworthy of his high reputation: he sided with Fabius Maximus, and was his friend for no other reason but in order to attack me. He wanted to prevent my passing into Afric. They were both timorous in their politics. Besides, Fabius knew only his old method of spinning out the war, of avoiding battles, of encamping in the clouds, of waiting till the enemies should waste themselves away. Cato, who out of pedantry loved old people, adhered to Fabius, and grew jealous of me, because I was young and daring. But the chief cause of his prejudice was his avarice: he would have the war carried on frugally, as he planted his cabbages and onions. I again was for having it waged with vigour, in order to bring it to a speedy and prosperous issue; and was desirous that the Public should consider, not what it would cost, but the actions I would perform. Poor Cato was quite forlorn, for he wanted always to govern the commonwealth as he did his cottage, and to gain victories at a reasonable rate. He did not see that Fabius' design would not succeed; never would he have driven Hannibal out of Italy. Hannibal was dextrous enough to subsist in it at the country's expence, and to preserve allies. He would also have brought over continual supplies of fresh troops from Afric by sea. Had not Nero defeated Asdrubal before he could join his brother, all had been gone. The dallier Fabius had been without resource; and Rome so pressed by such an enemy, must needs have yielded at the long-run. But Cato did not see that necessity of making a powerful diversion, in order to transport to Carthage the war, which Hannibal had found means to carry to Rome. I therefore demand reparation for all the wrongs Cato hath done me, and for the persecutions he hath raised against my family.

Cato. And I demand reward for having maintained justice and the public good against thy brother Lucius, who was a robber. Let us drop the African war, wherein thou wert more happy than wise; and let us come to the point. Was it not a base thing in thee, to extort from the republic the command of an army for thy brother who was incapable of it? Thou didst promise to follow him, and to serve under him. Thou wert his pedagogue in that war against Antiochus. Thy brother committed all manner of injustice and extortion. Thou didst shut thine eyes, that thou mightst not see it. A fraternal fondness had blinded thee.

Scipio. How! did not that war end gloriously? The great Antiochus was defeated, expelled and repulsed from the coasts of Asia. This was the last enemy that could dispute the sovereign power with us.

After him all kingdoms fell one upon another at the Romans feet.

Cato. 'Tis true, Antiochus might have given trouble enough, had he taken Hannibal's advice: but he only trifled his time away, and dishonoured himself by infamous pleasures. He married a young Greek in his old age. Then it was Philopemen said, that had he been protector of the Acheans, he would easily have defeated the whole army of Antiochus by surprizing them in the tippling-houses. Thy brother, and thou, Scipio, had no great difficulty to overcome enemies who had already overcome themselves by their sensuality and softness.

Scipio. The power of Antiochus was however formidable.

Cato. But let us return to our point. Did not Lucius, thy brother, rob, plunder, ravage? Wouldst thou have the face to say that he governed like an honest man?

Scipio. After my death thou hadst the severity to condemn him in a fine, and wouldst have had him seized by lictors.

Cato. He richly deserved it. And thou who hadst—

Scipio. As for me, I plucked up a spirit, when I saw the people turning against me. Instead of answering the accusation, I said: Come, let us go to the Capitol, and thank the gods that on a day like this I conquered Hannibal and the Carthaginians. After which I exposed myself no more to the caprice of fortune. I retired to Linternum, far from an ungrateful country, where I lived in a peaceful solitude, respected by all men of honour, and waited death like a philosopher. This it was that Cato the implacable Censor obliged me to: and this it is for which I demand justice.

Cato. Thou reproachest me with what constitutes my glory. I spared no body in point of justice. I made the most illustrious Romans tremble. I saw how manners were daily growing more corrupt through pride and pleasures. For instance, can I be refused immortal praises for having expelled the senate Lucius Quinctius (who had been Consul, and was brother to T. Q. Flaminius the conqueror of Philip king of Macedon) who had the cruelty to cause a man to be put to death before a young boy whom he loved, in order to gratify the child's curiosity with so horrid a spectacle.

Scipio. I own that action was just, and that thou didst often punish the guilty. But thou wert too violent against every body; and when thou hadst done a good action, thou boasted of it too grossly. Dost thou remember thy having formerly said, that Rome owed more to thee than thou owedst to Rome? Such a speech was ridiculous in the mouth of a man of gravity.

Rhadamanthus. What answerest thou, Cato, to this charge?

Cato. That I actually supported the Roman republic against the softness and pride of the women, who corrupted its manners; that I kept the great in awe of the laws; that I practised myself what I taught others; and that the republic did not in return take my part against those I had made my enemies only for her sake. As my estate lay in the neighborhood of that of Manius Curius, I proposed from my youth to imitate that great man in simplicity of manners, while, on the other hand, I took Demosthenes for my model of eloquence; insomuch that I was even called the Latin Demosthenes. Every day was I seen going naked with my slaves to labour the ground. But think not that this application to agriculture and eloquence diverted me from the military art. At the age of seventeen I shewed myself intrepid in the wars against Hannibal. Very early was my body covered with scars. When I was sent pretor into Sardinia, I abolished the luxury that all other pretors had introduced before me. I meant nothing but to ease the people, and to reject all bribes. Being made consul, I won a battle in Spain, on this side the Betis, over the Barbarians. After this victory, I took more towns in Spain than I was days in it.

Scipio. Another insupportable brag! but it is not new to us, for often hast thou made it, and many that have come hither within these twenty years have made me laugh with it. But, honest Cato, it is not before me thou shouldst talk so. I know Spain, and thy noble conquests.

Cato. It is certain, that four hundred towns surrendered to me almost at one and the same time, and thou never madest so many.

Scipio. Carthage alone is worth more than all thy four hundred villages.

Cato. But what wilt thou say of my conduct under Maximus Acilius, in marching over such precipices, and surprising Antiochus in the mountains between Macedonia and Thessaly?

Scipio. I approve that action, and it were unjust to refuse it commendations: they are all due to thee for having restrained evil manners; but nothing can excuse thy sordid avarice.

Cato. So thou talkest, because it was thou, that didst accustom the soldiers to live delicately. But it must be considered, that I found myself in a republic, which was daily growing more and more corrupted. Expences increased without measure; a fish gave now more money than an ox had done when I entered upon public affairs. 'Tis true, that things at the lowest price, to me appeared still too dear, when they were of no use. I said to the Romans: What avails it you to govern nations, if your vain and corrupted women govern you? Was I in the wrong to speak thus, when they lived in so shameless a manner? Every one ruined himself, and stuck at no baseness or dishonesty, to procure wherewithal to support his extravagant expences. I was censor: I had acquired some authority from my age and virtue; how then could I be silent?

Scipio. But why be still informer-general at fourscore and ten? A fine occupation for that age!

Cato. 'Tis the occupation of a man who hath lost none of his vigour, or of his zeal for the common weal, and who sacrificeth himself for its sake to the odium of the great, who want to lead disorderly lives with impunity.

Scipio. But thou hast been as oft accused as thou hast accused others. Thou hast been so, I think, as good as threescore and ten times, and that at the age of fourscore years.

Cato. 'Tis true; and I glory in it. It was not possible but the wicked should by calumnies wage a continual war against a man, who never passed them any thing.

Scipio. Thou hadst thy own difficulties to defend thyself against the last accusations.

Cato. I own it, and is it any wonder? 'Tis very hard to give account of one's whole life before men of another age. I was a poor old man exposed to the insults of the youth, who thought I doted, and who counted as fables all I had done formerly. When I would at any time be relating it, they did nothing but gape and laugh at me as an eternal Egotist.

Scipio. They were not far in the wrong. But after all, why wert thou so fond of reprehending others? Thou wert like a snarling cur that barks at all who go past.

Cato. I found all my life, that I learned much more by reproving fools, than by conversing with the wise. The wise are such but by halves, and give but faint lessons; but fools are thoroughly fools, and a person has but to see them to know how he should not behave.

Scipio. I allow it. But thou who wert so wise, why wert thou at first such an enemy to the Greeks?

Cato. Because I was afraid the Greeks would communicate to us their art much more than their wisdom, and their dissolute manners than their sciences. I did by no means like all those musicians, poets, painters, sculptors: all that tends only to an idle curiosity, and a voluptuous life. I thought it better to keep our rustic simplicity, our laborious and sober life in agriculture, to be more unpolished, and to live better, to talk less about virtue, and to put it more in practice.

Scipio. Why then didst thou afterwards take so much pains in thy old age to learn the Greek tongue?

Cato. I at last suffered myself to be enchanted by the Syrens, like the rest. I listened to the Grecian muses. But I am much afraid all those little Greek sophisters that come starving to Rome to make their fortune, will complete the corruption of the Roman manners.

Scipio. Thy fears are not without grounds: but thou shouldst also have been afraid of corrupting the Roman manners by thy avarice.

Cato. I avaritious! I was a good husband; I wanted to let nothing be lost, and yet I spent too much.

Rhadamanthus. O! the plain language of avarice, which thinks itself always prodigal.

Scipio. Was it not shameful for thee to forsake agriculture, in order to run into the most infamous usury? Thou thoughtst, towards thy latter days, as I have heard, that thy lands and flocks did not yield thee a sufficient income; and so didst turn usurer. Was that a trade for a Censor, who wanted to reform the city? What hast thou now to answer?

Rhadamanthus. Thou darest not speak, and I see plainly that thou art guilty. This is a cause pretty hard to judge. I must, my friend Cato, at once punish and reward thee. Thou puzzlest me vastly. Be this then my decision. I am touched with thy virtues and great actions in behalf of the commonwealth; but then what likelihood is there of an usurer's getting into the Elysian fields? No: that were too great a scandal. Thou shalt remain therefore, if it please thee, at the gate. But thy consolation shall be to keep others out also. Thou shalt controll all who present themselves. Thou shalt be censor here below as thou wast at Rome. Thou shalt have for smaller gratifications all the virtues of mankind to carp at. I deliver up to thee L. Scipio, L. Quintius, and all the rest, on whom to vent thy choler. Thou mayst also exercise it upon the other defuncts, who shall croud from all quarters of the universe, Roman citizens, great captains, barbarous kings, tyrants of nations: all shall be subject to thy spleen and satyr. But beware of L. Scipio; for I appoint him to censure thee, in his turn, without mercy. Here is money for thee to lend to all the dead, who shall have none in their mouth to pay their passage of Charon's ferry. If thou lend it out to any upon usury, Lucius will not fail to acquaint me of it, nor I to punish thee as the most infamous of thieves.

Sir Fleetwood Sheppard
(1634-1698)

The passage reprinted from this lively, posthumously published dialogue by a Restoration courtier constitutes nearly
half the work, which later becomes mainly an exchange of
broad abuse. Little, at most, is known of the saints in-
volved, aside from familiar George, Christopher, and Ursula. The Thebean Legion was a part of the Roman army,
commanded by Mauritius and said to be Christian to a
man, martyred by the Emperor Maximian in the third century. To escape imperial persecution, the Seven Sleepers
curled themselves up in a cave near Ephesus, in the middle
of the third century, and awoke late in the fourth. Longinus was a centurion who pierced the crucified Christ with
a spear. The Kings of Colen are the three Magi, whose rel-
ics were deposited in Cologne Cathedral. The most obscure
figure, Amphibalus, seems to have received his name when
Geoffrey of Monmouth, taking a Latin word for *cloak* to be
a proper noun, bestowed it on St. Alban's confessor (J. S. P.
Tatlock, "St. Amphibalus," *University of California Publications in English,* IV [1934], 249–57). The text of
the dialogue is from *Miscellaneous Works, Written by His
Grace, George, Late Duke of Buckingham* . . . (London,
1704), sigs. L1–M2, where it was first printed.

from *The Calendar Reform'd: or,*
A pleasant Dialogue between Pluto
and the Saints in the Elysian Fields
after Lucian's manner. Written by
Sir Fl. Sh——d in the Year 1687

Scene the Elysian Fields
Enter a Messenger to Pluto

Messenger. 'Tis well your Majesty's at hand to suppress the Riot newly begun in the Quarter of the Saints yonder: There is such calling of Names and giving the Lye, such Roaring and Screaming, such Swaggering and Bouncing, both among the Men-Saints and the Women Saints, that for my part I expected every minute, when it wou'd come to downright Kicking and Cuffing among 'em. If you don't give immediate Orders to have a stop put to this Hubbub, the Lord knows where it may end.—This is all Sir.

Pluto. Come, Friend, leave that Affair to my management.—But who are the Principal Bell-weathers of the Mutiny?

Messenger. Why first of all, an't please you, there's St. George of Cappadocia, a notable Fellow of his Inches, and Metal to the Back, I warrant him. A World of angry Words have pass'd between him and a huge two-handed Lubber St. Christopher, I think they call him; but unless I am mightily mistaken in my Man, I dare swear the dapper Cappadocian will bang half a dozen such hulky Rogues as t'other, and hardly sweat for't. Then there's a Termagant Fury, St. Ursula by Name, at the Head of eleven Thousand Red-hair'd

Bona Roba's, and every one of them Virgins forsooth, ready to fall
upon the Thebean Legion. The Soldiers call 'em Vagrants, threaten
to pluck up their Petticoats, and send them to the House of Correction. The Women on the other hand, exclaim against Lobsters and
Tatterdemallions, and defie 'em to prove 'twas ever known in any
Age, or Country in the World, that a Red-coat died for his Religion.

Pluto. This is odd enough; but go on.

Messenger. In another Corner of the Room there's nothing, but Fire
and Desolation denounc'd on both sides between the seven Sleepers
and the three Kings of Colen. The latter call the former a pack of
drowsy sleepy Sots, who getting Drunk with Poppy-water and
Brandy, fancied they slept several scores of Years at one go-down,
when 'twas all Whimsey and Imagination. Ay, ay, Gentlemen, cry
the Sleepers, you have great reason indeed to pick holes in your
Neighbours Coats, when if you were stript of your fine Names and
Titles, which never honestly belong'd to you, you'd be found to be
no better, nor no worse than three strowling Fortune-tellers. But
the oddest and most Comical Scene is still behind.

Pluto. Come, out with it then.

Messenger. A venerable old Gentleman, who they say had been high
Pontiff of Rome in the days of yore, pointing to a rusty Spear, and
a Cloak of singular Antiquity and Fashion, *I command you, good
People, says he, to pay your Respect to these two most incompara-
ble Saints and Martyrs, St. Longinus and St. Amphibalus. Upon my
Infallibility they have not their fellows in the Almanack.* Why
surely, reply'd I to him, you have a mind to banter Folks out of
their Senses. What is not this a Spear? *No, Sir, his Name is Longinus, and he was one of the earliest sufferers for the Christian Faith.*
Very well; but won't you own this to be a Cloak? *A Cloak Sir!
Have a care what you say. A Cloak! Why he was the undaunted
Companion of St. Alban, his Name Amphibalus, suffer'd with him
near Verulam, and for this I prefer'd him to the Calendar.*—But
why do I trouble your Majesty with these particulars? If you don't
send a Battalion or two of your Guards to reduce them out of

hand, these Revolters, for all I know, may prove a damn'd Thorn in your Royal Foot: Don't you hear, what a cursed Hurricane they make.

Pluto. Thou art more afraid than hurt. These Saints, thou talkest of, may do a damn'd deal of mischief at the Head of a parcel of Fools, that wou'd be led by the Nose by them; but by themselves they can do no more harm than a Physician without his Powders and Pills, or a Lawyer without his Parchments.—However since, as it happens, I have a spare Afternoon, no Business upon my Hands, and some of my disaffected Subjects may improve this Mole-hill into a Mountain, to the prejudice of my Affairs, I am resolved to try them my self; therefore order them to repair to me immediately: For all their Hectoring and making this boisterous Noise, I know they dare not disobey me. [*Exit.*

Enter St. George and St. Christopher

St. George plucking St. Christopher by the Nose.] Well, Insolence, I shall be even with you before I have done. Dark Nights will come, and then I'll substantially thrash your Jacket for you. What! such a Booby as thou art pretend to dispute the precedence with a person of my quality?

Pluto. Why, how now, Bully Royster! What's the meaning of this Outrage in the Face of Justice?

St. George. This over-grown Beast here, an't please your Highness, has not only reflected upon my Parentage, but calls my Valour in Question. 'Tis known to all the World, that I am the doughty Heroe that deliver'd the King of Ægypt's Daughter, kill'd the Dragon upon the spot, and carried off the Royal Virgin for my Reward. To justifie this Truth, I need urge no other Testimonies than the common Signs in most Towns of Europe, where I am to be seen most magnificently bestriding my Steed with the Dragon under my Feet.

St. Christopher. For all his bouncing and bragging, I believe your Majesty will put him strangely to his Trumps, if you'll but ask him where he was Born, what Profession he was of, and what sort of an Animal it was he Kill'd?

Pluto. Come hither, Friend, and resolve me a Question or two; Where were you Born?

St. George. Some say in Cappadocia, others in Coventry.

Pluto. Why truly Coventry lies very near Cappadocia. But what a plague, can't you tell where you were Born?

St. George. —And others have affirm'd, that Alexandria in Ægypt was the place of my Nativity: For my part I cannot precisely tell where I was Born, but that I was Born somewhere or other, I hope your Majesty has the Charity to believe.

Pluto. Most certainly: But what was thy Profession?

St. George. Some make me a great Officer in the Emperor's Army, and others an Arrian Bishop and a Persecutor.

Pluto. Thou art enough to distract the greatest patience. I'll allow thee indeed not to know the place of thy Birth, because Children don't use to come into the World with their Ink-horns and Pocket-books about them; but the Devil's in thee if thou canst not remember whether thou wer't a Bishop or a Soldier: Those two Professions are not so like one another, that there shou'd be any great danger of mistaking them.

St. George. 'Tis my misfortune, that I can not.—

Pluto. Come then, under what Emperor didst thou live?

St. George. Some say under the Emperor Dioclesian; some—

Pluto. How! At your *Some*'s again. Thou art a true original, I swear. Well, I have but one Question more to ask thee, What sort of an Animal was the Dragon which thou valuest thy self so much for slaying. Had it Wings, as 'tis commonly painted in the Signs, or was it a Reptile?

St. George. Not exactly resembling it in every particular, nor yet altogether different. As for Wings I can say nothing to the matter; for I confess I was under so great an agitation—

Pluto. I understand your meaning, you were so terribly scar'd in the time of Engagement, that you had not leisure to consider the shape of your Monster.—Come, come, honest Friend, these shams are too gross to pass upon the World any longer, your Dragons and flying Monsters won't go down at this time of day, therefore take my word for't I'll take care to see thee turn'd out of the Almanack.

St. George. Well then if it's my fate to be ejected out of my ancient Free-hold, I hope your Majesty will be so just, as to make that huge two-handed Fellow keep me Company. I dare engage, that if you ask him the same Questions you put to me, you'll find him as deficient.

Pluto. Nay, I won't favour one more than another, that I assure you. [*To his Officers.* Bring up that tall well-shaped Gentleman yonder to the Bar—Well, Sir, under whose Reign did you live? What Occupation did you follow? Who was your Father? Come resolve me immediately, for my Time's precious.

St. Christopher. I liv'd near an Arm of the Sea.

Pluto. Very particularly answer'd. And in what part of the World; for I suppose, you know there are more Arms of the Sea than one?

St. Christopher. I can't tell, an't please you.

Pluto. That's honest however. But proceed.

St. Christopher. I was a Ferry-man by my Calling, if I may call that a Calling, which never got me a Farthing; for I was so good Natured a Hackney, that I used to carry the Folks over for nothing.

Pluto. Why, how did you maintain your Boat and Tackle all this while?

St. Christopher. I kept none, but carried the good people upon my Shoulders.

Pluto. A very pretty story, and so you waded through this imaginary Arm of the Sea, and whipt over your Customers dry-shod. Well, I shall ask you no more Questions, for this has given me enough. Turn out both those Fellows there, and Mr. Recorder, pray remember to expunge their Names out of the Calendar.

William King (1663-1712)

These are the second and sixth dialogues of the *Dialogues of the Dead. Relating to the present Controversy Concerning the Epistles of Phalaris* (London, 1699), which King wrote against Richard Bentley, here called "Bentivoglio," and specifically against Bentley's *Dissertation upon the Epistles of Phalaris* (London, 1699) during the battle of the books. The two dialogues depend less than the other eight upon particular references to Bentley's text, though there are some, signified by four clusters of page numbers (omitted here) in King's margins. The passages in italics are imperfect but generally accurate quotations from the *Dissertation,* where Bentley had brought into play traditions—to King, trivia—about the cannibalism of Phalaris and Xerxes, about certain philosophers having boxed and wrestled in their youth, and about the cup associated with Hercules, and had mentioned some ancient foods, doing so primarily to identify and date ancient works, not, of course, to elevate the ancients above the moderns.

Modern Atchievements

Butcher and Hercules

Butcher. Well, for all your blustring, were we in the other World, I would not have turn'd my Back to you, and if I had but a Quarter-staff, I would have ventur'd you with your Club for coming in with me.

Hercules. Did not I cleanse the Augean Stables, and conquer the Bull of Marathon?

Butcher. And I have stav'd [1] and tail'd at the Bank-side when the stoutest He would not venture; Was it not I that when Tom Dove broke loose, and drove the Mob before him, took him by the Ring, and led him back to the Stake, with the universal Shouts of the Company? Besides, I question whether you ever saw a Bull-dog.

Hercules. You talk of mean Performances; But I subdu'd the Læstrigons, who us'd to Banquet upon Man's Flesh, and destroy'd Horses; that after they had eat the Meat from a Humane Body, would crash the Bones as other Palfries do Horse-beans. Perhaps, you never heard of these Stories.

Butcher. Not I.

Hercules. No, not you! Do you know what Authors say? That *Phalaris long'd to eat a Child,* and *at last came to devour sucking Children, taking them from their Mothers Breasts to eat 'em;* and that *his own Son did not escape his Hunger.* Do you know in what *Olympiad the famous Emperor* Xerxes *Butcher'd the Empress* Atossa, *Sister to* Cambyses, *Wife to* Darius, *and his own natural Mother, and then eat her?* No not you! Your Stature and Strength

---

[1] "slav'd" in the 1699 edition, corrected in King's *Miscellanies in Prose and Verse* (London, n.d. [1709?]); a term relating to bull-baiting (*OED*).

of Body makes you Proud, but your Ignorance in History renders you Contemptible. Read the Works of the Great Bentivoglio that are lately come over, and be Wiser.

Butcher. I don't know any thing about your Man-Eaters, but I know when, and where the Fellow run for the great Bag-Pudding, and eat it when he had done; and I am sure, if this Story was well told, it would seem the more probable.

Hercules. You enrage me! Now by the Gods I have taken the Thermodoontiack Belt from the Princess Thalestris.

Butcher. Hold a little, good Sir, I have flung down the Belt in Moorfields when never a Lincolns-Inn-Fields Wrestler durst encounter me.

Hercules. What think you of *Hyllus, Lycon,* and *Plato the Wrestlers, Cleanthes the Cuffer,* and twenty more of 'em. Oh the Glory of the former Ages! what Racing, what Running, what Wrestling, what Boxing at the *Olympiads,* the *Pythick* and *Nemean* Games, when the *Oak,* the *Pine* and *Parsly* Garlands remain'd the Reward of their Victories.

Butcher. In truth, Sir, I believe the Cornish Hug would have puzzl'd the Art of your Philosophers; and that a Prize at Back Sword, with the other Weapons, as Dagger, Faulchion, and the rest, may be as well worth admiration, as your hard nam'd 'Lympiads that you make such a rout with. Hereafter I would have all the Wenches that win the Smock at Astrop, and the Fellows that get the Hat and Feathers throughout England by Boxing and Cudgle-playing to be put in the Chronicle, and take place above the High-Constable.

Hercules. What can you have seen like the Horse-racing in Greece; for after the *Apene,* which *was drawn by Mules, and first was us'd at the Olympicks in the 70th Olympiad, was cried down in the 84th Olympiad;* the Race of Horses was improv'd to admiration.

Butcher. This may be true; but as poor a Fellow as I was, I could have laid my Leg over a good piece of Horse-Flesh, and with a hundred Guineas in my Pocket have rod to New-Market, where Dragon, or Why-not, Honey-cum-punch, or Stiff Dick, should have

run for it against any Grecian Horse that you, or any of your Fore-
fathers could have produc'd.

Hercules. You would still pretend to out-do the Ancients; but let me
tell you one thing, which I did, which I must own my Thanks to
Bentivoglio, is by him Recorded to Posterity. I had a mind to go to
Erythræa, an Island in the Western Ocean, and how do you think I
got thither? In a Ship, you will say; No! in a Brazen Ship? No, In
a Cauldron? No! In a Brazen Cauldron? No! In a Golden Bed?
No! How then, you will say in the Name of Wonder? Why, in
short, *I got the Sun to lend me his Golden Cup to sail in,* and I
scudded away as well as if I had had all the Wind and Sail imaginable.

Butcher. And no such great matter at last! I remember as I was
boasting one day of my Exploits to a good jolly Muscovite at the
Bear-Garden, he told me that St. Nicholas came to their Country
sailing upon a Mill-Stone, which I thought as humoursome a Passage as your Cup. But to be short and plain with you, I have Witnesses both on this side and t'other side of Styx, that saw me Row
my self from the Horse-Ferry to the other side of the Water in my
own Tray, with a couple of Trenchers; and there is a Tray and a
Mill Stone for your Cup and your Cauldron.

Hercules. I find you will have the last word.

Butcher. Well, since he is gone, I think I may say, That the Persons
who have liv'd lately, are only wanting to themselves, and that it is
the Negligence of our Ballad-Singers that makes us be talk'd of less
than others, for who almost, besides St. George, King Arthur,
Bevis, Guy, and Hickathrift, are in the Chronicles? Our great
Scholards are so much taken up with such Fellows as this Hercules,
Hyllus the Wrestler, Cleanthes the Cuffer, Phalaris and Xerxes the
Man-Eaters, that they never mind My Actions, nor several others of
their own Country-Men.

Affectation of the Learned Lady

Bellamira, Calphurnia

Bellamira. You seem, Madam, to have been strangely delighted with the *Belles Lettres* whilst you were in the other World.

Calphurnia. Why truly, Madam, I was thought to have had a Relish for 'em, and not to have been *Sans quelque goût* in the *Belle Maniere.*

Bellamira. Reading may be allowable in our Sex, when we have little else to do, especially if the Subject be diverting, but your *Toilette* us'd always to be heap'd with such Books as frighted me to look into 'em.

Calphurnia. Having an Acquaintance among the Learned, sometimes I had spread before me the Works of Jansenius, and Mr. Arnaud, Stephens's Thesaurus, des Cartes, Casaubon's Athenæus, Kircher, Lipsius, Taubmannus, with such like Authors and Manuscripts innumerable.

Bellamira. Indeed, Madam, you us'd to make such an appearance abroad, as if you bestow'd your time in your Dressing-Room different from other Ladies.

Calphurnia. I was so Visited in a Morning by the Virtuosi, Cricks, Poets, Booksellers, so taken up with my Correspondence with the Learned both at Home and Abroad, that I had little time to talk with my Milliner, Dresser, Mantua-Maker, and such Illiterate People.

Bellamira. Such a Levee for a Lady is not very common, but they who had a Capacity for such Company, must needs have been very well entertain'd.

Calphurnia. Oh infinitely! The Company most charming! I could have wish'd for your sake, Madam, that you had understood Latin and Greek, I could have recommended to your Acquaintance so profound a Scholar.

Bellamira. To what intent, Madam?

Calphurnia. Why you, Madam, were a Person very Nice and Exact in your Dress, your Table and Apartments. I have heard him, Madam, give such a Description of a Commode from a Satyr of Juvenal, that your Ladyship could not have found fault with the Air of it. Then he illustrated the Text with the Comments of Lubin, Holyday, and others, to that degree, Madam, *Compagibus altis ædificare Caput;* [1] Madam! Oh charming! beyond any thing, even of the *French* Madam.

Bellamira. You are obliging to assist me in this matter; for I ignorantly took the Fashion as I found it.

Calphurnia. A Gentleman came one Morning with several various readings upon Vitruvius, and from thence perswaded me that the Frame of my Looking-Glass was the most injudicious Piece of Architecture that could be, that the Bases were Dorick, the Capitals Corinthian, and the Architrave perfectly Barbarous, for which reason I went abroad without Patches, till such Absurdities were entirely Mended and Corrected by his Direction.

Bellamira. I remember in *Don Quixote,* one of my Authors, the Marquiss of Mantua, when he had sworn to revenge the Death of his Nephew Valdovinos, was not to Eat on a Table-cloth till he had perform'd it. But was not yours too severe a Mortification for the Ignorance of your Cabinet-maker? But, Pray, Madam, who was this knowing Person?

Calphurnia. It was the same great Virtuoso Signior Bentivoglio, a Person of the most known Merit then Breathing. I did nothing in my Family without his direction. He has often taken his Bill of Fare out of Athenæus, and cover'd my Table with the most surprizing Dishes imaginable. Ordinary Persons content themselves with modern Soupes, but after my acquaintance with him, nothing but

---

[1] Juvenal *Sat.* 6. 502–3: "Tot adhuc conpagibus altum / aedificat caput": "so numerous are the tiers and storeys [of curls] piled one another on her head!" (Loeb ed.). King's sense is that Bentley displayed the soaring honors of his head.

the Black Lacedæmonian Broth might be set before us. He gave the bravest sounding Greek Names from Simon's Art of Cookery, and the Gastronomia, such *Oulions, Groulions, Floios* and *Toios,* to the end of every thing, that it was most charming. He made the most delicious *Alphiton* of the Ancients, far exceeding our Hasty Pudding. I remember once at the sight of a Piece of Roast-Beef he repeated such a rumbling description out of Homer of the Beef sent up to Agamemnon, that I profess my Lady Cornelia's Children ran away frightened, long before the *Melimela* and *Mala Aurea,* which the Ignorant call the Desert, could possibly be set upon the Table.

Bellamira. I profess, Madam, I had rather have gone without a Desert, nay, a second Course, than have had things with such Hidious Names set before me. But, Madam, do Learned Men trouble themselves about such Affairs as these are?

Calphurnia. Oh! Madam, No Man can be a Scholar without being Expert in the whole method of Athenæus's Cookery. What Quarrels, Madam, do you think there have been between Grave and Learned Men, about spelling a Greek Word, that has been only one single Ingredient of a Patty-pan. Pray read Athenæus, Madam, and you will be convinc'd of it.

Bellamira. Sure, Learned Men won't quarrel about Trifles?

Calphurnia. Oh! Madam, rather than any thing. Why as I have read in several Authors, Timotheus, a Grammarian, upon a Dispute concerning a Greek word, laid his Beard to a Chechine,[2] with the great Scholar Philelphus. The old Gentleman lost, and his Adversary was so unmerciful as to cut it off, and hang it upon his Chair, as a Monument of his Victory.

Bellamira. A Cruelty in my Opinion too insulting.

Calphurnia. Oh! Madam, I had forgot one thing, I most heartily beg your Pardon. Bentivoglio one day show'd me the Name of a Pudding in one of Aristophanes his Plays; which, if it were wrote at its full length, would be as long as your Ladyship's Tippet.

Bellamira. I fancy this Outlandish way of furnishing your Table, was

[2] A chequeen or sequin, gold coin of Turkey and Italy (*OED*).

the reason why Persons of Quality avoided eating with you, especially having Company that discours'd so much above 'em.

Calphurnia. I was so involv'd in the Greek, that I protest, Madam, I had entirely forgot the necessary Ingredients for Lemmon Cream, and Jelly of Harts-horn.

Bellamira. Perhaps, that might be the reason you appear'd so seldom in the Park, and were so very long before you return'd a Visit that had been paid you.

Calphurnia. My Day for the Ladies was but once a Fortnight, but every day for the Virtuosi. But, pray, Madam, how did you spend your time, and fit your self for Conversation?

Bellamira. Why, Madam, my own Affairs took up some part of my time; Musick and Drawing diverted me now and then; I had sometimes a fancy for Work, I now and then went to see a Play, when I lik'd the Company I went with better than those I usually found there; I made my self as easie as I could to my Acquaintance, and I have still the vanity to think I was not disagreeable to them, and I did not find but if one of us make out in Civility what we want in Learning, we might pass our time well enough in the World.

Calphurnia. If you can satisfie your self with such Trifles, I am your Servant, Madam, and Adieu.

Matthew Prior (1664-1721)

The text of this, perhaps the subtlest of Prior's four dialogues of the dead (written *ca.* 1721, published in 1907), is reprinted by permission of The Clarendon Press from *The Literary Works of Matthew Prior,* ed. H. Bunker Wright and Monroe K. Spears, 2d ed. (Oxford, 1971), I, 640–55.

The legend of the vacillating Berkshire vicar had developed by the mid-seventeenth century. Dr. Burnet, mentioned in the vicar's antepenultimate salvo, is Gilbert Burnet, whose *History of the Reformation* disparages More. For further annotation, see Wright and Spears, II, 1017–21.

A Dialogue between the Vicar of Bray, and Sir Thomas More

Vicar. Farewell then to the Dear Vicarage, 'tis gone at last. I held it
bravely out however, Let me see, from the twentieth of Henry the
Eighth, and I Dyed in the twenty-ninth of Elizabeth, just Seven and
Fifty Years; Attacked by Missals and Common Prayer, Acts of Parliament opposed to Decrees of the Church, Mortuair'es in the Leg-
ates Courts, and Præmunire's in Westminster-Hall, Canon Law
and Statutes, Oaths of Obedience to the See of Rome, and of Supremacy to the King of England, Transubstantiation, real Presence,
Bulls and Premunires and that intricate question of Divorces. But is
not that my good Patron, Sir Thomas, who gave me the Living,
and charged the Clerks in his Office to take no Fees for expediting
the Writings, because I was Poor; Indeed I was so then, but God
be thanked, I took care of my Self after, as every prudent Man
should do: Aye, tis he indeed. O Dear Sir Thomas I was very sorry
for your Misfortunes; I was upon Tower-Hill when You sav'd Your
Beard, thô You lost Your head, but by our Lady I did not like such
Jesting. I saw you Executed. Oh that ugly Seam, Sir; that remains
stil about your Neck. O Sir a Head Sewed on again never sits well.
I pittyed You Sir, I prayed for You.

More. My Old Acquaintance, in good Truth, the Vicar of Bray very
well Friend, I am obliged to You for your Pitty and Your Prayers,
but You would have heightned the Obligation had You appeared
with Me upon the Scaffold. Your Spiritual Advice might have been
of Service to Mee.

Vicar. O Lord, Sir, I would have been there with all my heart, but
You remember the Times were so ticklish, and that point of the
Supremacy so Dangerous.

More. More Proper therefore for a Divine to have Assisted a Lay-man in so nice a Conjoncture.

Vicar. O, Lord help You, Sir, I thought You had known better than that, (at least since your Death). No Sir, more proper therefore for a Lay-man to have left the nicety of such a Matter to Divines.

More. Well; And did not some of the Clergy suffer upon the same Account with Me?

Vicar. And were they the Wiser for so doing? the greatest part of us were against your Suffering Doctrines, and, in good faith, We of the low Church thought it very Strange that with all your Law and Learning you should not have had Wit enough to keep your head upon your Shoulders.

More. It was that very Law and Learning that made me lay my head down patiently on the Block. My knowledge in Divine and Human Law gave me to understand I was born a Subject to Both. That I was placed upon a Bench not only to expound those Laws to others, but obliged to Observe them my Self with an Inviolable Sanction. That in some cases the King Himself could not change them. That I was commanded to Render to God the things that were of God, before I gave to Cæsar the things that are Cæsars, And when I was Accused upon a point, which I thought Strictly just, My Philosophy taught me to Dispise my Sufferings, and furnished me upon the Scaffold with the same Serenity of Mind and pleasantness of Speech with which I was used to Decide Causes at Westminster-Hall, or Converse with my Friends in my Gardens at Chelsea.

Vicar. Aye, Sir Thomas but it is a sad thing to Dye.

More. For ought Men know (I speak to Thee in the Language of People yet alive) it was an uneasy thing to be Born, and for ought they may know it will be no great Pain to dye. The Friend that stands by in full health may probably suffer more real Anguish than the Dying Man who raises His Compassion.

Vicar. Ay Sir Thomas but to Answer You in the same Language to Dye as You did to See the Headsman with the Ax after the Law had passed your Sentence and demanded the Execution of it.

More. No more than for the Patient to see the Apothecary bring the Quieting Draught after the Physician has given him over.

Vicar. But that Pomp and Apparatus of Death, the Black cloth and Coffin prepared, Your Relacions and Friends Surrounding You. You cannot but remember, Sir, Your Dear Daughter Roper following that Father, who always—

More. Hold good Vicar, Ay there indeed you did touch me to the Quick that beloved Daughter, Beautiful, Innocent, Learned, Pious, That Pride of my Life, that Idol of my Thought, But yet Reason and Religion soon got the better, and Armed Me as well against the Softness of Human Nature as against the Apprehension of Death. You See neither of these could as much as change or Debase even my good Humor.

Vicar. But yet, Sir.

More. But again, but yet what?

Vicar. Why methinks there is a great deal of difference between Dying and being put to Death. A Man must yeild to the call of Nature.

More. And can he resist the Decrees of Fate. A Man must do his Duty what soever may be the Event of it: in the high Station wherein I was placed I was keeper of the Kings Conscience, how then could I possibly dispence with the Dictates of my own?

Vicar. That was a pleasant employment indeed. Keeper of a Mans Conscience who never knew his own Mind half an Hour. What could the Chancellor think should become of him; if he contradicted his Highness, who Beheaded one of his best Beloved Wives upon meer Suspition of her being false to him, and had like to have played the Same trick upon another only for attempting to Instruct him. You that used to Puzzle Us with your Greek and Latin Should have minded what Your Friend Cicero said *in otio cum dignitate,* but to be sure *in negocio sine periculo.*[1]

More. And yet, Vicar, Cicero himself was beheaded as well as I.

---

[1] Cicero, *De Oratore* 1. i, referring to the varied possibilities of life available to statesmen in the golden days of the Roman republic. Prior's version of the Latin may be translated "in retirement, enjoying honor," "in political activity, safe from danger."

Vicar. Why that is just the thing I have often taken into my consideration, he lost his Life when he forsook his Maxime, to say the Truth on't his Case in some respect was not unlike Yours. He had his Head cutt off because he would be running it too far into Affairs, From which he had better to have Receeded. He Spoke so violently against Anthony that he could never hope in prudence to be forgiven by him, thô Anthony had good Nature enough, and You contradicted Henry who as to his temper was inflexible, and in his Anger never forgave any Man.

More. But did not Anthony deserve that and more from Cicero. And as to my Case if the King—

Vicar. Alas, Sir, let People Deserve or not deserve, that is not Sixpence matter, Have they Power or have they not. There's the Question. If they have, never provoke them. Let me tell You, my late Lord Chancellor, as there are a hundred Old Womens Receipts of more real use than any that the Physicians can prescribe by which the Vulgar live, while the Learned laugh at them, There are as many Common Rules by which We Ordinary People are Directed which You Wise Men (as You think your selves) either do not know, or at least never Practice; if you did it would be better for You.

More. Prethy good Vicar if thou hast any of these Rules to Spare, let us hear 'em.

Vicar. Attend then, never Strive against the Stream, always drive the Nail that will go, eat Your pudding and hold Your Tongue, dont pretend to be Wiser than your Master, or his Eldest Son.

> *Noli contradicere Priori*
> *Fungere officium taliter qualiter*
> *Sine Mundum vadere Sicut vult.*

and the never failing Reason of that most Excellent precept

> *Nam mundus vult vadere Sicut vult.*[2]

---

[2] "Don't argue with your master (or Prior).
Do your work adequately.
Let the world go as it likes.

    . . .

For the world will go as it wants."

You see I have not forgot all my Latin, will You have any more of them?

More. No Vicar if the whole hundred be such as these They will make but One great Tautologie which Signifies no more than take care of your Self, or keep out of harms way. A Maxim which I presume, you did most particularly Observe.

Vicar. You are in the Right on't else I should have made a pritty business of it, I'faith. I might have been Deprived of my Living by Old Harry, and perhaps not restored by his Son Edward for want of a Friend to the Protector. I might again have chanced to be Burned by Queen Mary, and if I had escaped that Storm I had been sure of Starving in the Reign of her Sister Elizabeth.

More. But what did You think was your business in the World, for what Cause did You Live?

Vicar. Why to teach my Parish and Receive my Tythes.

More. Oh, as to receiving Your Tythes I have no Scruple, but what did you teach your Parish?

Vicar. What a Question is that, Why, Religion.

More. What Religion?

Vicar. Again, Sometimes the Ancient Roman Catholic, sometimes that of the Reformed Church of England.

More. How came You to teach them the First?

Vicar. Why my Canonical Obedience, the Order of my Diocessan Bishop, the Missal and Breviary all injoyned it.

More. How happened it then that You taught the t'other?

Vicar. Why New Acts of Parliament were made for the Reformation of Popery. My Bishop was put into the Tower for Disobeying them, and our Missals and Breviarys were Burnt. You are not going to Catachise me, Are You?

More. And You continued Stil in Your Vicarage of Bray.

Vicar. Where would You have had me been? in Foxes Book of Martyrs?

More. Soft and fair, Vicar—Only one word more, did you make all these leaps and Changes without any previous Examination, as to the Essential good or ill of them.

Vicar. Why what Should I have done? the King had a mind to fall out with the Pope, would You have a single Man oppose either of these mighty Potentates? His Highness upon the Quarrel bids me read the Mass in English, and I do so. His Son Edward enjoins the same thing, and I continue my Obedience; Queen Mary is in Communion with the Church of Rome, and She commands me to turn my English Mass again into Latin. Why then things are just as they were when first I took Orders. Elizabeth will have it translated back into English, Why then matters stand as they did when I first reformed. You see, Sir, it was the Opinion of the Church of which I was a Member that changed, but the Vicar of Bray remained always the same Man.

More. What Colors do we put upon our Errors and our Fears? And You discharged your Duty all this while.

Vicar. Exactly: I never mist my Church, was civil to my Parishioners, and gave Something to the poor.

More. And You preached boldly and bravely without respect of Persons. You made Felix tremble.

Vicar. By Felix I suppose You mean Old Hall; No by our Lady He made us all tremble. To tell You the truth on't Sir Thomas, I always Preached in general at the Vices of the times, but took care not to be too particular upon those of any great Men. Sometimes indeed I ventured a little against Pluralities or Non-residence because if any man was touched he durst not openly show his resentment, and neither of these cases affected my Self, but I always took care to find Texts and deduce Doctrines from them a propos enough. When Harry went to the Seige of Bologne It was David that went out against the Jebusites or the Moabites. When he would be Divorced from Old Kate, and had a mind to Nanny Bullen; Why Vasthi was put away, and Esther was taken unto Ahasuerus into his House Royal. Little Edward was Josiah, who Destroyed the High Places. Then Mary again was Deborah or Judith, who Restored the Ancient Laws and Customs of the People of Israel. Elizabeth as She Succeeded to the Crown, had right to the same Texts, only with New Applications and with this difference that to Exalt her Praise I always clapt a little of the Jesabell or Athalia upon her Predecessor.

More. So that all this time You told no Body their Faults; put the Case now that You had been a Surgeon, you would never have applyed Medicaments to the proper wound. If You had been a Mariner you would not have stopped that part of the Ship where the Leake was sprung.

Vicar. But I was neither a Surgeon nor a Mariner, what Signifies putting cases? I was a Parson and Preached—

More. Rather Panegyrics I perceive than Sermons.

Vicar. No not quite So, but they were rather Sermons indeed than Satyrs.

More. How Sedulously do we endeavor to Shun the Exercise of Virtue, and what excuses do We make to cover Vice. You never Preach'd therefore against Ambition or Luxury before Cardinal Woolsey.

Vicar. No more than before You, I would have preached against Levity of Speech and vain Jesting.

More. But You ought to have done So, and we should both have been bound to thank You.

Vicar. Aye Sir Thomas but would either of You have prefered Me?

More. That indeed is the main Question. Alas how we Squander away our Days without doing our Duty. Desirous Stil to lengthen life, while we lose the very Causes for which it was given to Us; and thus You trifled fourscore Years without doing any good or intending it.

Vicar. Indeed, Sir, I thought that it was very well that I did not do much harm. Trifled away fourscore Years said You, Aye that I did indeed, and was very Sorry when they were passed.

More. But while they were Passing were you not under a thousand Apprehensions? did You not Suffer continual uneasiness in the frequent changes that happened as well in the Church as the State?

Vicar. O Sir, You may be sure I did: Every Body in the World we lived in had his troubles, I had one particularly that vext me mightily, the Constant fear of losing my Vicarage.

More. But I presume you Armed Your self against that fear.

Vicar. As well as I could, Sir, when I could not do as well as I would. When ever any new Law was made, or any harsh Injunction laid upon us, away went I to some Clergyman or Casuist who had a good repute for knowing these kind of things, and had himself already conformed as to the point in Question, and then I constantly carryed with me an Inclination to be convinced, which You know goes a great way in matters of this Nature, So admitting some things for truth without too Scrupulously Seeking for Demonstration, and Suppressing some Scruples that might have been troublesome I generally made the best of a Bad Market, and got safe again out of the Briars. If things looked bad one Day, I took a cup of Ale, and hoped they would be better the next. When they were very bad indeed, I concluded they were at the worst, and So I tell You on I Jogged.

More. How Naturally the Shallowness of thought in this Man increases the Severity of it in the mind of a Wiser. When we reflect upon our past Life, we find it charged with Misfortunes and Calamities. Yet we never think of the future but in Expectation of receiving it enlivened with Joy and pleasure. Our whole life all this while runs like the Current of the same River and to Morrow comes on just as Yesterday past, why therefore do we rather hope than Dread what it may bring. Why do we not think that in probability it may rather make us Miserable than happy. How is it that scarse enjoying the present we turn our thought forward into a Futurity, which the Will of Heaven in equal Wisdom and Pitty conceals from Us a futurity which may never be Ours; but suppose it shal be, suppose it coming with all the Delights that the Wildness of our Imagination can Suggest, Is it more durable is it less rapid in its course than the past, than the present? while I am Speaking it approaches and while I say it is arrived, Alas it is gone for ever: the fugitive never Stops, but we insensibly follow it 'till tyred with the pursuit we fall into our Grave.

Vicar. Aye, Sir, that Grave is an ugly hole indeed, when once a Man Slips his foot into it—

More. You have therefore thought of Death, I am glad at least I have brought you to this point.

Vicar. Thought of Death, Sir, aye that I have, and with different Agitations; Sometimes indeed with pleasure enough, for my Parish is of large extent, And when any Body Dyed in it that could pay, I had my Dirge and Funeral Fees, besides my Share of Ale, and the Company of a good many Friends, but then again when any of the poor Dyed whom I was forced to Bury Gratis especially in the Winter time, egad I did not like Death at all.

More. Drole, But did You think of your own Death?

Vicar. Very Seldom, and yet in good troth often enough. You must know I Buryed my Parish twice over, and I strove to forget every One of them as soon as I had laid them under ground. There was one Clergy-man in my Neighborhood who was four Years Older than my Self it was a great Comfort to me to see him in good health. Egad I lived at him. A t'other Side I never was heartily a Friend to my Curate. A lusty Young fellow with large white Teeth and a Vermillion Countenance: I was always apprehensive he'd Outlive me, and put in to be my Successor.

More. Strange Illusion! of which even Death has not cured this Wretch. We join Ideas which in Nature have no Coherence: Our fear of Death gives us not sufficient leizure to consider what Death it self is, we dare hardly think that it makes a total Separation between our Mind and our Body and We provide for our Selves after Death as if that Separation was not to be made. Are we to be alive and Dead at the Same time, Idle and Superstitious way of thinking. What was it to this Vicar who should enjoy that Benefice from which Death has given him an Eternal Quietus. Yet with regret he considers who shall possess the Tythes when he shal neither have Mouth to Receive or Stomach to Digest the produce. Yet with Envy he mentions that Man that shal present the Incense or adorn the Altar when he Shal neither Smel nor See. But why Should I blame him of an Error common to us all. Have not the greatest Men desired Monuments to be raised over them that the Eyes of all the world might gaze on, whilst they have Dreaded the thought that the Dust and Bones hid under the Marble Should be exposed to the Sight of their Surviving Friends.

Vicar. Why really Sir Thomas You preach very well; I begin to think there was some Mistake in Our Affairs while We were in the troublesome World of which you are Talking. We should e'en have changed Stations; if you had been Vicar of Bray the Parish might have had Excellent Sermons, and if I had been Chancellor of England, I'll give You my word for it, I would have kept my Head.

More. 'Tis true Vicar we Seldom are in life what we seem to be, I jested upon the Bench, yet guarded my Actions with the greatest Severity, and You looked gravely and talked Morally in the Pulpit without any Resolution of Living up to that You taught others, But Vicar what You all this while call Living is only Breathing. Did You think Morality was but Discourse, and that Virtue was not to be practised, did not you know that you must never prefer your Safety to Your Honor, or Your life to your Conscience. You said just now You had not forgot all your Latin, does not Horace tell You that neither the Fury of ill Men in Power nor the Frown of a Tyrant can alter the Resolution or bend the Mind of a Man Strictly just and honest; And Juvenal, that thô Phalaris stood by with his Brazen Bull, The Martyr should rather suffer Flames and Racks than Deviate the least Title from Truth.

> On Her own Worth true Virtue rear'd
> Nor Dreads Disgrace nor seeks reward:
> But from her higher Orb looks greatly down,
> On Life or Death, A Scaffold or a Throne.

Vicar. The meer Fancy of Poets, Ah Sir Thomas You are always too much Adicted to that sort of Reading. It is that which spoiled you: Egad those whimsical Fellows have done more Mischief in leading the Minds of Grave People aside by a Contempt of Pain and Death, than in Debauching Youth by too lively Discriptions of Love and Pleasure.

More. Come on then, You shal have some Prose-Men; I'l oblige You if I can: Has not Plato writ a whole Volumn to Explain how reasonable it is that we should rather consent to Die than to do evil? And has not his Imitator Cicero, commenting upon the Text, Instructed Us that we ought to be so far from fearing Death, in this case that we should contemn it. What think You of those Minds who have Practised what these Philosophers taught, of Socrates, Aristides, and Phocion, of Regulus, Cato and Brutus?

Vicar. Heathens, all by the Mass meer Pagan Heathens why I read Plutarch when I was a Young Man at the University, he is full of these People, when ever the Game did not go well they always threw up the Cards, and when they could not rule the World a Whim took Them that They would Stay no longer in it.

More. Now the Doctor is in for it indeed, well I hope Sir since You came from the University You have read of some Christians who were of this Opinion too: What think You of St: Polycarp who asserted what he thought was truth in opposition to the whole Roman Empire, and a growing Heresy in the Church, and that too in the moment he was sure to Dye for it? What of St Cyprian who when an Equivoque or Silence it self might have Saved him, Scorned even Deliberation in asserting his Belief and confirmed it in the Presence of an angry Judge, and in the Sight of that fire that was to consume him to Ashes.

Vicar. Aye, Sir, and St Laurence was broil on a Gridiron, and St. Protatius had his head cut off; and a great many more of them: Lord, there were Females too St: Ursula was Stabbed with a Poynard, and St: Catharine broke upon the Wheel, why do you think I am not acquainted with the Army of Martyrs. Oh Dear Sir, as their Holy days came I constantly did 'em Justice in my Prones, and set out their Relicts to be kist by the People. I had One Sermon You must know that Mutatis Mutandis did the Business for a great many of them. I clapt all the Praise I could upon the Saint of the Day, and e'en let the rest of the Calendar take it as they thought fit.

More. And as You Showed I suppose you respected the Relicks of these Saints.

Vicar. Aye marry did I.

More. Without any Resolution to follow their Example.

Vicar. Lord, Sir, They had their way to Heaven, which in all probability was the nearest; You were pleased to take That; very well, I had mine, it was a little about indeed, why very well again. We were not all Born to be Martyrs any more than Lord Mayors.

More. Strange is it, that after all that the Wisest and best Men of all Ages have said and writ on this subject of Life and Death, the great Majority of Mankind Stil argue and Act like this poor Vicar. Look You, my Old Friend without entering into any particular points of Religion, I repeat to You that we have two Duties One to our Selves, the other to the public. That either as we are private Persons or Members of the Commonweale our life on many occasions is not our Own, and our Conscience only is the guide, and the Disposer of it.

Vicar. Well, I do not flatly deny any thing of all this, Sir Thomas, but methinks we should make those many Occasions as few as we could. There may be certain times for those Tryals, but one must not Practise such Dangerous Experiments every Day. Our Duty may be Divided, and in that Case sure we may take the safer side. You that were a Judge Know very well that we are obliged to Conform to the Law of the Land. S'life it would be a Foolish mistake if a Man should fancy himself a Martyr to Religion, and be trus'd up in Fact as a Traytor to the King. A Man has but one Neck Sir Thomas, and I tell You it is a point that requires very mature Deliberation, good Sir, do but think a little.

More. Vicar, the beginning, Progress, and Ultimate end of Thought can only inform You that Truth is to Direct all your Actions, and that Courage is only a Virtue as Assistant to Truth, else You wander without a guide, and You Sail without a Compass. Your Caution is but Cowardise, and Your Discretion is double dealing: You scarse can pardon Your own fears to your Self, your Conscience therefore must direct Your prudence, and Your Virtue must be entire that your honor may be unspotted. Life and Death all this while are only things Accidental.

Vicar. Why Sir Thomas whilst You talk thus you are laying the

Model of Your own Utopia. Pray, is not self Preservation a Principle of Nature, is it necessary that we run Absolutely into Danger, should not we comparatively weigh Circumstances, and may not some Precepts which You take litterally be understood Figuratively; and consequently, may not Some Points be Essentiall only in relation to some cases, and may not others be indifferent as to other cases.

More. What are you got into the Old Cant, lurking behind Distinctions, and arming your Self with Adverbs. I said I would not enter into any Dispute of Religion with You, But take this at least as an Axiom that Your Scholemen have not only obscured their Texts but perverted them. Essentially, Absolutely, formally, comparatively, and Figuratively well engrafted upon Interest and Knavery, are sufficient to divide Five Nations, and produce as many different Heresies. Once for all Vicar every Man is obliged to suffer for what is right as to oppose what is unjust.

Vicar. Ay, but a Man may be mistaken in what he thinks Right, as I fancy you were in the point of the Popes Supremacy. Od Zooks Sir, to venture ones head in a doubtful cause—

More. Suppose the Cause to be false; when I had done my best to inform my self that what I did was Legal, and could not be convinced to the Contrary, I had nothing more to do but to Submit my Self to the Severity of the New made Law, and leave the Event to the Creator and Disposer of the World, So I tell Thee again that an Upright and unprejudiced Conscience is our Plea before any Human Tribunal, Nay, more that it is at once the Law and Judge that must Convict or Absolve Us in all we do or think thô We stand accused by no Man. The Basis of all Religion and the Bond of all Society is founded upon this Strict adherence to Truth, and constancy of Mind in the Defence of it.

> Conscience, Thou Solemn Bond of mutual Trust,
> Prop, to the Weak, and Anchor of the Just;
> Fructiferous Root whence human Virtues Spring,
> The Subjects Law, and safety of the King:
> Appeas'd by Thee our inward Tumults cease,

Thou guid'st our Feet into the Paths of Peace:
Fair Polar Star, whose influencing Ray
Directs our Toil, and Manifests our way;
Should Cloud or Storm Thy radiant beams obscure
Yet Those who hope They follow Thee are Sure:
Thô tyr'd by Day they pass the Night in rest,
And going wrong, yet seeking Right are Blest.

Vicar. Are those Verses of Your own making Sir Thomas? why really
they are pritty enough but a little hobbling in the Number.
More. They are not so much to be praised as practised, I'll give You
some translated from a Greek Epigram that carry almost the Same
Sense in a Style Something more flowing.

While thrô the Depth of Lifes tempestuous Sea
Our little Vessel cutts its destin'd way,
Now prosp'rous Insolence and wealthy Pride
With rolling Billows swell th'Impetuous Tyde;
Now care and want in hollow Tumult roar,
Threatning to Dash us on the Dangerous Shoar.
Around us and above with various rage
High and low Deaths alternately engage;
Fix'd on a Rock upon the distant Strand
Bright Virtue does our only Pharos Stand,
Contemns the Winds and Waves, and points us safe to Land.

Vicar. Pough, hang it, this is all but the Second part of the same tune.
Come Sir Thomas You used to Love a little Mirth, I'll repeat You
some Verses that a Friend of mine brought down heither with him
t'other Day.

Your Conscience like a Firy Horse
Shou'd never know His native force
Ride him but with a Moderate Rein
And stroke him down with Worldly gain;
Bring him by Management and Art
To every thing that made him Start;
And strive by just degrees to Settle
His native warmth and height of mettle;
And when by use he once has got
An honest canting low Church Trott

He'll carry You thrô thick and thin
Secure thô dirty to your Inn.
But if You give the Beast his head
And prick and Spur him to His Speed,
The Creature Strait begins his tricks,
He Foams and Neighs Curvets and Kicks,
He gets the Bitt between his Teeth
And runs His Rider out of Breath:
Better You ne'r had rid abroad,
For down You come as sure as LAUD.

We may be allowed to know who Laud was thô he lived since our time, for sure it is as reasonable for Us here to mention a Man that was born Since we Dyed as it is for those in the t'other World to quote an Author that Dyed before They were born.

More. I like your thought well enough, but the Verses You repeat were meant as a Satyr upon that very sort of Conduct, which You seem to Commend. You put me in mind of some German Doctors that reading the little Book of my Friend Erasmus fancyed he wrote a real Panegyrick upon the Folly he was laughing at.

Vicar. Be it as it will with the Verses; In honest Prose I must tell You, Sir Thomas, that in difficult cases there must be some Allowances made; if we cannot bring the thing to our Conscience, we must e'en Strive as much as we can to bring our Conscience to the thing. Mahomet and the Mountain seems to me not so unreasonable as some Strait laced Christians think it.

More. Go to, I contemn You now. If I were to be Chancellor again, and had all the Livings in the Land to dispose I would not give You one of them.

Vicar. If all Succeeding Chancellors were of Your Opinion your Livings would want Incumbents, and the Civil Power might send out Press Gangs for Priests to supply the Parishes.

More. How few are there that dare Exercise a true and Active Virtue, too many indeed there are that live in the open Practice of impudent and Successful Vice but the Mass of Mankind is a Multitude of Such Animals as this Vicar, the Burden of the Earth, who only feed upon it without endeavoring to deserve the Bread it affords them, Wretches, who in having done nothing have done ill. Negative Ideots who Sink into Folly for want of Courage to aspire to Wisdom, and think nothing bad or hurtfull except they may be Indicted for it at the next Quarter Sessions. This Man now would not commit any famous Wickedness, yet how far is he from being honest; Well; as bad as they say the World is, there are fifty Idle Knaves in it for one determined Villain.

Vicar. Twenty for One is as much as I can grant You; Ah Sir Thomas, tis very true what Dr: Burnet says of You, that you mix't too much Gall with your Ink. Egad with these Maximes of Your's you would raise both Court and Country against You, and if You had as many heads as there are Loops upon Your Gown You might run a fair risk to have 'em all cut off.

More. What then! many better heads would have been Confirmed by my Example, and I should have Answered the end for which life was given me.

Vicar. Admirable Philosophy indeed, in the Practice of which you were Beheaded on Tower Hill at fifty-three, whereas without it I Dyed quietly in my bed at eighty. Since I am afraid your Lordship may grow Angry, which would be a little against Your Stoicism, and since You may be assured that if we were to live again I should never be a Convert to your Doctrine, it is time we should part.

More. Withal my heart, Adieu, thou poor Spirited Parson with thy Vicarage of Bray.

Vicar. Thou Great Chancellor of England, without a head, Adieu.

George, Lord Lyttelton
(*1709-1773*)

Of these dialogues first published in 1760, the latter two
recall Lucian's confrontation of Alexander and Hannibal;
in fact, Charles XII here uses some of Hannibal's arguments, and Alexander's introducing the example of Peter
the Great at the end may remind readers of Scipio's belated entry into the Greek dialogue. "Arthur's," mentioned by the duelist in Dialogue VI, was a gaming club
in London. Arria's husband (Dial. XV), Caecina Paetus,
was condemned to death after being implicated in a plot
against the Emperor Claudius (A.D. 42); she stabbed herself and then handed Paetus the dagger. Dialogues XV and
XX bear twelve marginal notes, omitted here, which include six references to various works of Plutarch; one
reference to Pope's *Essay on Man,* IV, 219–20, where
Charles and Alexander are called madmen; and three references to Voltaire's *Charles XII,* the source of that
king's popularity as a cautionary example in the eighteenth
century. For my text I have used the last edition published
in Lyttelton's lifetime: *Dialogues of the Dead. The Fifth
Eition, Corrected* (London, 1768).

Dialogue VI. Mercury—An English Duellist—A North-American Savage

The Duellist. Mercury, Charon's Boat is on the other side of the Water. Allow me, before it returns, to have some conversation with the North-American Savage, whom you brought hither with me. I never before saw one of that Species. He looks very grim.—Pray, Sir, what is your Name? I understand you speak English.

Savage. Yes, I learnt it in my Childhood, having been bred for some years among the English of New York. But, before I was a Man, I returned to my valiant Countrymen, the Mohawks; and having been villainously cheated by one of yours in the sale of some Rum, I never cared to have any thing to do with them afterwards. Yet I took up the Hatchet for them with the rest of my Tribe in the late War against France, and was killed while I was out upon a Scalping Party. But I died very well satisfied: for my Brethren were victorious; and, before I was shot, I had gloriously scalped seven Men, and five Women and Children. In a former War I had performed still greater Exploits. My Name is *the bloody Bear:* it was given me to express my Fierceness and Valour.

Duellist. Bloody Bear, I respect you, and am much your humble Servant. My Name is Tom Pushwell, very well known at Arthur's. I am a Gentleman by my Birth, and by Profession a Gamester and Man of Honour. I have killed Men in fair Fighting, in honourable single combat, but don't understand cutting the Throats of Women and Children.

Savage. Sir, that is our way of making War. Every Nation has its Customs. But by the Grimness of your Countenance, and that Hole in your Breast, I presume you were killed, as I was, in some scalping

Party. How happened it that your Enemy did not take off your Scalp?

Duellist. Sir, I was killed in a Duel. A friend of mine had lent me a sum of Money. After two or three years, being in great Want himself, he asked me to pay him. I thought his Demand, which was somewhat peremptory, an Affront to my Honour, and sent him a Challenge. We met in Hide-Park. The Fellow could not fence: I was absolutely the adroitest Swordsman in England. So I gave him three or four Wounds; but at last he run upon me with such Impetuosity, that he put me out of my Play, and I could not prevent him from whipping me through the Lungs. I died the next day, as a Man of Honour should, without any sniveling Signs of Contrition or Repentance: and he will follow me soon; for his Surgeon has declared his Wounds to be mortal. It is said that his Wife is dead of Grief, and that his Family of seven Children will be undone by his Death. So I am well revenged, and that is a Comfort. For my Part, I had no Wife.—I always hated Marriage: my Whore will take good care of herself, and my Children are provided for at the Foundling-Hospital.

Savage. Mercury, I won't go in a Boat with that Fellow. He has murdered his Countryman: he has murdered his Friend: I say positively, I won't go in a Boat with that Fellow. I will swim over the River: I can swim like a Duck.

Mercury. Swim over the Styx! it must not be done; it is against the Laws of Pluto's Empire. You must go in the Boat, and be quiet.

Savage. Don't tell me of Laws: I am a Savage: I value no Laws. Talk of Laws to the Englishman: there are Laws in his Country, and yet you see he did not regard them. For they could never allow him to kill his Fellow-subject, in time of Peace, because he asked him to pay a Debt. I know indeed, that the English are a barbarous Nation; but they can't possibly be so brutal as to make such things lawful.

Mercury. You reason well against Him. But how comes it that you are so offended with Murder; you, who have frequently massacred Women in their Sleep, and Children in the Cradle?

Savage. I killed none but my Enemies: I never killed my own Countrymen: I never killed my Friend:—Here, take my Blanket, and
let it come over in the Boat; but see that the Murderer does not sit
upon it, or touch it. If he does, I will burn it instantly in the Fire I
see yonder. Farewell.—I am determined to swim over the
Water.

Mercury. By this touch of my Wand I deprive thee of all thy
Strength.—Swim now if thou canst.

Savage. This is a potent Enchanter.—Restore me my Strength, and
I promise to obey thee.

Mercury. I restore it; but be orderly, and do as I bid you: Otherwise
worse will befal you.

Duellist. Mercury, leave him to me. I'll tutor him for you. Sirrah Savage, dost thou pretend to be ashamed of my company? Dost thou
know that I have kept the best company in England?

Savage. I know thou art a Scoundrel.—Not pay thy debts! kill thy
Friend who lent thee Money for asking thee for it! Get out of my
sight. I will drive thee into Styx.

Mercury. Stop.—I command thee. No Violence.—Talk to him
calmly.

Savage. I must obey thee.—Well, Sir, let me know what Merit you
had to introduce you into good company? What could you do?

Duellist. Sir, I gamed, as I told you.—Besides, I kept a good table.
—I eat as well as any Man either in England or France.

Savage. Eat! did you ever eat the Liver of a Frenchman, or his Leg, or
his Shoulder! There is fine Eating! I have eat twenty.—My table
was always well served. My Wife was esteemed the best Cook for
the dressing of Man's Flesh in all North-America. You will not
pretend to compare your Eating with mine?

Duellist. I danced very finely.

Savage. I'll dance with thee for thy Ears.—I can dance all day
long. I can dance the War-Dance with more spirit than any Man
of my Nation. Let us see thee begin it. How thou standest like a
Post! Has Mercury struck thee with his enfeebling Rod? Or art
thou ashamed to let us see how aukward thou art? If he would per-

mit me, I would teach thee to dance in a way that thou hast never yet learnt. But what else canst thou do, thou bragging Rascal?

Duellist. O Heavens! must I bear this! What can I do with this Fellow? I have neither Sword nor Pistol. And his shade seems to be twice as strong as mine.

Mercury. You must answer his Questions. It was your own Desire to have a conversation with him. He is not well bred; but he will tell you some truths which you must necessarily hear, when you come before Rhadamanthus. He asked you what you could do besides Eating and Dancing.

Duellist. I sung very agreeably.

Savage. Let me hear you sing your Death Song or the War Whoop. I challenge you to sing.—Come, begin.—The Fellow is mute. —Mercury, this is a Liar.—He has told us nothing but Lies. Let me pull out his tongue.

Duellist. The Lie given me!—and alas! I dare not resent it. What an indelible Disgrace to the family of the Pushwells! This indeed is *Damnation*.

Mercury. Here, Charon, take these two Savages to your Care. How far the Barbarism of the Mohawk will excuse his horrid Acts I leave Minos to judge. But what can be said for the other, for the Englishman? The Custom of Duelling! A bad Excuse at the best! but here it cannot avail. The spirit that urged him to draw his Sword against his Friend is not that of Honour; it is the Spirit of the Furies, and to them he must go.

Savage. If he is to be punished for his wickedness turn him over to me. I perfectly understand the Art of tormenting. Sirrah, I begin my Work with this *kick on your Breech*.

Duellist. Oh my Honour, my Honour, to what Infamy art thou fallen!

Dialogue XV. *Octavia—Portia—Arria*

Portia. How has it happened, Octavia, that Arria and I, who have a higher Rank than you in the Temple of Fame, should have a lower here in Elysium? We are told, that the Virtues, you exerted, as a Wife, were greater than our's. Be so good as to explain to us what were those Virtues. It is the Privilege of this Place, that one can bear Superiority without Mortification. The Jealousy of Precedence died with the rest of our Mortal Frailties. Tell us then your own Story. We will sit down under the shade of this Myrtle Grove, and listen to it with Pleasure.

Octavia. Noble Ladies, the Glory of our Sex and of Rome, I will not refuse to comply with your desire, though it recalls to my Mind some Scenes, my Heart would wish to forget. There can be only one reason why Minos should have given to my conjugal Virtues a Preference above your's; which is, that the Trial assigned to them was harder.

Arria. How! Madam; harder than *to die* for your Husband! We *died* for ours.

Octavia. You did, for Husbands who loved you, and were the most virtuous Men of the Ages they lived in; who trusted you with their Lives, their Fame, their Honour. To *outlive* such Husbands is, in my judgment, a harder effort of Virtue, than to die for them or with them. But Mark Antony, to whom my Brother Octavius, for reasons of State, gave my Hand, was indifferent to me, and loved another. Yet he has told me himself, I was handsomer than his Mistress Cleopatra. Younger I certainly was; and to Men that is generally a charm sufficient to turn the Scale in one's favour. I had been loved by Marcellus. Antony said he loved me, when he pledged to me his Faith. Perhaps he did for a time: a new hand-some Woman might, from his natural Inconstancy, make him forget an old Attachment. He was but too amiable.—His very Vices had charms beyond other Mens Virtues. Such Vivacity! such Fire! such a towering Pride! He seemed made by Nature to command; to govern the World; to govern it with such Ease, that the Business of it did not rob him of an hour of Pleasure! Nevertheless, while his Inclination for me continued, this haughty Lord of Mankind, who could hardly bring his high Spirit to treat my Brother, his Partner in Empire, with the necessary Respect, was to me as submissive, as obedient to every Wish of my Heart, as the humblest Lover that ever sighed in the Vales of Arcadia. Thus he seduced my Affection from the Manes of Marcellus, and fixed it on himself. He fixed it, Ladies, (I own it with some Confusion) more fondly than it had ever been fixed on Marcellus. And when he had done so, he scorned me, he forsook me, he returned to Cleopatra. Think who I was:—the sister of Cæsar, sacrificed to a vile Egyptian Queen, the Harlot of Julius, the Disgrace of her Sex! Every Outrage was added that could incense me still more. He gave her, at sundry times, as public Marks of his Love, many provinces of the empire of Rome in the East. He read her Love-letters openly, in his Tribunal itself; even while he was hearing and judging the Causes of Kings. Nay he left his Tribunal, and one of the best Roman Orators pleading before him, to follow her Litter, in which she happened to be passing by, at that time. But, what was more grievous to me than all these demonstrations of his extravagant Passion for that infamous Woman, he had the Assurance, in a letter to my Brother, to call her his Wife. Which of you, Ladies, could have patiently borne this treatment?

Arria. Not I, Madam, in truth. Had I been in your Place, the Dagger with which I pierced my own bosom, to shew my dear Pætus how easy it was to die, that Dagger should I have plunged into Antony's Heart, if Piety to the Gods, and a due Respect to the Purity of my own Soul, had not stopped my Hand. But, I verily believe, I should have killed myself; not, as I did, out of Affection to my Husband, but out of Shame and Indignation at the Wrongs I endured.

Portia. I must own, Octavia, that to bear such Usage was harder to a Woman than to swallow Fire.

Octavia. Yet I did bear it, Madam, without even a Complaint, which could hurt or offend my Husband. Nay, more; at his return from his Parthian Expedition, which his Impatience to bear a long Absence from Cleopatra had made unfortunate and inglorious, I went to meet him in Syria, and carried with me rich Presents of clothes and money for his Troops, a great Number of Horses, and two thousand chosen Soldiers, equipped and armed like my Brother's Prætorian Bands. He sent to stop me at Athens, because his Mistress was then with him. I obeyed his orders: but I wrote to him, by one of his most faithful Friends, a Letter full of Resignation, and such a Tenderness for him as I imagined might have power to touch his Heart. My Envoy served me so well, he set my Fidelity in so fair a light, and gave such reasons to Antony, why he ought to see and receive me with Kindness, that Cleopatra was alarmed. All her Arts were employed to prevent him from seeing me, and to draw him again into Egypt.—Those Arts prevailed. He sent me back into Italy, and gave himself up more absolutely than ever to the Witchcraft of that Circé. He added Africa to the States he had bestowed on her before, and declared Cæsario, her spurious Son by Julius Cæsar, Heir to all her Dominions, except Phœnicia, and Cilicia, which, with the Upper Syria, he gave to Ptolemy, his second Son by her; and at the same time declared his eldest Son by her, whom he had espoused to the Princess of Media, Heir to that Kingdom, and King of Armenia, nay, and of the whole Parthian Empire, which he meaned to conquer for him. The Children I had brought him he entirely neglected; as if they had been Bastards. —I wept. I lamented the wretched Captivity he was in;—but I never reproached him. My Brother, exasperated at so many Indignities, commanded me to quit the House of my Husband at Rome, and come into his.—I refused to obey him.—I remained in Antony's House, I persisted to take care of his Children by Fulvia, the same tender care, as of my own. I gave my Protection to all his Friends at Rome. I implored my Brother not to make my Jealousy

or my Wrongs the cause of a Civil War. But the Injuries done to
Rome by Antony's conduct could not possibly be forgiven. When
he found he should draw the Roman Arms on himself, he sent Orders to me to leave his House. I did so, but carried with me all his
Children by Fulvia, except Antyllus, the eldest, who was then with
him in Egypt. After his Death and Cleopatra's, I took her Children
by him, and bred them up with my own.

Arria. Is it possible, Madam? the Children of Cleopatra?

Octavia. Yes, the Children of my Rival. I married her Daughter to
Juba, King of Mauritania, the most accomplished, and the hand-
somest Prince in the World.

Arria. Tell me, Octavia, did not your Pride and Resentment entirely
cure you of your Passion for Antony, as soon as you saw him go
back to Cleopatra? And was not your whole conduct afterwards
the effect of cool Reason, undisturbed by the Agitations of jealous
and tortured Love?

Octavia. You probe my Heart very deeply. That I had some help
from Resentment and the natural Pride of my Sex, I will not deny.
But I was not become indifferent to my Husband. I loved the Antony who had been my Lover, more than I was angry with the Antony who forsook me, and loved another Woman. Had he left
Cleopatra and returned to me again with all his former Affection, I
really believe I should have loved him as well as before.

Arria. If the Merit of a Wife is to be measured by her Sufferings, your
Heart was unquestionably the most perfect model of conjugal Virtue. The Wound I gave mine was but a scratch in comparison to
many you felt. Yet I don't know, whether it would be any benefit
to the World, that there should be in it many Octavias. *Too good
Subjects are apt to make bad Kings.*

Portia. True, Arria; the Wives of Brutus and Cecinna Pætus may be
allowed to have Spirits a little rebellious. Octavia was educated in
the Court of her Brother. Subjection and Patience were much better taught there than in our Houses, where the Roman Liberty
made it's last abode. And though I will not dispute the judgment
of Minos, I can't help thinking that the Affection of a Wife to her

Husband is more or less respectable in proportion to the Character of that Husband. If I could have had for Antony the same friendship as I had for Brutus, I should have despised myself.

Octavia. My Fondness for Antony was ill placed; but my Perseverance in the performance of all the Duties of a Wife, notwithstanding his ill Usage, a Perseverance made more difficult by the very excess of my Love, appeared to Minos the highest and most meritorious effort of female Resolution against the Seductions of the most dangerous Enemy to our Virtue, offended Pride.

Dialogue XX. Alexander the Great — Charles the Twelfth, King of Sweden

Alexander. Your Majesty seems in great Wrath! Who has offended you?

Charles. The Offence is to you as much as me. Here is a Fellow admitted into Elysium, who has affronted us both: an English Poet, one Pope. He has called us *two Madmen!*

Alexander. I have been unlucky in Poets. No Prince ever was fonder of the Muses than I, or has received from them a more ungrateful Return! When I was alive, I declared that I envied Achilles, because he had a Homer to celebrate his Exploits; and I most bountifully rewarded Chœrilus, a Pretender to Poetry, for writing Verses on mine: but my Liberality, instead of doing me Honour, has since drawn upon me the Ridicule of Horace, a witty Roman Poet, and Lucan, another Versifier of the same nation, has loaded my Memory with the harshest Invectives.

Charles. I know nothing of these; but I know that in my time, a pert French Satirist, one Boileau, made so free with your character, that I tore his book for having abused my favourite Hero. And now this saucy Englishman has libelled us both.—But I have a Proposal to make to you for the Reparation of our Honour. If you will join with me, we will turn all these insolent Scriblers out of Elysium, and throw them down headlong to the bottom of Tartarus, in spite of Pluto and all his Guards.

Alexander. This is just such a Scheme as that you formed at Bender, to maintain yourself there, with the aid of three hundred Swedes, against the whole Force of the Ottoman Empire. And I must say, that such Follies gave the English Poet too much cause to call you a Madman.

Charles. If my Heroism was Madness, your's, I presume, was not Wisdom.

Alexander. There was a vast difference between your Conduct and mine. Let Poets or Declaimers say what they will, History shews, that I was not only the bravest Soldier, but one of the ablest Commanders the World has ever seen. Whereas you, by imprudently leading your Army into vast and barren Deserts, at the approach of the Winter, exposed it to perish in it's march for want of Subsistence, lost your Artillery, lost a great number of your Soldiers, and were forced to fight with the Muscovites under such disadvantages, as made it almost impossible for you to conquer.

Charles. I will not dispute your Superiority as a General. It is not for me, a mere Mortal, to contend with the Son of Jupiter Ammon.

Alexander. I suppose you think my pretending that Jupiter was my Father as much intitles me to the name of a Madman, as your extravagant behavior at Bender does you. But you are greatly mistaken. It was not my Vanity, but my Policy, which set up that Pretension. When I proposed to undertake the conquest of Asia, it was necessary for me to appear to the People something more than a Man. They had been used to the Idea of Demigod Heroes. I therefore claimed an equal Descent with Osiris and Sesostris, with Bacchus and Hercules, the former Conquerors of the East. The Opinion of my Divinity assisted my Arms, and subdued all Nations before me, from the Granicus to the Ganges. But, though I called myself the Son of Jupiter, and kept up the Veneration that name inspired, by a Courage which seemed more than human, and by the sublime Magnanimity of all my Behaviour, I did not forget that I was the Son of Philip. I used the Policy of my Father, and the wise Lessons of Aristotle, whom he had made my Preceptor, in the conduct of all my great Designs. It was the Son of Philip who planted Greek Colonies in Asia, as far as the Indies; who formed Projects of Trade more extensive than his Empire itself; who laid the foundations of them in the midst of his Wars; who built Alexandria, to be the Centre and Staple of Commerce between Europe, Asia, and Africk; who sent Nearchus to navigate the unknown Indian Seas, and intended to have gone himself from those Seas to the Pillars of Hercules, that is, to have explored the Passage round Africk, the Discovery of which has since been so glorious to Vasco de Gama. It was the Son of Philip, who, after subduing the Persians, governed them with such Lenity, such Justice, and such Wisdom, that they loved him even more than ever they had loved their natural Kings; and who, by Intermarriages, and all Methods that could best establish a Coalition between the Conquerors and the Conquered, united them into one People. But what, Sir, did you do, to advance the Trade of your Subjects, to procure any Benefit to those you had vanquished, or to convert any Enemy into a Friend?

Charles. When I might easily have made myself King of Poland, and was advised to do so, by Count Piper, my favourite Minister, I generously gave that Kingdom to Stanislaus, as you had given a great part of your Conquest in India to Porus, besides his own Dominions, which you had restored to him entire, after you had beaten his Army and taken him Captive.

Alexander. I gave him the Government of those Countries under me, and as my Lieutenant; which was the best method of preserving my Power in Conquests, where I could not leave Garrisons sufficient to maintain them. The same Policy was afterwards practised by the Romans, who of all Conquerors, except me, were the greatest Politicians. But neither was I, nor were they so extravagant, as to conquer only for Others, or dethrone Kings with no view, but merely to have the pleasure of bestowing their Crowns on some of their subjects, without any advantage to Ourselves. Nevertheless, I will own, that my Expedition to India was an Exploit of the Son of Jupiter, not of the Son of Philip. I had done better if I had staid to give more Consistency to my Persian and Græcian Empires, instead of attempting new Conquests, and at such a distance, so soon. Yet even this War was of Use to hinder my Troops from being corrupted by the Effeminacy of Asia, and to keep up that universal Awe of my Name, which in those Countries was the great Support of my Power.

Charles. In the unwearied Activity with which I proceeded from one

Enterprize to another, I dare to call myself your equal. Nay, I may pretend to a higher Glory than you, because you only went on from Victory to Victory; but the greatest Losses were not able to diminish my Ardour, or stop the Efforts of my daring and invincible Spirit.

Alexander. You shewed in Adversity much more Magnanimity than you did in Prosperity. How unworthy of a Prince who imitated me was your behaviour to the King your Arms had vanquished! The compelling Augustus to write himself a Letter of Congratulation to one of his Vassals, whom you had placed in his Throne, was the very reverse of my treatment of Porus and Darius. It was an ungenerous insult upon his ill fortune! It was the Triumph of a little and a low Mind! The Visit you made him immediately after that Insult was a farther contempt, offensive to him, and both useless and dangerous to yourself.

Charles. I feared no Danger from it.—I knew he durst not use the Power I gave him to hurt me.

Alexander. If his Resentment, in that instant, had prevailed over his Fear, as it was likely to do, you would have perished deservedly by your Insolence and Presumption. For my part, intrepid as I was in all Dangers, which I thought it was necessary or proper for me to meet, I never put myself one moment in the Power of an Enemy whom I had offended. But you had the Rashness of Folly as well as of Heroism. A false Opinion conceived of your Enemy's Weakness proved at last your Undoing. When, in answer to some reasonable Propositions of Peace, sent to you by the Czar, you said, You would "come and treat him with at Moscow;" he replied very justly, "That you affected to act like Alexander, but should not find in him a Darius." And, doubtless, you ought to have been better acquainted with the Character of that Prince. Had Persia been governed by a Peter Alexowitz when I made war against it, I should have acted more cautiously, and not have counted so much on the Superiority of my Troops, in Valour and Discipline, over an Army commanded by a King, who was so capable of instructing them in all they wanted.

Charles. The Battle of Narva, won by eight thousand Swedes against fourscore thousand Muscovites, seemed to authorize my Contempt of the Nation and their Prince.

Alexander. It happened that their Prince was not present in that Battle. But he had not as yet had the time, which was necessary to instruct his barbarous Soldiers. You gave him that time, and he made so good a use of it, that you found at Pultowa the Muscovites become a different Nation. If you had followed the Blow you gave them at Narva, and marched directly to Moscow, you might have destroyed their Hercules in his Cradle. But you suffered him to grow, till his strength was mature, and then acted as if he had been still in his Childhood.

Charles. I must confess you excelled me in Conduct, in Policy, and in true Magnanimity. But my Liberality was not inferior to your's; and neither you nor any Mortal ever surpassed me in the Enthusiasm of Courage. I was also free from those Vices which sullied your Character. I never was drunk; I killed no Friend in the Riot of a Feast; I fired no Palace at the Instigation of a Harlot.

Alexander. It may perhaps be admitted as some Excuse for my Drunkenness, that the Persians esteemed it an Excellence in their Kings to be able to drink a great quantity of Wine, and the Macedonians were far from thinking it a Dishonour. But you were as frantic, and as cruel, when sober, as I was, when drunk. You were sober when you resolved to continue in Turkey against the Will of your Host, the Grand Signior. You were sober when you commanded the unfortunate Patkull, whose only crime was his having maintained the Liberties of his Country, and who bore the sacred Character of an Embassador, to be broken alive on the Wheel, against the Laws of Nations, and those of Humanity, more inviolable still to a generous Mind. You were likewise sober when you wrote to the Senate of Sweden, who, upon a Report of your Death, endeavoured to take some care of your Kingdom, *That, you would send them one of your Boots, and from That they should receive their Orders, if they pretended to meddle in Government:* An Insult much worse than any the Macedonians complained of from me, when I was most heated with Wine and with Adulation! As for my Chastity, it was not so perfect as your's, though on some Occasions I obtained great Praise for my Continence: but, perhaps, if you had been not quite so insensible to the Charms of the fair Sex, it would have mitigated and softened the Fierceness, the Pride, and the Obstinacy of your Nature.

Charles. It would have softened me into a Woman, or, what I think still more contemptible, the Slave of a Woman. But you seem to insinuate that you never were cruel or frantic unless when you were drunk. This I absolutely deny.—You were not drunk, when you crucified Hephæstion's Physician, for not curing a Man who killed himself by his Intemperance in his Sickness; nor when you sacrificed to the Manes of that favourite Officer the whole Nation of the Cusseans, Men, Women, and Children, who were entirely innocent of his Death; because you had read in Homer, that Achilles had immolated some Trojan Captives on the Tomb of Patroclus. I could mention other Proofs that your Passions inflamed you as much as Wine: but these are sufficient.

Alexander. I can't deny that my Passions were sometimes so violent as to deprive me for a while of the Use of my Reason; especially when the Pride of such amazing Successes, the Servitude of the Persians, and Barbarian Flattery, had intoxicated my Mind. To bear, at my Age, with continual Moderation, such Fortune as mine, was hardly in human Nature. As for you, there was an Excess and Intemperance in your Virtues, which turned them all into Vices. And one Virtue you wanted, which in a Prince is very commendable, and beneficial to the Public, I mean the Love of Science and of the elegant Arts. Under my Care and Patronage they were carried in Greece to their utmost Perfection. Aristotle, Apelles, and Lysippus were among the Glories of my Reign: Your's was illustrated only by Battles.—Upon the whole, though, from some Resemblance between us, I should naturally be inclined to decide in your favour, yet I must give the Priority in Renown to your Enemy, Peter Alexowitz. That great Monarch *raised* his Country; You *ruined* your's. He was a *Legislator;* you were a *Tyrant.*

Elizabeth Montagu (1720-1800)

The first dialogue by Mrs. Montagu reprinted here is one of the three she contributed to Lyttelton's *Dialogues of the Dead* (1760) and reflects his admiration for Plutarch. The text is from the fifth edition (1768). *Artamiène; ou Le Grand Cyrus,* the romance mentioned by the bookseller, was written by Madeleine de Scudéry; "Monsieur Scuderi" is her brother George, whose name, not hers, appeared on the title page. Among the chief authors of "secret History" were Mary Delariviere Manley (1663–1724) and Eliza Haywood (1693?–1756).

The dialogue "Berenice & Cleopatra," so different in spirit from Lyttelton's "Octavia—Portia—Arria," was not included in the *Dialogues of the Dead,* though it might have been: Lyttelton added four dialogues in 1765, and Mrs. Montagu had shown the conversation to Edward Young in 1761. It was first printed, imperfectly transcribed, in Emily J. Climenson's *Elizabeth Montagu, the Queen of the Blue Stockings; Her Correspondence from 1720 to 1761* (London, 1906), II, 238–40, with letters to and from Young. I have reproduced it from a photocopy of Mrs. Montagu's manuscript (HM MS. MO 2998), by permission of The Huntington Library, San Marino, California; my single departure from the manuscript is in spelling "managment" (i.e., management) correctly the two times it occurs.

The Jewish princess Berenice, whom the Emperor Titus considered marrying after the destruction of Jerusalem in the year 70, was decidedly not the tyro she is called here: accused of incest, thrice married, she had not confined her affections to Titus. But Racine had restored her virginity in the tragedy *Bérénice* (1670), and Lyttelton explicitly followed his example in Dialogue XI, which compares Titus' renunciation of Berenice with Scipio Africanus' delicacy regarding the captive Celtiberian maiden. Berenice's calling herself *"l'amante* of Titus" reflects her origin in Racine. The quotation, "all the mighty names by love undone," is from Dryden's "Palamon and Arcite: Or, The Knight's Tale, from Chaucer," II, 504, *The Poems of John Dryden,* ed. James Kinsley (Oxford, 1958), IV, 1496. The last words of the dialogue have the ambiguity they possess in the alternate title of Dryden's tragedy concerning Antony and Cleopatra, *All for Love.*

Dialogue XXVIII. Plutarch—Charon— And a modern Bookseller

Charon. Here is a fellow who is very unwilling to land in our Territories. He says he is rich, has a great deal of Business in the other world, and must needs return to it: He is so troublesome and obstreperous I know not what to do with him. Take him under your care therefore, good Plutarch; you will easily awe him into order and decency by the superiority an Author has over a Bookseller.

Bookseller. Am I got into a world so absolutely the reverse of that I left, that here Authors domineer over Booksellers? Dear Charon, let me go back, and I will pay any price for my passage. But, if I must stay, leave me not with any of those who are stiled Classical Authors. As to you, Plutarch, I have a particular animosity against you, for having almost occasioned my ruin. When I first set up shop, understanding but little of Business, I unadvisedly bought an Edition of your *Lives;* a pack of old Greeks and Romans, which cost me a great sum of money. I could never get off above twenty sets of them. I sold a few to the Universities, and some to Eaton and Westminster; for it is reckoned a pretty book for Boys and Undergraduates; but, unless a man has the luck to light on a Pedant, he shall not sell a set of them in twenty years.

Plutarch. From the merit of the subjects I had hoped another reception for my works. I will own indeed, that I am not always perfectly accurate in every circumstance, nor do I give so exact and circumstantial a detail of the Actions of my Heroes, as may be expected from a Biographer who has confined himself to one or two Characters. A Zeal to preserve the memory of Great Men, and to extend the influence of such noble examples, made me to undertake more than I could accomplish in the first degree of perfection: but surely the Characters of my illustrious Men are not so imperfectly sketched, that they will not stand forth to all ages as Patterns of Virtue, and Incitements to Glory. My reflections are allowed to be deep and sagacious; and what can be more useful to a reader than a wise man's judgment on a great man's conduct? In my writings you will find no rash censures, no undeserved encomiums, no mean compliance with popular opinions, no vain ostentation of critical skill, nor any affected finesse. In my Parallels, which used to be admired as pieces of excellent Judgment, I compare with perfect impartiality one great man with another, and each with the rule of Justice. If indeed latter ages have produced greater men and better writers, my Heroes and my Works ought to give place to them. As the world has now the advantage of much better rules of morality than the unassisted reason of poor Pagans could form, I do not wonder, that those vices, which appeared to us as mere blemishes in great Characters, should seem most horrid deformities in the purer Eyes of the present Age: a delicacy I do not blame, but admire and commend. And I must censure you for endeavouring, if you could publish better examples, to obtrude on your Countrymen such as were defective. I rejoice at the preference which they give to perfect and unallayed Virtue; and as I shall ever retain an high veneration for the illustrious men of every age, I should be glad you would give me some account of those persons, who in Wisdom, Justice, Valour, Patriotism, have eclipsed my Solon, Numa, Camillus, and other Boasts of Greece or Rome.

Bookseller. Why, Master Plutarch, you are talking Greek indeed. That work which repaired the loss I sustained by the costly Edition of your Books, was, *The Lives of the Highwaymen:* but I should never have grown rich, if it had not been by publishing *the Lives of men that never lived.* You must know, that though in all times it was possible to have a great deal of Learning and very little Wisdom, yet it is only by a modern improvement in the art of writing, that a man may read all his Life and have no learning or knowledge at all, which begins to be an advantage of the greatest importance. There is as natural a War between your men of Science and Fools, as between the Cranes and the Pigmies of old. Most of our young men having deserted to the Fools, the Party of the Learned is near being beaten out of the field; and I hope in a little while they will not dare to peep out of their Forts and Fastnesses at Oxford and Cambridge. There let them stay and study old musty Moralists, till one falls in Love with the Greek, another with the Roman Virtue: but our men of the world should read our new Books, which teach them to have no Virtue at all. No book is fit for a Gentleman's reading which is not void of Facts and of Doctrines, that he may not grow a Pedant in his morals or conversation. I look upon History (I mean real History) to be one of the worst kinds of study. Whatever has happened may happen again; and a well-bred man may unwarily mention a parallel instance he had met with in History, and be betrayed into the aukwardness of introducing into his discourse a Greek, a Roman, or even a Gothic Name. But when a Gentleman has spent his time in reading Adventures that never occurred, Exploits that never were atchieved, and Events that not only never did, but never can happen, it is impossible that in Life or in Discourse he should ever apply them. A secret History, in which there is no Secret and no History, cannot tempt indiscretion to blab or vanity to quote; and by this means modern conversation flows gentle and easy, unincumbered with matter and unburthened of instruction. As the present studies throw no weight or gravity into discourse and manners, the women are not afraid to read our Books, which not only dispose to Gallantry and Coquetry, but give rules for them. Cæsar's Commentaries, and the Account of Xenophon's Expedition, are not more studied by military Commanders, than our Novels are by the Fair; to a different Purpose indeed; for their military maxims teach to conquer, our's to yield; Those inflame the vain and idle Love of Glory, These inculcate a noble contempt of reputation. The women have greater obligations to our writers than the men. By the commerce of the world men might learn much of what they get from Books; but the poor women, who in their early Youth are confined and restrained, if it were not for the friendly assistance of Books, would remain long in an insipid purity of mind, with a discouraging reserve of Behaviour.

Plutarch. As to your Men who have quitted the study of Virtue for the study of Vice, useful Truth for absurd Fancy, and real History for monstrous Fiction, I have neither regard nor compassion for them: but I am concerned for the Women who are betrayed into these dangerous studies: and I wish for their sakes I had expatiated more of the character of Lucretia and some other Heroines.

Bookseller. I tell you, our Women do not read in order to live or to die like Lucretia. If you would inform us, that a *Billet-doux* was found in her Cabinet after her Death, or give an hint as if Tarquin really saw her in the Arms of a Slave, and that she killed herself not to suffer the shame of a discovery, such Anecdotes would sell very well. Or if even by tradition, but better still, if by papers in the Portian family, you could shew some probability that Portia died of dram drinking; you would oblige the world very much; for you must know, that next to new-invented Characters, we are fond of new Lights upon ancient Characters; I mean such Lights as shew a reputed honest man to have been a concealed knave; an illustrious hero a pitiful coward, &c. Nay, we are so fond of these kinds of information, as to be pleased sometimes to see a character cleared from a Vice or Crime it has been charged with, provided the person concerned be actually dead. But in this case the Evidence must be authentic, and amount to a demonstration; in the other a detection is not necessary; a slight suspicion will do, if it concerns a really good and great Character.

Plutarch. I am the more surprised at what you say of the Taste of your contemporaries, as I met with a Frenchman who assured me that less than a century ago he had written a much admired life of Cyrus under the name of Artamenes, in which he ascribed to him far greater Actions than those recorded of him by Xenophon and Herodotus; and that many of the great Heroes of History had been treated in the same manner; that Empires were gained and Battles decided by the valour of a single man, Imagination bestowing what Nature has denied, and the system of human affairs rendered impossible.

Bookseller. I assure you these Books were very useful to the Authors and their Booksellers: and for whose Benefit beside should a man write? These Romances were very fashionable and had a great Sale: They fell in luckily with the humour of the Age.

Plutarch. Monsieur Scuderi tells me they were written in the times of Vigour and Spirit, in the evening of the gallant days of Chivalry, which, though then declining, had left in the hearts of Men a warm glow of Courage and Heroism; and they were to be called to Books as to Battles, by the sound of the Trumpet: he says too, that, if writers had not accommodated themselves to the Prejudices of the age, and written of bloody battles and desperate encounters, their works would have been esteemed too effeminate an amusement for Gentlemen. Histories of Chivalry, instead of enervating, tend to invigorate the mind, and endeavour to raise human nature above the condition which is naturally prescribed to it; but as strict Justice, patriot motives, prudent counsels, and a dispassionate choice of what upon the whole is fittest and best, do not direct these heroes of Romance, they cannot serve for instruction and example, like the great Characters of true History. It has ever been my opinion, that only the clear and steady light of Truth can guide Men to Virtue, and that the Lesson which is impracticable must be unuseful. Whoever shall design to regulate his Conduct by these Visionary Characters will be in the Condition of Superstitious People, who chuse rather to act by Intimations they receive in the Dreams of the Night, than by the sober counsels of Morning Meditation. Yet I confess it has been the practice of many nations to incite men to Virtue by relating the Deeds of fabulous Heroes; but surely it is the custom only of your's to incite them to Vice by the History of fabulous Scoundrels. Men of fine imagination have soared into the regions of Fancy to bring back Astrea: you go thither in search of Pandora; Oh Disgrace to Letters! O Shame to the Muses!

Bookseller. You express great indignation at our present race of Writers; but believe me the fault lies chiefly on the side of the Readers. As Monsieur Scuderi observed to you, Authors must comply with the manners and disposition of those who are to read them. There must be a certain Sympathy between the Book and the Reader to create a good liking. Would you present a modern fine Gentleman, who is negligently lolling in an easy Chair, with the *Labours of Hercules* for his recreation? Or make him climb the Alps with Hannibal when he is expiring with the fatigue of last Night's Ball? Our readers must be amused, flattered, soothed; such adventures must be offered to them as they would like to have a share in.

Plutarch. It should be the first object of writers to correct the vices and follies of the age. I will allow as much compliance with the Mode of the times as will make truth and good morals agreeable. Your love of fictitious Characters might be turned to good purpose, if those presented to the Public were to be formed on the rules of Religion and Morality. It must be confessed, that History, being employed only about illustrious Persons, public Events, and celebrated Actions, does not supply us with such instances of Domestic Merit as one could wish: Our Heroes are great in the Field and the Senate, and act well in great Scenes on the theatre of the World: but the Idea of a man, who in the silent retired path of Life never deviates into Vice, who considers no spectator but the omniscient Being and sollicits no applause but His approbation, is the noblest model that can be exhibited to mankind, and would be of the most general use. Examples of Domestic Virtue would be more particularly useful to Women than those of great Heroines. The virtues of Women are blasted by the breath of public fame, as flowers that grow on an Eminence are faded by the Sun and Wind, which expand them. But true female Praise, like the Music of the Spheres, arises from a gentle, a constant, and an equal Progress in the Path marked out for them by their great Creator; and, like the heavenly Harmony, it is not adapted to the gross ear of mortals, but is reserved for the delight of higher Beings, by whose wise Laws they were ordained to give a silent light, and shed a mild benignant influence on the world.

Bookseller. We have had some English and French writers who aimed at what you suggest. In the supposed character of Clarissa, (said a Clergyman to me a few days before I left the world) one finds the dignity of Heroism tempered by the meekness and humility of religion, a perfect purity of mind and sanctity of manners: in that of Sir Charles Grandison, a noble pattern of every private Virtue, with sentiments so exalted as to render him equal to every public Duty.

Plutarch. Are both these characters by the same Author?

Bookseller. Ay, Master Plutarch; and what will surprise you more, this Author has printed for me.

Plutarch. By what you say, it is pity he should print any work but his own. Are there no other Authors who write in this manner?

Bookseller. Yes, we have another writer of these imaginary Histories; One who has not long since descended to these regions; his Name is Fielding, and his Works, as I have heard the best judges say, have a true spirit of Comedy, and an exact representation of Nature, with fine moral touches. He has not indeed given lessons of pure and consummate Virtue, but he has exposed Vice and Meanness with all the powers of Ridicule; and we have some other good Wits who have exerted their Talents to the Purposes you approve. Monsieur de Marivaux, and some other French writers, have also proceeded much upon the same Plan, with a spirit and elegance which give their works no mean rank among the *Belles Lettres.* I will own that, when there is wit and entertainment enough in a book to make it sell, it is not the worse for good morals.

Charon. I think, Plutarch, you have made this Gentleman a little more humble, and now I will carry him the rest of his Journey. But he is too frivolous an Animal to present to wise Minos. I wish Mercury were here; he would damn him for his Dulness. I have a good mind to carry him to the Danaïdes, and leave him to pour water into their vessels, which, like his late readers, are destined to eternal emptiness. Or shall I chain him to the rock, side to side by Prometheus, not for having attempted to steal celestial fire, in order to animate human forms, but for having endeavoured to extinguish that which Jupiter had imparted? Or shall we constitute him *Friseur* to Tisiphone, and make him curl up her locks with his Satires and Libels?

Plutarch. Minos does not esteem any thing frivolous that affects the Morals of mankind; He punishes Authors as guilty of every Fault they have countenanced, and every Crime they have encouraged; and denounces heavy Vengeance for the Injuries which Virtue or the Virtuous have suffered in consequence of their writings.

Berenice & Cleopatra

Berenice. The similitudes & dissimilitudes of our fortune have long made me wish to converse with you, if the charming the victorious Cleopatra, by her Lover prefer'd to glory, to empire, to life, will deign to hold converse with the forsaken, the abandon'd, the discarded Berenice.

Cleopatra. The scorns of Octavius, the bite of the aspic, & the waters of Lethe have so subdued my female vanity, that I will own to you I greatly suspect my better success with my Lover did not arise so much from my charms being superior to yours, as my skill in the management of them.

Berenice. I can scarce understand you. Beauty and love I thought to be the greatest attractions. In the first you must have excell'd me, but in the second you certainly could not. I had beauty, youth, regal dignity, & an elevated mind. I was distinguish'd by many qualities and accomplishments, which were so dedicated to my Lover, that of all I had been, & all I could be, I was, I would be only *l'amante* of Titus. I thought the next person in merit & dignity to Titus himself was the woman who ador'd him; and I was more proud of the homage I paid him, than of all I had receiv'd from lovers or subjects. But you, Cleopatra, had loved Cæsar before Anthony, and other passions besides the gentle one of love seem'd still to share your heart. Yet for you, Anthony despised the dangers of war, the competition of a rival in Empire, the motives of military glory, and the resentment of a Senate & people not yet taught to submit to and flatter the passions of a master. Over these you triumph'd; but I was sacrificed to the low murmurs of the people, & the cautious counsels of grey headed statesmen. Was it that Minerva desired to triumph over Venus in the noblest and gentlest

heart that ever was contain'd in the breast of a mortal? Tell me
Cleopatra: for 1700 years have not made me forget my love and
my grief!

Cleopatra. I have often with attention listen'd to your story; and your
looks on which still remain the sadness of a lovers farewell move
my compassion. I wish I could have assisted you with my counsels
when Titus was meditating your departure; I would have taught
you those arts by which I enslaved the soul of Anthony, and
brought ambition and the Roman Eagles to lye at my feet.

Berenice. Alass! your arts would have been of little service to me. I
had no occasion to counterfeit love. From Titus's perfections one
learn'd to love in reality beyond whatever fiction pretended; no
feign'd complaisance could imitate my sympathy: if he sigh'd I
wept, if he was grave I grew melancholly, if he sicken'd I dyed. My
heart echoed his praises, it beat for his glory, it rejoyced in his fortunes, it trembled at his dangers.

Cleopatra. Indeed Berenice you talk more like a shepherdess than a
great queen. You might perhaps in the simplicity of pastoral life
have engaged some humble swain, but there was too much of nature & too little of art in your conduct, to captivate a man used to
flattery, to pleasures, to variety. I find you was but the mirror of
Titus; you gave him back his own image, while I presented every
hour a new Cleopatra to Anthony. I was gay, voluptuous, haughty,
gracious, fond, and indifferent by turns; if he frown'd on me, I
smiled on Dollabella; if he grew thoughtfull, I turn'd the banquet
to a riot; I dash'd the soberness of counsels by the vivacity of
mirth, and gilded over his disgrace by shew and magnificence; if
his reason began to return I subdued it by fondness or disturb'd it
by jealousy. Thus did I preserve my conquest, establish my fame,
and put Anthony first in the list of

> all the mighty names by love undone.

Had I only wept when Honour & Octavia call'd him home I might
have been the burthen of a love ballad, or subject of a tender elegy,
who now am the glory of our sex, and the great instance of beautys

power. Do not you wish you had used the same managements?

Berenice. I might have used them had I loved the same man. Cleopatra the coquette was a proper mistress for the reveller Anthony; but the godlike Titus, the delight as well as master of mankind, left no part of the heart unengaged and at liberty to dissemble. What had not yielded to his wisdom submitted to his witt, was subdued by his magnanimity, or won by his gentleness. When affection does not vary behaviour cannot change; and methinks Anthony should have quitted you from distrust of your love, and Titus have retain'd me from confidence in mine. After what you have told me I am more than ever surprized at your fate & my own.

Cleopatra. If you want this explain'd ask Eneas, Theseus, Jason, & the infinite multitude of faithless lovers: but if my authority will pass, believe me when I tell you, Anthony was preserved by his doubt of my love, and Titus was lost by his confidence in yours. Do not look so concern'd. From the era of your disaster to this very day, you will find every faithfull & fond Berenice discarded, while the gay, vain, and capricious fair one is to her Anthony a Cleopatra & *the world well lost.*

William Weston (1711?-1791)
and John Green (1706-1779)

Uneven and unlordly, the seventeen conversations in the anonymous *New Dialogues of the Dead* (London, 1762) were evidently published to capitalize on the popularity Lyttelton had won for the genre. The dialogue reprinted here, with its speculations about Lucretia, calls to mind Mrs. Montagu's account, as delivered by her bookseller, of what the reading public wanted. Marie de Bourgogne (1457–82) was the daughter of Charles the Bold, the last reigning duke of Burgundy. Louis XI sought her hand for the dauphin, Charles, in order to consolidate French claims to Burgundy as well as the Low Countries, part of Marie's legacy. Instead she married the Hapsburg prince Maximilian, later the first Emperor of that name. She died after suffering a fall from a horse. Charles the Bold, Louis, and Maximilian are speakers in Fénelon; Fontenelle's debate between Hadrian and Margaret of Austria on the subject of which faced death more calmly, entailing invidious comparison with Cato the Younger, may have suggested the topic.

Dialogue IV. Mary of Burgundy and Montaigne

Montaigne. You may say what you please, but certainly your's was a very ridiculous death: because you had hurt yourself in a certain part, which it naturally gave you offence to name, you would hinder its being looked at, and so take pet and die.

Mary. I wonder to see a man of your education so dim-sighted here. Why my pet was no more than thousands have taken before me; and you of all people should know it, who had seen the manners of a court, and the refined turn of thinking which frequently prevails there.

Montaigne. Let me have seen them as much as you please, yet I know of no such example at all; there certainly was not one in all the courts of my time; and, as far as I can judge of those since, they have not even a chance of ever producing another.

Mary. Indeed you do me a great deal of honour; I did not think this piece of female heroism so singular as never to be matched again, even in those higher spheres of life, where exalted notions should be common.

Montaigne. Nay, this second mistake is still greater than your first; in the higher spheres you mention, where exalted sentiments prevail, the very species of these examples is extinct; and if any one of them is ever seen, it is in some obscure and homely shed, the simple mistress of which complains of she knows not what, and dies she knows not why.

Mary. I do not think your reflection just; but pray, for my sake, be less severe in your censures on this occasion.

Montaigne. No; you of all others have the least claim to clemency here: What! an heiress of the Low Countries; one that was sought

for as a wife by all the world;—one that was given backwards
and forwards in marriage an hundred times;—one that from her
very infancy had been used to the gross idea of an husband, and to
have his several qualifications canvassed and laid open;—one
that was to lie in state, and to have herself and children exposed to
grave statesmen and uxorious senators—

Mary. You may spare the sequel; for though you aggravate the matter ever so much, what would it all shew, but that my delicacy was
very excessive, and that I died a martyr to this, as others had done
to more shameful passions?

Montaigne. But yet, in some other things, your delicacy was not so
excessive, if what your confidante said, came, as it is probable, immediately from you; for her answer to Lewis the XIth's ambassador
was, that her mistress was fit for a man, and did not choose a boy.

Mary. Would it puzzle my ingenious opposer much, if I was to take
upon myself all that an unpolished maid of honour was pleased to
say for me?

Montaigne. I confess it is a little embarassing.

Mary. Why? Does it require so much sagacity to see, that chastity
and delicacy need not always subsist together, and that I might
have one of these to excess, and yet have but an inconsiderable portion of the other?

Montaigne. This is just possible, but certainly not very common.

Mary. No; nor the counter-part of it in the maid of honour just-men-
tioned: for though her enemies allow that she had one of these virtues in perfection, yet her very friends cannot allow her the other;
and the numerous obscenities in her conversation, and intire freedom from them in her life, justified the observations of both: in
short, I might, for aught you know, be delicate, but not chaste; as
she was chaste, but not delicate.

Montaigne. This indeed may be: but why should you die on this account?

Mary. I do not wonder at your putting this question so often. A man
of no delicacy himself cannot feel the sentiments of those that
have.—But suppose I had died for chastity?

Montaigne. That would have been more commendable, and more easily solved.

Mary. Suppose for love?

Montaigne. More common, and more to be expected still.

Mary. Suppose for pain, for captivity, or dishonour?

Montaigne. All of them more justifiable causes of death than yours.

Mary. To vulgar and undistinguishing eyes it should seem so, but in the clear and unprejudiced eye of reason it is far otherwise: let us bring this matter to the test. What does a duellist die for?

Montaigne. Because he cannot bear reproach.

Mary. So did I.—What did Cato leave the world for?

Montaigne. Because he could not bear captivity.

Mary. And why not captivity, but because it ended in one sort of infamy, as my disorder did in another? and neither he nor I were able to support our shares. But if this example be thought of too great dignity to be compared with mine, what think you of that shade who now walks before you with a bleeding bosom?

Montaigne. O! it is Lucretia, the pride and boast of the Roman world, that admirable pattern of fortitude and chastity to all succeeding ages.

Mary. Bless me! what a profusion of applause ought I to expect, if you begin already with such encomiums on her.

Montaigne. No: her cause of death was real and substantial; your's whimsical and imaginary: her's had its foundation in nature and custom; your's in neither: at least, if we cannot go so far, we may say with great justice, that she could not after such a misfortune live with a proper degree of credit amongst her virtuous countrymen, and therefore it was reasonable for her to die.

Mary. This last is the whole of what can be said in her praise, and the preferring an honourable death to unavoidable infamy was all the merit of this so much applauded act.

Montaigne. And do you call this all the merit? was it not a great deal for a woman to have such an extraordinary degree of courage, to prefer death to a reproach she did not deserve?

Mary. Undoubtedly it was; and on this account her example will be memorable and illustrious to the latest posterity. But suppose now, that by some favourable circumstances she had made her escape from Tarquin, in the very moment he was about to perpetrate his intended villainy, and afterwards suffered the same martyrdom to honour.

Montaigne. No: here the martyrdom to honour would end, and the martyrdom to folly must begin.

Mary. Why so? what is that nice and undistinguishable barrier, that can separate actions so much alike?

Montaigne. The custom of the country just now mentioned, in which Lucretia would have met with no reproach if she had escaped without pollution.

Mary. And yet certain of these very countrymen of her's have delivered it down to us in their writings, that it is some reflection on a woman to be solicited; and therefore she could not even then have avoided the censures of all.

Montaigne. Of all the wise and honest she would; and what could the idle jeers of a few wanton and capricious wits avail?

Mary. Just as much with some tempers, as those of a whole people, equally wanton and capricious in loading ingenuous minds with infamy for what they never could help: at least there is only this difference, that the degrees of infamy, all of them undeserved, would be greater or less.

Montaigne. Well, this is however something.

Mary. Yes, a great deal with me; for even I in my misfortune might not have escaped the censures of some: that jester, or that clown, that historian, or that poet, who could say that there were the signs of frailty in a woman's face, which led her lover to tempt her virtue, might see some of the same marks in me for suffering myself to be cured.—If I died therefore to be free from these reflections, my courage is as much superior to Lucretia's, as the censure of a nation is superior to a single man's.

Montaigne. So, you bring yourself off with flying colours; and however modest you was in some points above, you make ample amends for it in some others below: I could never have expected from one of your character such an eulogy on herself.

Mary. That I may appear therefore to you to keep up some consistency in my character, I will lower this eulogy as much as possible, by confessing, that the sum of the whole matter is, that the causes of pain are frequently more imaginary than real; more relative than absolute. A Cato could not bear captivity, nor an Atticus endure sickness; yet a Cato could have endured sickness, and an Atticus have borne captivity: and to come still nearer to the point, a Lucrece could not live after a rape, nor I after my fall; yet it is possible, that Lucrece might have lived after my misfortune, and I after her's: nay, what is more remarkable yet, the very same person at different times and in different circumstances would wonder at himself for his strange resolutions, either of living or dying; and if you will not peevishly deny me the just praises I deserve, I will confess to you, that if I had continued some years longer in the world, I might not have proved so great a heroine as I was.

The Sentimental Magazine

From Lucian's time through the eighteenth century, no classical personage turns up in dialogues of the dead more frequently than Scipio Africanus Major. In Lyttelton's twenty-ninth dialogue, for example, Scipio beats back Caesar's criticism and emerges only slightly scathed, still worthy of historical consecration as an unsurpassed hero and patriot. Lyttelton's favorite Fénelon devoted one of his two conversations between Scipio and Hannibal to praise of the Roman for his continence on the occasion discussed in the following anonymous dialogue from the *Sentimental Magazine,* II (April, 1774), 137–39, where a notable and unconventional series of such pieces appeared. Mahomet is the Ottoman Sultan Mohammed II (1429–81), Irene the heroine of Samuel Johnson's tragedy. There is some precedent for the sultan's blunt attitude in the first of Fontenelle's second series of dialogues between modern shades, where Mohammed's great-grandson Suleiman I argues that love need not be requited to be satisfactory. In the fifth dialogue of that group Roxelana, the wife of Suleiman II, boasts that Turkish directness in matters of love is better than French courtesy.

Dialogue between Scipio Africanus and Mahomet the Great, in the Regions of the Dead

Scipio. So you laugh at me for resigning my fair captive.

Mahomet. Can I avoid it?—For what did you conquer?

Scipio. For the glory of the Roman name.

Mahomet. Sounding words:—how pretty in the mouths of school boys!—And I, as every Mussulman will tell you, to extend the glorious light of the Koran. But I need not tell you, that we had both some other motives of a less disinterested nature. Ambition, pleasure, or avarice, had to share in all our actions; and as you were too young to hoard, and the servant of a state, which you would not hope to rule, I should have thought pleasure would have been your predominant passion. But some people, it would seem, never have any passions.

Scipio. I was not insensible to the charms of beauty, but had too much delicacy to owe them to force.

Mahomet. To force?—How strangely you talk! What beauty would not have been proud to bestow them on the conqueror of Carthage?

Scipio. My captive would not, nor on the conqueror of the world; for she was betrothed to the man she loved: and I had more pleasure in restoring her to him, than I could possibly have had in enjoying her charms, by taking advantage of her condition.

Mahomet. You are welcome to think so. One would imagine you had been dragged into the world against your will, (for the idea of violence is still before you) and educated in a dungeon. Are female affections unalterable? Would the Celtiberian bride have been the first woman who has fallen in love with one man, while betrothed to another?—I dare swear she was heartily mortified, to find that her charms made so little impression on the youthful conqueror; and that she thought you an unfeeling cub for parting with what she considered as more valuable than all your other conquests.

Scipio. She might think what she pleased. I acted properly; and the world has given me credit for my conduct.

Mahomet. The foolish part of it: old women, girls and boys, and men of Scipionian continence.

Scipio. Say rather, Roman virtue.

Mahomet. As you please; for the one is about as respectable to me as the other. The man of no passions, and he who restrains them to avoid the censure, or obtain the applause of mankind, without any impulse from within, stand equally high in my estimation: the one is a coward, and the other a flatterer; flattery is but cowardice disguised. Give me the man who acts from interest or passion, regardless of censure or applause.

Scipio. What barbarous maxims!—By such a conduct you would deprive yourself of the most delightful of human pleasures, and for the want of which not all the rest will atone; the approbation of your species.

Mahomet. By no means: I did not incur so much censure as you may imagine, and yet I never avoided it for its own sake only. There is a sympathy in human affections; and, when we do not act unnaturally, or absurdly, we are seldom subject to blame. Had you, for instance, taken the fair captive to your arms instead of restoring her to her lover, or selling her, as was your Roman custom, nobody would have blamed you; your youth, her beauty, and a thousand other circumstances, would have pleaded your apology.—But your character, indeed, would have been somewhat altered: you would have been the amorous Scipio, instead of the chaste; which would not, in my opinion, have been less to your honour.

Scipio. Still returning to the same sentiment!—Had I not been

otherwise informed, I should have taken you for a voluptuous tyrant, whose sole pursuit was pleasure.

Mahomet. There indeed you would have been mistaken, though not
altogether; for pleasure was always one of my pursuits: and to the
love of pleasure I owed my conquests. I set before my followers fine
women, as the reward of their valour in this world, and immortal
transports in the arms of the eternal Houris in the next, according
to the promise of our great prophet and predecessor: and the success was answerable to my expectations; the Greeks fled before us,
like timorous doves from the hawk. We were lions let loose upon a
herd of deer. The nations were scattered at our approach; and, such
is the influence of beauty! that, in a few years, we acquired a
greater empire than your countrymen, the boasted Romans had
done, in many ages, by their stoical maxims.

Scipio. You astonish me. I should have thought pleasure would have
enervated both the minds and the bodies of your soldiers.

Mahomet. That is a vulgar mistake. The love of women is one of the
greatest incentives to human action; and is seldom productive of
any emasculating effects, unless when accompanied with the use of
wine, which is wisely prohibited by our religion. We, therefore,
freely indulged in amorous delights, and found every fine woman
only a new spur to conquest. Valour seemed to gather strength in
the arms of Pleasure, while Beauty was the reward of heroism.

But, voluptuous as I was, I gave as striking a proof of my command over my passions as any Roman that ever lived; and that too
with regard to a captive not less fair than yours.

Scipio. I am glad to hear it, and should be happy to learn the particulars; for my heart still glows at the recital of a great or a generous
action.

Mahomet. You shall judge of its generosity. The world has allowed it
to be great.

In the sacking of Constantinople, the beautiful Irene fell into
my hands, whom I valued more than all the wealth it contained. I did
every thing possible to make myself dear to her; but the difference
of our religions rendered her a long time deaf to my fond solicita-

tions, whatever impression I might have made on her heart. She was likewise under engagements to a young Greek; the christian faith did not permit her to be any thing but a wife; and we sultans never marry: but, notwithstanding these objections, she at last consented to make me happy; and I really was, for once, intoxicated with pleasure. I neglected my military affairs, and shewed a thousand indulgencies to the Christians. The zealous Mussulmen were offended at such lenity being shewn to infidels, and my whole army was prepared for a revolt. I was apprised of my danger, and awoke from my delirium. I ordered all my forces to be assembled, and presented my lovely captive before them, arrayed in all the riches of the East: (how contemptible, in comparison of her inestimable beauty!)—And, when they had viewed her sufficiently, I said in a solemn tone, "Is this, ye faithful! the cause of your dissatisfaction, and it shall speedily be removed?"

They hung down their heads in silence, over-awed by the presence of so much beauty; but well did I see what rankled in their hearts: I therefore drew my scymeter; and, while the sweet angel looked ineffable delight, I severed her head from her body.

Scipio. Frightful blow!

Mahomet. What cannot ambition?—My troops trembled at my fury: instead of shouting, they seemed to implore forgiveness, and were ready to kneel at my feet. My heart swelled with triumph, while my tenderness expired in a sigh. I ordered the leaders of the mutiny to immediate execution, and began anew the career of glory, of conquest, and of love.

Scipio. I admire your fortitude; but would not have possessed your feelings for all the delights of love, and all the trophies of ambition.

Mahomet. But I was a Turk, you know, and therefore thought otherwise; and those who estimate men more by the vigour, than the lenity of their minds, will not see less to admire in my conduct than in yours.

Thomas Tyers (*1726-1787*)

At once pedantic and dilettante, Johnson's amiable friend wrote thirty dialogues of the dead. This dialogue, from *Conversations Political and Familiar* (London, 1784), is more dramatic than most of his productions, a piece after Lyttelton's manner: Lyttelton's fourth dialogue supplied Addison's penultimate remarks, Swift there opening the conversation by observing that Addison should have been a bishop. Here Gondamor (Gondomar) is the Spanish ambassador to James I who demanded Raleigh's execution. Keymis is the sea-captain Lawrence Kemys, for some years an aide of Raleigh, who gave Kemys command of an unsuccessful expedition up the Orinoco to take possession of a gold mine. The venture resulted in the loss of several Englishmen including Raleigh's son Walter, and Kemys committed suicide after reporting his failure.

Conversation XXVIII. Sir Walter Raleigh and Mr. Addison

Raleigh. Men were not designed to live *by* themselves, nor *for* themselves; to grow old in a monastic cell, or to moulder away in a college library.

Addison. It is impossible for every one to act a principal part upon the theatre of the world. Some are only intended by nature for the shade of retirement. No doubt, society has its demands upon us. But every ploughman is not fit to be made a dictator; nor every butcher's or blacksmith's son capable of being a Wolsey or a Cromwell. The temper of some men is too fine for business, and the faculties of others are found to be even below it. I mean not this as an excuse for idleness and inactivity.

Raleigh. For my part, I launched out very early into the tempestuous ocean of an active life. I still remember the line I wrote in the window, on my first going to court:

> "Fain would I climb, yet fear I to fall;"

and the queen underwriting:

> "If thy heart fail thee, climb not at all."

All this added spurs to my ambition, that already wanted a bridle.

Addison. Such a martial spirit, and so enterprizing a disposition as yours, could not be kept long at home.

Raleigh. No: I travelled into France, into the Netherlands, and into Ireland. After passing several years abroad, and seeing a great deal of military service, I returned with wreaths of glory, but without making my fortune. I performed several voyages to the new world;

for the success and high deeds of Columbus, Cortez, and Pizarro, heated my imagination to an extravagant degree. I discovered and planted the colony of Virginia, that has since turned out so beneficial to my country. All this I atchieved before I was thirty-two years of age.

Addison. I know your activity of mind and person determined you rather to wear out, than to rust out. When you gave up the land service, and confined yourself to the command at sea, you distinguished yourself against the Armada in eighty-eight, and came to be considered as one of the first men in England. The death of Queen Elizabeth was a great blow to Sir Walter Raleigh.

Raleigh. I outlived all the seamen of her illustrious reign. Drake and Hawkins left me their hatred against the Spaniards. I have no doubt, I should have been sent by the Queen to take possession of Guiana, a country that might have proved equal in value to Mexico or Peru, and which might have been as compleatly discovered and settled as Virginia itself. Essex was removed out of the way, who stood between me and the Queen, and I might have succeeded to her esteem and favour.

Addison. But, whilst you was indulging your thirst for fame, and exerting every nerve to the utmost, were you not engaged in all the violence and malevolence of faction? Were not your rivals constantly endeavouring to keep you down as fast as you were striving to rise? The progress of your life presented a continual scene and series of perturbations, and to those who were at leisure to view things narrowly, pointed out a situation rather to be avoided as a rock, on account of its perils, than to be envied for its splendour.

Raleigh. Sequestered men, and superficial observers, are apt to think every commotion in affairs a storm and a hurricane. Great spirits, who thrust themselves forward into notice, and are called into public direction, have their abilities polished by the collision of parties, and invigorated by state bustle. The perpetual industry and predominant passion of my soul, like the boasted talent of Themistocles, was to make a little city become a great one.

Addison. Though yours was the age of heroes, yet there was room for people of another sort to become objects of distinction. Spenser obtained your patronage by his poetry. You loved the Muses too well, and was too well beloved by them, to have formed a wish, that his pen or his laurels should be taken from him. According to the opinion of the age in which I flourished, I was not thought to have mis-spent my time, nor to have lived in vain. I did not indeed contend for the military nor the civic crown; but I endeavoured to become useful in another way. I had not the smallest ambition of performing heroic services; but was content with the secondary praise of recording and commending them. A poem on Marlborough, our great captain, was esteemed so meritorious a composition, that it introduced me to Godolphin our first minister. I did not wear the lazy academic habit for half my time, nor pass the remainder in barren speculations, nor in matters irrelative to human life. I devoted myself to the literary service of my country, and endeavoured, by some periodical essays, to meliorate our manners, and to smooth and fix our fluctuating language. If I do not set too great a value on my pursuits, I made myself as useful by my pen, as another could have done by the sword. But every one could not write as well as fight, like Xenophon, Cæsar, and Sir Walter Raleigh.

Raleigh. If you allude to my History of the World, I can tell you, that the writing it only occupied my moments and thoughts when I could do nothing else, and had nothing else to do. It would have increased my misery to have had my mind as well as my body cooped up in the narrow prison of the Tower. As soon as I could get out, I braved the thunder and lightning I struggled with upon the Atlantic, in my endeavour to enrich my country from the gold mine of Guiana.

Addison. Alas, Sir Walter! the present age, as well as the past, consider your promise to fetch gold from thence, as the unmanly pretence for obtaining your liberty. Your Eldorado, or golden city, that you described with so much luxuriance in print three and twenty years before your last voyage, is treated as a city in Utopia and a Romance of your fertile brain. If gold was to be had, I believe you was determined to bring it with you. But I am afraid you had no reason to expect it, but by plundering the Spaniards at St. Thomas, by which you intended to make your peace at court. For though you went out with the power of life and death, you knew you had not a compleat pardon. The commission, which is still visible, wanted the emphatical expression, of trusty and well-beloved. Your son, just before he was killed, declared to his followers, "they were fools who thought there was any other gold mine than what was to be had for fighting for."

Raleigh. Let me not stand so low in your estimation, to be considered as earning my life or liberty by the fraud of fiction or the meanness of a lie. I had brought a specimen of the gold of Guiana to court in the Queen's time, which I helped to dig out of the rocks with my dagger; and I undertook they should produce more of that metal. My proposal was so plausible, and the king's necessities so pressing, that I speedily set out with a good equipment, and with many adventurers and volunteers. Gondamor's notification, and my confidential letter to the King, containing the particulars of my hopes from the expedition, arrived in America before me. This you may have read in books; and I affirm the truth of it to you now, by word of mouth. The death of my eldest son, and the precipitate conduct of Keymis, who, upon my declaring to him that he had ruined me by his hostilities, pistolled himself in his cabin, the disaffection on board the ships, and my engagement to my bondsman to return, like another Regulus to Carthage, made me sail for England, which ended in the exposing me to the vengeance of the Spaniard, and the fearfulness and even the policy of the king, who had begun to think of the infanta for his son, and scrupled not to make me the sacrifice.

Addison. I am ready to acknowledge your hard fate, and even the injustice done you upon your trial, for a treason, which has never been made out, nor legally proved against you.

Raleigh. Attorney Coke talked me to death on that day.

Addison. The King's bringing you to the block, after the punishment of thirteen years captivity, was pusillanimous, and one of the many blemishes of his reign. Your patron Prince Henry used to say, that none but his father would have kept such a bird so long in a cage.

Raleigh. I condescended to ask my life; being willing, as I expressed it, to die *for* the king, but not *by* the king. In truth, I abased myself even to Gondamor; though I believe and trust, that it is not generally known. But all would not do. When I came to die upon the scaffold, did I not perform my last part well? Did I not confess the vanity and sinfulness which my several callings, as a soldier, a sailor, and a courtier, subjected me to? Did I not assert the mode of dying by the sharpness of the axe to be less ungrateful than by a burning fever? Did I not shew great indifference to life and contempt of death? Did I not solemnly protest my innocence at the moment when falsehood could do me no good? And did I not take the last revenge of an injured man, to blacken those who had defamed me, and sworn falsely against me?

Addison. Your death made all the errors of your life forgiven or forgot. Can you bear to be told, that at one time you were the most unpopular man in England? that Lord Burlegh, amongst his cautionary precepts to his son Lord Salisbury, thus expresses his exception to you: "Seek not to be Essex; shun to be Raleigh."

Raleigh. Neither the censure of the ill-judging populace, nor the notions of a crafty statesman, should influence my conduct, were I to return to earth again. I would live and die my own way, in contradiction to them both. But it is high time to have done with my own story, the greatest part of which you must have been informed of already, that I may hear, without concealment of any circumstances, as I have done, what you have to say for yourself. Though we know a great deal of each other by reports and tradition, the present free conference will make us better acquainted, and set many things to rights in our character. What apology can you offer to remove my pity or reproach, for being nothing more than a poet and philologer, when your talents were considerable enough to have raised you to the lustre of a public character; for employing yourself in writing when you should have been in action; and for consulting your ease instead of your importance and your dignity?

Addison. Come, Sir Walter, I will discover myself to you. As great a secret as I find it is to you, and I reserved it to the conclusion of your narration, I have to tell you, that I was dragged, by those who most intended my interest, into the public eye of observation and into the responsibility of office. According to a sentiment in my own popular tragedy of Cato, I was placed on high, "to make my virtues or my faults conspicuous." I was elected a member of the House of Commons, and I took my seat for Malmsbury. But I did not distinguish myself there so much to my credit as you did; for I got up twice to speak to a question in favour of my party (for I was of a party as well as yourself, though not at the head of one), and raised the eager attention of the House to that pitch, and became so much embarrassed by their calling out, "Hear him! hear him!" that I could not proceed, but I was obliged to sit down, and never hazard the making another attempt. I was promoted to be secretary to a lord lieutenant of Ireland; and, some years after my return home, to my utter astonishment, I had the seals of secretary of state delivered into my hands.

Raleigh. I rejoice that your merit was rewarded with such advancement. I am impatient to hear, that time and practice got the better of your diffidence.

Addison. I found myself every day more unequal to my station; and what was worse, my most determined friends, and those who had the greatest hopes of me, saw my insufficiency, and blushed for me. I had not the presence of mind, like Sir Walter, to look all men full in the face, and reject their insolent petitions with a frown and a sturdy denial. I felt myself unfit for the coarse labour of official business, and the weight of state affairs. The distemper of an increasing asthma furnished me with an excuse for resigning the seals, and of retiring, upon a pension of two thousands pounds a year, to privacy and to my books.

Raleigh. It is enough to make my blood boil in these regions, to be told, that Addison, the man raised by the steadiness of his patrons to a principal post in the government, who was possessed of the opportunities of providing for his dependents, and of taking ample revenge upon his enemies, should plunge himself into inextricable disgrace. That he should suffer his heart to fail him, and his tongue to faulter in the cause he rose up to support: that a person, whose pen was equal to all subjects, whose name was in high reputation with all men, whose elevation was thought an ornament and ought to have been a blessing to his country, should secede from the public, desert his party, and shrink into nothingness and oblivion.

Addison. Lay the blame on my innate aukwardness and invincible modesty. Conscious I always was of the failings imputed to me. One of my best friends, and in high employment, continued to complain of my forbearance in the midst of senetorial debate, and was angry with me "for letting a forward fellow, who had not half my sense, prate for an hour together, without my taking him up." Fortune, who sometimes makes a laughing-stock of mankind, may be supposed, in a frolic, to have made Addison a secretary of state, when he could have discharged the function of a bishop with applause.

Raleigh. I marvel, under the disadvantages of an habitual silence, and an unprovocable temper, how you preserved yourself from insult and ridicule; that opposition did not roar like a lion when your tongue was fascinated into silence; that malignancy did not invent difficulties against you, and perplex even the current of public affairs, when the timidity of your disposition was so well known; and that every little Matchiavel in politics did not attempt to confound so feeble a minister, and expose so insignificant a tool of state.

Addison. If confidence were not the virtue of my mind, turbulence, I assure you, was not the pernicious vice of my heart. It is the first time I ever thought myself justified in being pert to a great man; but upon this provocation I cannot help observing, that I always had wit and sense enough to keep my head upon my shoulders.

Henry Duff Traill
(*1842-1900*)

H. D. Traill's discursive but meaty dialogues of the dead, published in magazines and in two editions of *The New Lucian* (1884, 1900), display the journalist's attention to current events, here the unveiling of a bust of Fielding by Margaret Thomas at Taunton, Somersetshire, in 1883, and the man of letters' consciousness of the resonance of the past in such events. Most pieces in *The New Lucian* have at least one nineteenth-century speaker, often paired with a more authoritative figure from Traill's beloved eighteenth century—"Richardson and Fielding," printed in both editions, constitutes an exception only insofar as Richardson, in the context of the dialogue, is not a Victorian. The preeminent eighteenth-century authority in dialogues of the dead, Samuel Johnson, censures newfangled folly in another of Traill's conversations. Here he becomes all but present as Fielding mentions Richardson's lending him money (see the Hill-Powell edition of Boswell's *Life,* III, 303*n*) and later quotes from "The Vanity of Human Wishes." E. L. McAdam, Jr. surveyed the personal relations of Fielding and Richardson in the course of "A New Letter from Fielding," *Yale Review,* XXXVIII (1948), 300–10.

Richardson and Fielding

Richardson. Sir! Mr. Fielding! This is mighty ill manners! I would
have you to know, sir, that I prefer my own company to yours.

Fielding. I cannot believe it. Death does not so change men's natures.
Your known conviviality of disposition—

Richardson. Again, sir! You pass all bounds! 'Tis strange that you
should suppose yourself entitled to use this freedom with me. Were
we on earth I should impute your rudeness to an excitement in
which you were said to indulge yourself something too freely.

Fielding. I know you would: and as a backbiter you deserve to be pit-
ied for the loss of so useful a tooth.

Richardson. I shall suffer less by my loss, Mr. Fielding, I am well assured, than you will by yours.

Fielding. Perhaps so; but you will suffer in the same way. Tea and
tittle-tattle must be almost as bad to go without as a bottle of
Burgundy and a rousing catch; though I dare say, by the way, that
you manage to get the most favourite of all your drinks even down
here.

Richardson. I know not what you would be at, sir.

Fielding. There is a beverage which intoxicates more hurtfully than
wine and makes a greater fool of the drinker. Ladies' parlours are
its taverns and old maids its tapsters. *You* know its taste, Mr.
Richardson,—no man better; its name is flattery.

Richardson. 'Tis in vain, sir, that you would attempt by ridicule to
make me ashamed of having earned the approbation of virtuous
women. If that is your object let me tell you that—

Fielding. That my object, Mr. Richardson! You are vastly mistaken.
The praises bestowed upon you by virtuous women, so far from ex-
citing my ridicule, inspired me with emulation. I sought to rival

you among the other sex, and began the composition of *Joseph Andrews* in the hope of winning the approbation of virtuous men.

Richardson. I marvel, Mr. Fielding, that you should have the hardihood to speak of that offence against morality and good manners. Ah, sir, you have much to answer for in so thoughtless an endeavour—for thoughtless I hope it was—to raise a laugh against chastity.

Fielding. The chastity which a laugh could put out of countenance is not worth much. But for my own part I see nothing more ridiculous in the manly continence of Joseph than in the virginal purity of his sister.

Richardson. Then you were unfortunate, sir, in your manner of describing it. *The Adventures of Joseph Andrews*—I speak from hearsay only, for I confess I never had the patience to read the book—did more to divert than edify the town.

Fielding. I am not to answer for the levity of my readers. It is enough to provide them with a serious moral; the seriousness to profit by it they must find for themselves. Besides, sir, you are setting up a ticklish test of the morality of authors. I have seen an unthinking reader smile over the sufferings of Mrs. Pamela.

Richardson. That is like enough, sir. Your acquaintance lay chiefly among those who would naturally make a jest of virtue. A work of morality, however, is not to be judged by its effects on the rakehells of Covent Garden.

Fielding. No; nor by its acceptance among the precise spinsters of Fleet Street. If the one be beyond the reach of reform, the others are beyond the need of it. I think we may fairly lay both of them out of the account.

Richardson. Nay, sir; I may boast at any rate of having confirmed the virtuous in their virtue: while you were doing all that lay in your power to cocker the vicious in their vice.

Fielding. 'Fore Gad, Mr. Richardson, there is one virtue to which you do not seem to show much favour; though the Scripture tells us, I think, that charity is the greatest of them all.

Richardson. Charity, sir? Charity? I—I—find nothing to—But no!

I was wrong. The warmth of our dispute betrayed me into error. I had no right to charge you with any deliberate design of corrupting morals, and I ask your pardon.

Fielding. Say no more, Mr. Richardson! You are an honest little fellow with all your—

Richardson. Sir! Mr. Fielding!

Fielding. Pray excuse me. A warmth of another kind has betrayed me into error. I should have said, sir, that I did not need this proof of your generosity and Christian spirit. You do me no more than justice, however. I have never knowingly left a line unblotted which I thought could injure the cause of morality, though, I own, I believed I could serve it bettter by describing men and women as I saw them rather than as I could have wished them to be. After all, Mr. Richardson, we live among realities. It is among them that virtue has to be practised; and I doubt whether it is possible to teach it by examples drawn from a wholly ideal world, where the personages live and move as it were in another and different element altogether. As soon might one understand the art of swimming by watching men perform its movements, belly downwards, on a bowling-green. The men and women of my romances may not all of them swim like Leander, but they are at least in the water, and worth watching on that account.

Richardson. Your parable, if you mean to apply it to the most ingenious of your romances, is indeed a rash one. Your hero there is assuredly no Leander.

Fielding. My hero no Leander! (I forbear to laugh, you see, though there are few things more diverting than gravity stumbling on a clench.) No sir; Tom is certainly no Leander: his head is pretty often under water before he contrives to make his way to the haven of his Sophia's arms. But he gets there, however; he does not sink; he swims.

Richardson. Swims! Mr. Fielding! Nay, sir, he struggles somehow to land, and that is all. He is a profligate roisterer—I speak from report, sir, for I would not have you to suppose that I have read his adventures—who is altogether unworthy of the beautiful and

virtuous young gentlewoman (as she is described to me) who rewards him with her hand: and what sort of lesson in morality is
that, I would ask?

Fielding. No better than life affords us, sir, I grant you that. I never
could bring myself to improve upon the instructions which the
great Disposer of events vouchsafes to His creatures.

Richardson. I grieve, sir, that you should add impiety to license. Providence does not reward the vicious as you have dared to do.

Fielding. What? Do you mean to tell me that all the loose fellows
are condemned to marry ugly women? Or is it Sophy's virtue that
they have to do without—as indeed they have but too often
made shift to do in their wilder days?

Richardson. Your talk, sir, is becoming something too free for my
taste; but you are only affecting to misunderstand me. The Al-
mighty may well allow vice to prosper in this life, if such be His
inscrutable will, seeing that He has the power of rewards and punishments after death: but a writer of romances has but this world
to deal with. His judgment-day is in his last chapter, and the good
must be rewarded and the evil punished before he pens his "Finis,"
or not at all.

Fielding. True enough, sir; but if you believe in the infinite mercy of
the Supreme Being—you need not interrupt me; I see you do
from your manner—you ought not to be so shocked at the leni-
ency of the romancer. He also, if I may say it without irreverence,
is a creator: and none can know so well as he what allowances are
to be made for the infirmities of his creatures.

Richardson. I have no patience, sir, with such profane trifling. Do you
not encourage youth to believe that recklessness and riotous living,
dicing and drinking, chambering and wantonness are after all but
venial irregularities, and that if a man be bold and open-handed,
good-natured, and good-humoured with it all, he shall come to no
great harm? And is not that corrupting?

Fielding. Is it more corrupting than life itself? I protest, sir, that I
cannot see it. If good and evil impulses be mixed in all men, and if
their fellows see that sometimes the good is allowed in this life to

atone for the evil, shall we say that those who are rather embold-
ened by contemplating the impunity of vice than humbled by observing how lamentably it defaces and chequers virtue, have been
corrupted by the world? Or that they are self-corrupters? Unless we
give the latter account of them, we must declare, as I said but now,
that divine mercy is itself an instrument in the demoralisation of
mankind.

Richardson. You seem mighty well content, sir, with that sophism,
but it cannot serve you. I must remind you again that you did not
stand towards your characters as a man stands towards his fellow,
but on another foot. You were, as you said with too little rever-
ence, their creator, and you were also their judge. Why did you
shrink then from making a wholesome example? Why teach young
men that vice may escape punishment and even attain to happi-
ness. How can you tell but that many a youth may have been
tempted to intrigue with a Lady Bellaston—if that is the hussey's name—while yet hoping to be rewarded with a Sophia
Western at last?

Fielding. Well, Mr. Richardson, and why teach waiting-maids that
virtue will always be rewarded by £10,000 a year and a couple of
country houses? How can you tell but that many an ambitious abi-
gail, disappointed of becoming the wife of her first amorous master,
has jumped at the situation of mistress to the second?

Richardson. Sir, I see no pertinence in your question.

Fielding. Do you not? It seems to me very much to the point. I cannot see that virtue is any better served by feigning a false certainty
for its earthly prizes, than by teaching men what is strictly true,
—that it need not despair of its recompense even though it be
mingled with vice. Besides, sir, to come back to my old position,
how is it possible for a faithful delineator of human life to do otherwise than I have done? Are not good and evil mingled in life,
and are not those who look upon life—I speak not now of
boarding-school misses, but of men and women of the world—
are they not, I say, perpetually conscious of the mixture? Do they
not see too that the tares and wheat—or is it tares and oats? no!

wheat—tares and wheat are allowed to grow together until the harvest, and that the tares sometimes flourish a plaguy deal better than the wheat? [1] If they do see all these things in life, they would not recognize the romancer's picture if it omitted them all.

Richardson. I am amazed, sir, at the shallowness of such reasoning. Good and evil are indeed mingled in this life, but it is not therefore for an honest and Christian writer to fling down the things and persons of this world chance-medley before his readers, like so much unsorted goods and leave them to pick out the fair or foul as best suits their taste. It is his duty sir to put them upon contemplating only what is good, and to encourage them to the pursuit of it by showing what advantages it brings.

Fielding. Is that his duty? Then egad, let him throw aside his pen and quit his closet, clap on a cassock and bands and get him to the pulpit, for that, sir, is the proper place for him. Once there, however, he will do better to drop this life altogether, so far as rewards and punishments are concerned, and to seek to fortify the virtuous, and alarm the vicious by dwelling on the comforts of a good conscience, and the agonies of an evil one, on the joys of heaven and the terrors of hell. That, Mr. Richardson, is his business—the business of a man whose concern is with the future world, and not like my own, as I conceived it, with the present.

Richardson. I cannot believe it either necessary or right to divide one of these concerns from the other. It was my own endeavour—in which I humbly trust to have succeeded—to write both for a future and for the present world. I was insensible I hope to the vanity of authorship, and deemed it by far a higher honour to have been a teacher of morals than an inventor of romances. But I judged, and I think rightly, that I could do more for morality as a delineator of life than as a pulpit homilist.

Fielding. Why then did you make a pulpit homilist of yourself? Plague take it, Mr. Richardson, a pulpit is but a wooden box, and an arm-chair will serve one's turn as well at a pinch. You preached

[1] Matthew 13. 24–30.

sitting instead of standing, and hammered out your periods over an escritoir instead of thumping them out on a velvet cushion. But preacher you were always, and delineator of life, never. I doubt indeed whether you ever saw more of it than could be seen from your shop door: but whatever you saw of it, you never drew it.

Richardson. Never drew it! No delineator of life! Mr. Fielding, you are uncivil.

Fielding. Am I? I thought you set so little store by your fame as an author that you would take it as a compliment to be regarded solely as a preacher of morals.

Richardson. No man takes it as a compliment, sir, to hear that he has failed in anything which he has attempted. However, I need not allow myself to be vexed by your mean opinion of my writings: nor will I. I thank Heaven that a man's reputation is not to be made or marred to all time by the wits of Covent Garden. There are others sir, besides the coxcombs who were scrambling for the chair of Dryden, to whose judgment—

Fielding. Mr. Richardson! Mr. Richardson! I beg of you to compose yourself. Such earthly trifles as the fame of ingenious authorship are beneath the care of a moralist. Besides, as you have well said, there is nothing which need vex you in the expression of my poor opinion. I never laid claim to the chair of glorious John, out of which indeed I should have first had to hoist a heavy—

Richardson. You are right there, sir, and I spoke in forgetfulness. The seat of John Dryden was filled, and well filled, at the time when we two entered the court of letters.

Fielding. Well filled indeed! amply, tightly filled, Mr. Richardson; and by a judge, too, as much your friend as he was my enemy.

Richardson. I know not in what sense you can call him your enemy, but I accept with pride the title of his friend. I am prouder indeed of Dr. Johnson's friendship than even of his praise.

Fielding. The one, maybe, had a good deal to do with the other. If report speaks truly you were the greater Samuel's banker.

Richardson. I have given no man a right to circulate any such report.

Fielding. Of that I am sure. You were as much too magnanimous to speak of your benefactions as the Doctor was too generous to conceal them. I say that in all sincerity, believe me. Your left hand, I dare swear, would never have known what your right hand had done, had he not come between them and let out the secret. But there it is: you were the great censor's friend in need.

Richardson. And what if I were, Sir? would you charge one of the proudest and most upright of men with corrupt motives?

Fielding. Not I, faith! The old bear was as honest as one of his own hugs. But then his heart was as warm as his skin, and he was full of goodwill to all who showed him any kindness. You had proved your friendship to him in the most effectual of fashions—by lending him money. With me he had but slight acquaintance, and if we had improved it I should probably have borrowed money of him. What wonder then if his critical foot-rule should have meted to you a little fuller, and to me a little shorter, measure than we deserved?

Richardson. Suppose him then to have been somewhat disbalanced by partiality: he is not the only admired critic who has thought highly of my work. One of the ingenious though, I lament to say, atheistical editors of the Encyclopedia has spoken of me in language which too many will regard as that of extravagant laudation. Mr. Diderot has ventured to compare me with our immortal Shakespeare.

Fielding. Mr. Diderot had better settle the value of that compliment with his friend Mr. Voltaire.[2] For if I mistake not he commends you for that very quality of cultivation in which Mr. Voltaire dared to find our illustrious countryman deficient. But I do not know after all that the Frenchman's compliment is inconsistent with my censure.

Richardson. Nay, sir, how can that be? Was Shakespeare no delineator of life?

Fielding. Not in the humble sense in which I lay claim to that title

---

[2] Diderot exalts the English novelist in the *Eloge de Richardson* (1761); Voltaire attacked Shakespeare in a letter to the French Academy (August 25, 1776) and elsewhere.

for myself. I studied the men and women among whom I moved, and strove to represent their lineaments with fidelity on my canvas. I drew from the life and with my models always before me. Shakespeare had surveyed all life and had his models by heart if he had cared to work in that fashion. But when he sat down to write he looked within and found there the imaginative types of perfect form upon which he worked. I drew my characters as Reynolds painted his portraits, but Shakespeare created his as Phidias modelled his Jove.

Richardson. To what does all this tend, Mr. Fielding? Am I really to conclude that you are ascribing the superior mode of workmanship to me?

Fielding. You are fluttered, I see, by the mere anticipation; but it is a correct one. You did not study from the life, though perhaps you thought you did, but you had a certain power of imagining types. It was not, I am sorry to say, till I had roundly ridiculed you that I found it out: but I confessed it when I did. For your *Clarissa Harlowe* I had a great value, and you will do me the justice to remember that I was not slow to express it. You possessed deep insight, sir, into the female heart, and in one instance you have most powerfully idealised the wickedness of a man. It matters nothing that neither Clarissa nor Lovelace are representations of any possible human being: they have a truth of their own. I should like to say the same of Pamela, but I cannot. She is neither an ideal waiting-maid nor a real one.

Richardson. What, sir, you profess to find no reality in Pamela?

Fielding. My experience of her is in two respects the reverse of Mr. B's. I find her neither of flesh-and-blood, nor resisting to the touch. Come, Mr. Richardson, is there any truth to nature in the preaching little baggage, or in her sanctified parents—hedgers and ditchers with a longer string of long words in their mouths than they had ever had onions. Is there any reason and probability in her restraint by the wicked Mrs. Jukes? Can we believe in the real inability of so virtuous a maiden to escape from so ill-guarded a prison? Or in the sudden conversion of so hardened a profligate as her master?

Richardson. I see no great violation of probability, sir, in any of these things. I know not why a squire or a waiting-maid should not comport themselves as they do in *Pamela.*

Fielding. Then take the word of a squire who has had some experience of waiting-maids, that they would not. One would have been less pertinacious or the other more approachable. And what do you think of Lovelace? Do you suppose that the rake-hells of Covent Garden, as you call them, numbered any such audacious and triumphant villain among them as he?

Richardson. The selfishness of long self-indulgence, sir, and the insolence of rank and wealth and the visitation of God upon a godless life, may produce, nay, I think they must produce, a Lovelace.

Fielding. Ay, as hatred and suspicion and callous contempt for his kind may produce the undoer of Othello. But for all that, I should not expect to meet with an Iago on the Piazza at Venice, and I can assure you that you would meet no Lovelace at its namesake in Covent Garden. The spot is too near Bow Street for that.

Richardson. You mean that—

Fielding. I meant, sir, to remind you that I had been a magistrate as well as a writer, and that in the former of these characters I should have made short work of the most famous of your personages. One of my runners would have laid "Captain" Lovelace and his lawless lieutenants by the heels in a very short time. What! to abduct a young lady of quality under pretence of escorting her to the house of a kinswoman, and then to detain her for weeks against her will, to say nothing of attempting and finally accomplishing yet worse outrages—and all this to go on unchecked under the very noses of his majesty's commission of the peace! Upon my conscience, Mr. Richardson, your magistrates and constabulary vastly needed a call over the coals.

Richardson. On such a matter, sir, you speak with an authority which it does not become me to question.

Fielding. Believe, then, on that authority, sir, that no such man as Lovelace was possible in England in the reign of his gracious majesty George II., and still less so, I suppose, at any time since. Nor do I know whether one could have met with so unredeemed a scoundrel in any country or time. But one may say the same of the blacker villains of Shakespeare; and it does not prevent Lovelace from possessing what I have already allowed to him, a reality of his own. His is a powerfully conceived and awe-striking figure of the Satanic sort, as Clarissa is a most affecting picture in the angelic order of portraiture, and both of them deserved to live. Have I atoned, Mr. Richardson, for speaking of you as no delineator of life?

Richardson. You have at any rate said some vastly civil things, sir, and I thank you for them. My regret is the greater that I cannot return your civilities in kind. But I could not honestly say anything in praise of *Tom Jones*—which is—I mean, which I understand to be your masterpiece; and I know you would not have me sacrifice conscience to courtesy.

Fielding. Not for the world, Mr. Richardson: particularly when I should derive so little pleasure from what would give you so much pain. I will strive to do without your good opinion on my writings, consoling myself as best I may, by the imaginative contemplation of my effigy.

Richardson. Hey? what? what say you, Mr. Fielding, your effigy?

Fielding. 'Tis even so, sir. How does your friend the great doctor turn it?

> "See nations slowly wise and meanly just
> To buried merit raise the tardy bust;
> If dreams. . . ."

But what ails you, Mr. Richardson? You seem agitated.

Richardson. 'Tis nothing sir—nothing. But I confess I had thought that. . . .

Fielding. You hardly need tell me what. But, plague take it, sir, these empty honours can profit us nothing.

Richardson. True, Mr. Fielding, very true—

> "Can storied urn or animated bust
>   Back to its mansion call the fleeting breath?
> Can Honour's voice provoke the silent dust?
>   Or flattery soothe the dull cold ear of death?"

My venerable friend Dr. Johnson thought meanly of Mr. Gray, I remember, but to me he seemed to have considerable merit.

Fielding. He can put unpleasant questions at any rate, if that be a merit in a poet.

Richardson. A bust is not wanted by any man who lives in the memory of his countrymen.

Fielding. And useless to any man who does not.

Richardson. I refrained, Mr. Fielding, from adding that.

Fielding. Why did you then? It is your own consolation on the want of a statue. You are not mocked, and I am.

Richardson. I do not understand you.

Fielding. I will whisper my meaning, so that it may not get abroad: for you keep your court of admirers here, though I do not. They have raised a statue to me, and for aught I know they may raise one to you, but—*they do not read either of us.*

Richardson. Great Heaven! You jest, Mr. Fielding.

Fielding. Not now. I have given it up. I did all my jesting on earth, and I fear that my works are suffering for it.

Richardson. Ah! I perceive how it stands with you, sir. It is as I feared. Your freedoms have excluded you from polite hands. I always somewhat marvelled at the hardihood of the gentlewomen in my own day who could be seen perusing your works. But the neglect of my own romances, which were thought to have done so much for the cause of virtue, is both strange and mortifying.

Fielding. Nevertheless it is complete, or so I am assured on the best authority. They tell me that a young woman would be almost as likely to be seen giggling over the temptations of Joseph Andrews, as fluttering over the trials of Pamela. As to the men, I am perhaps a little better off than you, for some few of them have still a certain acquaintance with me, and the others think it right to pretend it. But for the ladies, Mr. Richardson—well, we must do our best to console each other with the reflection that since they are too straitlaced to relish my romances, they may perhaps be too virtuous to need your sermons.

Part III

CHECK LIST

Original Dialogues of the Dead
in English, 1641-1907

       The following list is exclusive rather than inclusive, containing the titles of works the eighteenth century recognized, or would have recognized, as "dialogues of the dead" because of their close resemblance to the work of Lucian so named. Virtually every speaker in every dialogue is either a god of the Greek underworld or a shade, the setting of every dialogue being Hades or a place like it; additional fieldmarks—as well as mention of significant works related to, but not quite within the pale of, the genre—may be found in the text and notes of my history, particularly Chapters I-II. The list stops with 1907, the year Matthew Prior's dialogues were finally published. Dialogues of any note published later, for which bibliographical detail is unwarranted, are mentioned in the history, as are significant works translated into English and also important reprintings. One exception: the dialogue dated 1658 is included here because it is a translation of an Englishman's Latin.

    Title-page information is recorded with as few changes as possible in spelling and punctuation, though without any attempt to indicate italicization or variations of typography. Where whole words or lines were found in capitals, I have substituted small letters, except for the initials of words capitalized in present-day usage. For the most part, entries for each year are arranged alphabetically; components of series in periodicals, however, are listed chronologically, as are works related sequentially (e.g., Brown's reply to Lyttelton, 1760). After titles of rare books and pamphlets I have supplied abbreviated references to the owner library:

Bod.   The Bodleian Library, Oxford University
BM   British Museum
Bost.   Boston Public Library
Col.   Columbia University
Chi.   University of Chicago
Harv.   Harvard University
HL   The Henry E. Huntington Library, San Marino, California
Il.   University of Illinois
NL   The Newberry Library, Chicago
NYPL   New York Public Library
Tex.   University of Texas
UT   Union Theological Seminary
Yale   Yale University

My efforts to locate several works have been in vain; their titles, and information lacking on title pages of works I have examined, are supplied in brackets, with—where necessary—specification of my source at the end of the entry. Sources referred to more than once are:

CBEL   *The Cambridge Bibliography of English Literature.* Ed. F. W. Bateson. 4 vols. Cambridge, 1941.

CR   *The Critical Review.*

GM   *The Gentleman's Magazine.*

Halkett and Laing   Samuel Halkett and John Laing. *Dictionary of Anonymous and Pseudonymous English Literature.* Ed. James Kennedy and others. 9 vols. Edinburgh, 1926–62.

Nichols   John Nichols. *Literary Anecdotes of the Eighteenth Century.* 9 vols. London, 1812–15.

PMLA   Benjamin Boyce. "News from Hell: Satiric

Communications with the Nether World in English Writing of the Seventeenth and Eighteenth Centuries," *PMLA,* LVIII (1943), 402–37.

1641

A Description of the Passage of Thomas late Earle of Strafford, over the River of Styx, with the conference betwixt him, Charon, and William Noy. Printed in the yeare 1641. (BM)

1642

Strange Apparitions, or The Ghost of King James, With a late conference between the ghost of that good King, the Marquesse Hameltons, and George Eglishams, Doctor of Physick, unto which appeared the Ghost of the late Duke of Buckingham concerning the death and poysoning of King James and the rest. London printed for J. Aston, 1642. (Yale)

1658

A Messenger From the Dead, or, Conference Full of stupendious horrour, heard distinctly, and by alternate voyces, by many at that time present. Between the Ghosts of Henry the 8. and Charles the First of England, in Windsore-Chappel, where they were both Buried. In which the whole Series of the Divine Judgments, in those infortunate Ilands, is as it were by a Pencil from Heaven, most lively set forth from the first unto the last. London, Printed for Tho. Vere, and W. Gilbertson, and are to be sold at their Shops, at the Signe of the Angel, and the Signe of the Bible without Newgate, 1658. (UT) A translation of Richard Perrinchief's *Nvntius a Mortvis. . . .* London, 1657.

1659

A Dialogue Betwixt the Ghosts of Charls the I, Late King of England: and Oliver The late Usurping Protector. London, Printed in the year, 1659. (Harv.)

A New Conference Between the Ghosts of King Charles and Oliver Cromvvell. Faithfully Communicated by Adam Wood. London, Printed for Robert Page, living in Barbican, 1659. (UT)

1660

Bradshaw's Ghost; A Poem: or, A Dialogue between John Bradshaw, Ferry-man Charon, Oliver Cromwel, Francis Ravilliack, and Ignatius Loyola. 1660. (BM)

1683

A Dialogue between Anthony Earl of Shaftsbury, and Captain Thomas Walcott, Upon their Meeting in Pluto's Kingdome. London, Printed by William Downing, 1683. (BM)

1684

Pluto, the Prince of Darkness, His Entertainment of Coll. Algernoon Sidney, Upon His Arrival at the Infernal Palace. With the Congratulations of the Fanatick Cabal for his Arrival There. To the Tune of, Hail to the Mirtle shade, &c. London: Printed for a warning to all Traytors, 1684. (Harv.)

1687

See the second entry under 1704.

1692

Gildon, Charles. *Nuncius Infernalis: or, A New Account From Below. In Two Dialogues. The First From the Elizium Fields, Of Friendship. The Second From Hell of Cuckoldom, Being the Sessions of Cuckolds. By Charles Gildon, Gent. With a Preface by Mr. Durfey.* London, Printed for Thomas Jones near Essex-street in the Strand, 1692. (NL)

1699

[King, William.] *Dialogues of the Dead. Relating to the present Controversy Concerning the Epistles of Phalaris. By the Author of the*

Journey to London. London: Printed, and Sold by A. Baldwin, near the Oxford-Arms-Inn in Warwick-Lane. 1699. (Yale)

1701

Dialogues of the Living and the Dead: In Imitation of Lucian and the French. London, Printed in the Year 1701. (Chi.)

1702

"A Dialogue between the Late L— L—, Doctor Con—st and Charon," *A Pacquet from Parnaseus: or, A Collection of Papers, viz. . . . Vol. 1. Numb. I.* London Printed by J. How, in the Ram-Head-Inn-Yard in Fanchurch-street; and Sold by J. Nutt, near Stationers-Hall, 1702. Pp. 13–17. (BM)

1704

[Brown, Thomas.] "The Belgic Heroe Unmasked: or, The Deliverer set forth in his proper Colours. In a Dialogue Between Sir Walter Raleigh and Aaron Smith," *Miscellaneous Works, Written by His Grace, George, Late Duke of Buckingham. Collected in One Volume from the Original Papers. . . . Also State Poems. . . .* London: Printed for and Sold by J. Nutt near Stationers-hall. 1704. Sigs. M8-O3 (Col.) Author not specified; accepted as Brown's by Benjamin Boyce, *Tom Brown of Facetious Memory: Grub Street in the Age of Dryden,* Harvard Studies in English, XXI (Cambridge, Mass., 1939), p. 165.

Sheppard, Fleetwood. "The Calendar Reform'd: or, A pleasant Dialogue between Pluto and the Saints in the Elysian Fields after Lucian's manner. Written by Sir Fl. Sh—d in the Year 1687," *Miscellaneous Works, Written by His Grace, George, Late Duke of Buckingham. Collected in One Volume from the Original Papers. . . . Also State Poems. . . .* London: Printed for and Sold by J. Nutt near Stationers-hall. 1704. Sigs. L1-M2. (Col.)

1708

[Hughes, John.] "Two New Dialogues Written in the Manner of Monsieur Fontenelle," *Fontenelle's Dialogues of the Dead, in Three*

Parts. I. Dialogues of the Antients. II. The Antients with the Moderns. III. The Moderns. Translated from the French. With a Reply to some Remarks in a Critique, call'd The Judgment of Pluto &c. And Two Original Dialogues. London: Printed for Jacob Tonson, within Grays-Inn Gate next Grays-Inn Lane. 1708. Pp. 195–209. (Col.) Dedication signed by Hughes.

ca. 1708–1709

King, William. "A Dialogue, Shewing the Way to Modern Preferment, between Signior Inquisitivo, Don Sebastiano des los Mustachiero's, Signior Cornaro, and Mustapha," *Miscellanies in Prose and Verse. By William King.* London: Printed for B. Lintott between the two Temple Gates, and H. Clements at the Half-Moon in St. Paul's Church-yard. Pp. 469–81. (Col.) Dated by Colin J. Horne, "Dr. William King's *Miscellanies in Prose and Verse*," *The Library,* 4th ser., XXV (1944), 37, 43.

1715

A Dialogue of the Dead; Between the very Eminent Signor Glibertini and Count Thomaso, in the Vales of Acheron. London; Printed and Sold by E. Berrington in Silver-street Bloomsbury. 1715. (Yale)

1721

Matthew Prior's dialogues composed at about this time. See entry under 1907.

1723

Sheffield, John, first Duke of Buckingham. "A Dialogue between Augustus Cæsar, and Cardinal Richelieu" and "A Dialogue between Mahomet and the Duke of Guise," *The Works of John Sheffield, Earl of Mulgrave, Marquis of Normanby, and Duke of Buckingham.* London: Printed for John Barber, and Sold by the Booksellers of London and Westminster, 1723. 2 vols. I, 172–94. (Yale)

1725

"Julius Cæsar and Jack Shepherd," *The British Journal*, December 4, 1725, p. [1].

News from the Dead: or, a Dialogue. Between Blueskin, Shepperd, and Jonathan Wild. London: Printed by J. Thompson, in the Strand. (BM) Date from *PMLA*, p. 434.

1738

"A Dialogue between the Queen of Sweden and the Czarina," *The Gentleman's Magazine*, VIII (November, 1738), 594.

1744

Siris in the Shades: a Dialogue Concerning Tar Water; Between Mr. Benjamin Smith, lately deceased, Dr. Hancock, and Dr. Garth, at Their Meeting upon the Banks of the River Styx. London: Printed for C. B. and Sold by A. Dodd, at the Peacock, near Essex-Street, in the Strand. MDCCXLIV. (Bod.)

1745

A Dialogue in the Shades: between Mrs. Morley and Mrs. Freeman. Containing, A Review of all the most material Incidents in their past Lives. London: Printed for M. Cooper at the Globe in Pater-Noster-Row. 1745. (BM)

1747

"Dialogue between Augustus II. King of Poland, and Catherine Opalinska, Queen of Poland, and Duchess of Lorrain, in the Elysian Fields," *The Museum*, XXVIII (April 11, 1747), 45–48.

1749

A Dialogue in the Shades Below: Manag'd by Mrs. Phill—ps, Mrs. Pilk—nton, Dean Swift, Galilæo, Lais the Courtezan, and Several other Persons of Taste and Distinction. Together with the Trial and Sentence of Mrs. Phill—ps and Mrs. Pilk—nton. Accurately taken down by a Stander-by, and sent last Post to a Correspondent Above by the Hands of Mercury. London: Printed for W. Owen, at Homer's Head, near Temple-Bar. (HL) Date from *GM,* XIX (1749), 384.

1752

The Inspector in the Shades. A New Dialogue In the Manner of Lucian. London: Printed for J. Swan, in the Strand, near Northumberland-House. MDCCLII. (Yale) Attributed to John Kennedy by Halkett and Laing, III, 160.

Sola, Sylviana. "Dialogues of the Dead," *Various Essays By Sylviana Sola.* Printed for the Author in 1752. Pp. 83–164. (BM)

1753

A Dialogue between Dean Swift and Tho. Prior, Esq; in the Isles of St. Patrick's Church, Dublin, On that memorable Day, October 9th, 1753. By a Friend to the Peace and Prosperity of Ireland. Dublin: Printed for G. and A. Ewing, at the Angel and Bible in Dame-Street, 1753. (Col.) Attributed to Samuel Madden by Charles A. Stonehill, Jr. and others, *Anonyma and Pseudonyma* (London, 1926–27), I, 422.

1759

A Dialogue betwixt General Wolfe, and the Marquis Montcalm, in the Elysian Fields. Printed in the Year 1759: And Sold by E. Jopson, in Coventry; Messrs. Rivington and Fletcher, at the Oxford-Theatre, in Pater-noster-Row, London; and the other Booksellers in Town and Country. (BM)

1760

[Lyttelton, George, first Baron Lyttelton.] *Dialogues of the Dead.* London: Printed for W. Sandby, in Fleet-street. M.DCC.LX. (Yale) Dialogues XXVI–XXVIII are by Elizabeth Montagu.

An Additional Dialogue of the Dead, between Pericles and Aristides: Being a Sequel to the Dialogue between Pericles and Cosmo. London, Printed for L. Davis and C. Reymers, opposite Gray's-Inn-

Gate, in Holbourne. MDCCLX. (BM) Written in response to Lyttelton's Dialogue XXIII. Attributed to John Brown by Nichols, II, 339.

1761

Elizabeth Montagu includes "Berenice & Cleopatra" in a letter (April 28). See entry under 1906.

1762

"Dialogue between Mr. Gay and Mr. Rich," *The Universal Museum*, I (July, 1762), 395–97.

New Dialogues of the Dead. London: Printed for R. and J. Dodsley, in Pall-Mall. M. DCC. LXII. (Col.) Attributed to William Weston and John Green by Nichols, IX, 668.

Il Tasso. A Dialogue. The Speakers John Milton, Torquato Tasso. In which, New Light is thrown on their Poetical and Moral Characters. London: Printed for R. Baldwin, in Pater-Noster-Row. M. DCC. LXII. (BM)

1763

"A Dialogue between the Late Earls of Orford and Granville," *The Universal Museum*, II (June, 1763), 318–20.

1765

[*A Dialogue among the Dead, occasioned by some late Transactions in Gaming and Duelling*. Wilkie.] *CR*, XIX (June, 1765), 475.

[*A Dialogue in the Elysian Fields, between Two D—k—s*. Hooper.] *CR*, XX (July, 1765), 72.

[Lyttelton, George, first Baron Lyttelton.] *Four New Dialogues of the Dead*. London: Printed for W. Sandby, in Fleet-street. M.DCC.LXV. (Tex.)

Pye, Samuel. *Moses and Bolingbroke; A Dialogue in The Manner of the Right Honourable *******, Author of Dialogues of the Dead. By Samuel Pye, M.D.* London: Printed for William Sandby, in Fleet-street. MDCCLXV. (BM)

1766

A Dialogue in the Shades, Between the Celebrated Mrs. Cibber, And the no less Celebrated Mrs. Woffington, Both of Amorous Memory; Containing Many Curious Anecdotes of the Dramatic and Intriguing World; the Amours of the Modern Roscius; the real State of the Case for which Theophilus Cibber prosecuted Mr. S.*****, &c. &c. &c. London: Printed for S. Bladon, in Pater-noster-Row, MDCCLXVI. (HL)

1770

"A Dialogue in the Shades," *The Repository,* I (April, 1770), 452–54. Reprinted (according to a note) from *The Morning Chronicle,* April 5, 1770, which I have not seen.

"A Dialogue of the Dead; betwixt Lord Eglington, and Mungo Campbell," *The Universal Museum,* VI (April, 1770), 153–57. Attributed to John Langhorne by *CBEL,* II, 369.

Voltaire in the Shades; or, Dialogues on the Deistical Controversy. London: Printed for G. Pearch, (No. 12.) Cheapside; T. and J. Merril, in Cambridge; and D. Prince, in Oxford. MDCCLXX. (BM) Attributed to William Julius Mickle by *CBEL,* II, 374.

1773

"Dialogue between Eloisa and Lady Mary Wortley Montague, in the Regions of the Dead," *The Sentimental Magazine,* I (December, 1773), 433–36.

1774

"Dialogue between Cervantes and Lord Herbert, of Cherbury, in the Regions of the Dead," *The Sentimental Magazine,* II, (January, 1774), 1–4.

"Dialogue between Messalina and Lord Rochester, in the Regions of the Dead," *The Sentimental Magazine,* II (February, 1774), 58–60.

"Dialogue between Scipio Africanus and Mahomet the Great in the Regions of the Dead," *The Sentimental Magazine*, II (April, 1774), 137–39.

"Dialogue between Zeno and Epicurus in the Regions of the Dead," *The Sentimental Magazine*, II (May, 1774), 185–89.

Candaliensis. "Dialogue in the Shades between Charles XII. of Sweden, and Oliver Cromwell," *The Sentimental Magazine*, II (June, 1774), 244–46.

1775

"Dialogue between the late Queen of Denmark, and Mary, Queen of Scots, in the Regions of the Dead," *The Town and Country Magazine*, VII (May, 1775), 267–68.

"A Dialogue in the Shades, between the late Lord Chesterfield, and the late Doctor Goldsmith," *The London Magazine*, XLIV (December, 1775), 632–33.

1776

Crito. "A Dialogue in the Shades between James Quinn and Tom Weston," *The Town and Country Magazine*, VIII (February, 1776), 98–99.

1777

[Combe, William.] *A Dialogue in the Shades between an Unfortunate Divine, and a Welch Member of Parliament, lately deceased.* London: Printed for J. Bew, No. 28, Pater-Noster-Row; and Sold by B. Bristow, No. 85, Great Tower-Street. (BM) Harlan W. Hamilton, *Doctor Syntax: A Silhouette of William Combe, Esq. (1742–1823)* (London, 1969), p. 307.

Dialogues in the Shades, between General Wolfe, General Montgomery, David Hume, George Grenville, and Charles Townshend. London: Printed for G. Kearsley, No 46, in Fleet Street. M. DCC. LXXVII. (NL)

1778

"A Dialogue in the Shades, between Sir Robert Walpole and Mr. Pelham," *The Town and Country Magazine,* X (February, 1778), 59–60.

"A Dialogue in the Shades between Mrs. Woffington and Kitty Fisher," *The Town and Country Magazine,* X (September, 1778), 455–56.

[Knox, Vicesimus.] "Essay XII. Dialogue between Drs. Swift and Bentley," *Essays Moral and Literary.* London: Printed for Edward and Charles Dilly. M DCC LXXVIII. Pp. 79–86. (Yale) Became Vol. I of the last work listed under 1779.

A Philosophical and Religious Dialogue in the Shades, between Mr. Hume and Dr. Dodd. With Notes by the Editor. London: Printed for the Editor, and Sold by Hooper and Davis, No. 25, Ludgate-Hill, London; Charles Elliott, Edinburgh, and T. Wilson, York. MDCCLXXVIII. (Harv.)

1779

"A Dialogue in the Shades between Lord Littleton and Earl Temple," *The Town and Country Magazine,* XI (September, 1779), 489–90.

"A Dialogue of the Dead. Milton and Pope," *The Public Advertiser,* July 3, 1779, p. [2]. Probably by Thomas Tyers.

Garrick in the Shades; or, A Peep into Elysium; a Farce: Never Offered to the Managers of the Theatres-Royal. London: Printed for J. Southern, in St. James's Street. MDCCLXXIX. (BM)

Knox, Vicesimus. Essay XXXVIII. "On the Superior Value of Solid Accomplishments. A Dialogue between Cicero and Lord Chesterfield," *Essays Moral and Literary. By the Reverend Mr. Knox, Master of Tunbridge School, and Late Fellow of St. John's College, Oxford. Volume the Second.* London; Printed for Charles Dilly, in the Poultry. MDCCLXXIX. Pp. 379–88. (NYPL)

1780

Francklin, Thomas. "On the Life and Writings of Lucian. A Dialogue, between Lucian, and Lord Lyttelton, In the Elysian Fields," *The Works of Lucian, from the Greek, By Thomas Francklin, D. D. Some time Greek Professor In the University of Cambridge.* London, Printed for T. Cadell in the Strand. MDCCLXXX. 2 vols. I, i–xvii. (NYPL)

1782

"A New Dialogue of the Dead," *The Westminster Magazine,* XI (August, 1782), 417–18.

[Tyers, Thomas.] "Conversation VI. In the Shades. The Marquis of Rockingham, and the Earl of Chatham," *Dramatic Conversations.* London, Printed by J. Nichols for the Author. MDCCLXXXII. Pp. 82–96. (NYPL)

1783

"Dialogue of the Dead. Lord Herbert, Mr. Hume, Mercury," *The London Magazine,* LII (February, 1783), 65–68.

1784

[Tyers, Thomas.] *Conversations Political and Familiar.* London. Printed in the Year 1784. (Il.)

1785

A Dialogue between Dr. Johnson and Dr. Goldsmith, in the Shades, Relative to the Former's Strictures on the English Poets, Particularly Pope, Milton, and Gray. London: Printed for Debrett, in Picadilly; Egerton, at Charing Cross; Flexney, in Holborn; Kearsley, in Fleet Street; Bew, in Paternoster Row; and Sewell, in Cornhill. (Tex.) Date from *The English Review,* V (1785), 199.

A Dialogue between The Earl of C——d and Mr. Garrick, in the Elysian Shades. London: Printed by J. Nichols, and Sold by T.

Cadell, in the Strand. M DCC LXXXV. (BM) Attributed to George Butt by *GM,* LV (February, 1785), 126.

"Dialogue betwixt Diocletian Emperor of Rome, and Abdolonymus King of Tyre," *The Edinburgh Magazine,* I (February, 1785), 139–41.

1790

Seymore, J. C. "A New Dialogue of the Dead. Horace and Pope in the Elysian Shades," *The Scots Magazine,* LII (December, 1790), 601–2.

1791

A New Dialogue of the Dead: or, a Supposed Debate between the Crucified Thief and the Apostle Paul, upon this Question, Who was the greater Sinner before Conversion? London: Printed for M. Trapp, No. I, Paternoster-Row. M DCC XCI. (NYPL) Attributed to Ambrose Serle by Halkett and Laing, IV, 170.

1793

Rickman, Thomas Clio. "Dialogue in the Shades between Churchill and Collins," *The European Magazine,* XXIV (November, 1793), 345.

1794

Beattie, James Hay. "Dialogues of the Dead," *Essays and Fragments in Prose and Verse. By James Hay Beattie. To Which is Prefixed an Account of the Author's Life and Character.* Edinburgh: Printed by J. Moir, Paterson's Court. M,DCC,XCIV. Pp. 233–97. (Yale) A label pasted on the verso of the title page and signed "J. B." (James Beattie, author of *The Minstrel* and father of James Hay Beattie) indicates that "this Book is not published" but printed for distribution to friends.

A Dialogue in the Shades, between Mercury, a Nobleman, and a Mechanic. London: Printed for J. S. Jordan, No. 166, Fleet-Street. 1794 (NYPL)

1798

"A Dialogue in Empyreum. Louis XVI. and Charles I," *The Monthly Magazine,* V (May, 1798), 351–55.

"Dialogue of the Dead. A Fragment," *The Spirit of the Public Journals,* II (1798), 116–23. Thus listed by Anthony E. Brown, *Boswellian Studies: A Bibliography,* 2d ed., rev. (Hamden, Conn., 1972), p. 122. I have seen the dialogue as reprinted in *The Spirit of the Public Journals for 1798,* new ed. (London, 1805), II, 116–23, where a bracketed subtitle, "From the Telegraph," indicates original publication in a newspaper unavailable to me.

Ferriar, John. "Dialogue in the shades. Lucian.——Neodidactus," *Illustrations of Sterne: with Other Essays and Verses. By John Ferriar, M.D.* Printed for Cadell and Davies, London, by George Nicholson, Manchester. M.DCC.XCVIII. Pp. 289–302. (NYPL)

1802

"Dialogue between Boswell and Johnson, in the Shades," *A Critical Enquiry into the Moral Writings of Dr. Samuel Johnson. In Which the Tendency of Certain Passages in the Rambler, and other Publications of That Celebrated Writer, is Impartially Considered. To Which is Added an Appendix. Containing a Dialogue between Boswell and Johnson in the Shades. By Attalus.* London: Printed by C. Corrall, 38, Charing Cross. Sold by Messrs. Cobbett and Morgan, Pall Mall, and R. Faulder, Bookseller to the King, New Bond Street. 1802. (NYPL) Attalus (William Mudford) was not the author of the dialogue, which J. B.—allegedly the author—reprinted in the book dated 1804 below.

1804

Two New Dialogues of the Dead. The First, Between Handel and Braham. The Second, Between Johnson and Boswell. By J.B. Printed for J. Johnson, St. Paul's Church-yard. 1804. By J. Crowder, War-wick-Square. (Yale) The second dialogue is that first published in 1802.

1805

Perry, William. *A Dialogue in the Shades, Recommended to Every Purchaser of Dr. Kinglake's Dissertation, &c. as an Appropriate Tailpiece For Embellishment and Illustration. Number 1. By Sir John Floyer's Ghost.* Uxbridge: Printed and Sold by T. Lake. Sold also in London by T. Cox, at the Medical Library, St. Thomas's Street, Borough, and J. Harris, St. Paul's Church Yard. 1805. (NYPL) Dedication signed "William Perry, M.D." Succeeded in the same year by four additional pamphlets with the same title containing dialogues 2–9.

1809

[*A Dialogue in the Elysian Fields, between the Right Honourable Charles James Fox, and some of his Royal Progenitors.*] *The Edinburgh Review*, XIII (1809), 505.

"Dialogue of the Dead. The 1st Earl of Chatham and William Pitt," *Amusements of Solitude.* Clonmel: Printed by T. Gorman, Bookseller and Stationer, Shakspeare's-Head, Main-Street. 1809. Pp. 29–41. (BM)

1814

[Beasley, Frederick.] *American Dialogues of the Dead; and Dialogues of the American Dead.* Philadelphia: Published by Edward Earle. William Fry, Printer. 1814. (Col.) *PMLA,* p. 436.

1817–1819

A Dialogue in the Shades, Between William Caxton, Fodius, a Bibliomaniac, and William Wynken, Clerk, a descendent of Wynken de Worde:—To which is added, the Story of Dean Honywood's Grubs. With explanatory Notes, by W. W. Published July 1, 1817, by W. Clarke, New Bond Street. (Col.) Bound with *Repertorium Bibliographicum; or Some Account of the Most Celebrated British Libraries* (London: William Clarke, New Bond Street. MDCCCXIX), where, in an addendum to the Advertisement (p. vii), one William

Wynken attributes the dialogue to his late uncle the Reverend William Wynken and offers it to subscribers to *Repertorium* who apply for it during the month beginning June 10, 1819.

1822

"Dialogues of the Dead. No. 1," *The New Monthly Magazine and Literary Journal,* supplement to N.S., V (1822), 140–45. Signed "Y."

ca. 1824

Translation of a Fragment of the Works of Lucian Lately Found In a Bog near Enniskillen, in Ireland, Containing a Full and True Account of the Interesting Trial of Purple Ghost & Green Ghost, Before Chief Baron Æacus, and his brethren Barons Rhadamanthus and Minos. By Lucian Erigena. (BM) Dated in *PMLA*, p. 436.

1825

Barbauld, Anna Laetitia. "Dialogue in the Shades," *The Works of Anna Lætitia Barbauld. With a Memoir By Lucy Aikin.* London: Printed for Longman, Hurst, Rees, Orme, Brown, and Green, Paternoster-Row, 1825. II, 338–49. (Col.)

1826

Barbauld, Anna Laetitia. "A Dialogue of the Dead, between Helen, and Madame Maintenon," *A Legacy for Young Ladies, Consisting of Miscellaneous Pieces, in Prose and Verse, By the Late Mrs. Barbauld.* London: Printed for Longman, Hurst, Rees, Orme, Brown, and Green, Paternoster Row. 1826. Pp. 241–50. (Il.)

"Napoleon and Franklin. Dialogue of the Dead," *The United States Literary Gazette,* III (February 1, 1826), 339–44.

1832

"Dialogues of the Dead. On Sepulchral Rites and Rights," *Fraser's Magazine,* VI (December, 1832), 728–46.

1854

Landor, Walter Savage. "A Dialogue of the Dead. Nicholas and Diogenes," *The Examiner,* February 11, 1854, p. 84.

1856

[Townsend, Frederic.] *Ghostly Colloquies. By the Author of "Letters from Rome," "Clouds and Sunshine," etc.* New York: D. Appleton and Company, 346 & 348 Broadway. M.DCCC.LVI. (Chi.) *British Museum General Catalogue of Printed Books,* XLI (1966), 1154.

1868

"Dialogues of the Dead. I. —Between Lords Palmerston and Brougham," "II. D'Orsay, Jerrold, and a Stranger," "III. Shakespeare, Thackeray, and a Critic," "IV. Johnson, Macaulay, Boswell, Goldsmith, Goethe, Thackeray, Richardson, Fielding, Sterne, Addison, Voltaire, Bacon," "V. Artists,—Ancient and Modern," "VI. Amongst the Musicians," *Once a Week,* October 3, 1868, pp. 271–74; October 17, 1868, pp. 315–18; November 7, 1868, pp. 377–80; November 21, 1868, pp. 423–26; December 5, 1868, pp. 465–68; December 19, 1868, pp. 509–12.

1879

[Linton, William James.] "Charlotte Corday and Marat," *Voices of the Dead.* [Hamden, Conn. Appledore Private Press, 1879.] Pp. 1–5. (Bost.) R. Malcolm Sills, "W. J. Linton at Yale—the Appledore Private Press," *The Yale University Library Gazette,* XII (1938), 46.

1884

Traill, H. D. *The New Lucian Being A Series of Dialogues of the Dead by H. D. Traill.* London: Chapman and Hall Limited 1884. (Col.)

T[raill], H. D. "Wilkes and Lord Sandwich: A Dialogue," *Macmillan's Magazine,* L (September, 1884), 334–43.

1889

Watson, William. "Dr. Johnson on Modern Poetry. An Interview in the Elysian Fields. A.D. 1900," *The National Review,* XIII (July, 1889), 593–604.

1892

Traill, H. D. "Parnell and Butt. A Dialogue in the Shades," *The Fortnightly Review,* N.S., LI (January, 1892), 115–26.

1896

Percival, William. "A Conversation in Hades. Interlocutors, Lord Byron and M. Honoré de Balzac," *The Sewanee Review,* IV (May, 1896), 377–80.

1900

Traill, H. D. *The New Lucian Being a Series of Dialogues of the Dead by H. D. Traill / New Edition, Revised and Enlarged.* London: Chapman & Hall, Ld. 1900. (NYPL)

1902

McIlwraith, Jean N. "A Dialogue in Hades. Omar Khayyám and Walt Whitman," *The Atlantic Monthly,* LXXXIX (June, 1902), 808–12.

1906

Montagu, Elizabeth. "Berenice and Cleopatra," *Elizabeth Montagu the Queen of the Blue-Stockings Her Correspondence from 1720 to 1761 by Her Great-Great-Niece Emily J. Climenson* . . . 2 vols. London John Murray, Albemarle Street 1906. II, 238–40.

1907

Prior, Matthew. "Four Dialogues of the Dead," *Dialogues of the Dead and Other Works in Prose and Verse,* ed. A. R. Waller. Cambridge: at the University Press 1907. Pp. 205–69.

Index